NUMBER TWENTY-THREE
The Walter Prescott Webb Memorial Lectures

Essays on
Sunbelt Cities
and Recent Urban America

[THE WALTER PRESCOTT WEBB MEMORIAL LECTURES]

Essays on Sunbelt Cities and Recent Urban America

BY RAYMOND A. MOHL, ROBERT FISHER,
CARL ABBOTT, ROGER W. LOTCHIN,
ROBERT B. FAIRBANKS, AND ZANE L. MILLER

Introduction by KENNETH T. JACKSON
Edited by ROBERT B. FAIRBANKS
and KATHLEEN UNDERWOOD

Published for the University of Texas at Arlington by
Texas A&M University Press : College Station

The paper used in this book meets the minimum requirements
of the American National Standard for Permanence of Paper
for Printed Library Materials, Z39.48–1984. Binding materials
have been chosen for durability.

Library of Congress Cataloging-in-Publication Data

Essays on sunbelt cities and recent urban America / by Raymond A. Mohl . . . [et al.] ;
    introduction by Kenneth T. Jackson ; edited by Robert B. Fairbanks and Kathleen
    Underwood. — 1st ed.
        p.   cm. — (Walter Prescott Webb memorial lectures ; 23)
    ISBN 0-89096-396-7 (alk. paper)
        1. Cities and towns—Sunbelt States.   2. Cities and towns—United States.
    I. Mohl. Raymond A.   II: Fairbanks, Robert B. (Robert Bruce, 1950–   .
    III. Underwood, Kathleen, 1944–   .   IV. Series.
    HT123.5.S86E87   1990
    307.76'0973 — dc20   89-32498
                                                                        CIP

Manufactured in the United States of America
First Edition

For Wendell H. Nedderman

Contents

Preface

THIS VOLUME owes its origins to the twenty-third annual Walter Prescott Webb Memorial Lectures held at the University of Texas at Arlington to honor Texas' most celebrated historian. Participants in that lecture series of March 17, 1988, included Professors Carl Abbott, Robert B. Fairbanks, Roger W. Lotchin, and Zane L. Miller. The setting for these lectures, in the heart of the Dallas–Fort Worth Metroplex, seemed particularly appropriate for the subject matter, "Sunbelt Cities and Recent Urban America."

Not only does this volume contain the papers given at the public lectures, it also includes essays by Raymond Mohl and Robert Fisher, who authored the co-winning entries for the 1988 Webb-Smith Essay competition. Kenneth T. Jackson introduces the volume. The result of this cooperative venture is a work that illustrates the rich diversity of approach and methodology which now characterizes urban history.

Raymond Mohl's essay provides a broad context for the rest of the volume by examining major developments — demographic, spatial, economic, and political — characteristic of recent urban America. Utilizing a comparative approach to study Houston, the "buckle" of the Sunbelt, Robert Fisher examines traits that distinguish sunbelt cities from the rest of urban America, as well as from western European cities. Carl Abbott also investigates the peculiar characteristics of southwestern cities. In contrast to Fisher's emphasis on political economy, Abbott examines what he calls the "distinctive cityscape" of southwestern cities. His three-dimensional analysis of urban form helps clarify the distinguishing physical characteristics of these cities. Two additional case studies provide specific examples of the growth and development of the Sunbelt. In his examination of San Diego, Roger W. Lotchin explores the special relationship that some sunbelt cities have had with the military. He not only adds to our understanding of the impact of the military and defense on urban growth, but provides new insight into the rapid rise of military spending after World War II. Robert B. Fairbanks' study of Dallas politics between 1930 and 1960 explores still another characteristic of sunbelt cities—the dominance of business leadership. Moreover, Fairbanks provides a new perspective on the changing political climate that characterized sunbelt cities in the 1950s. In the concluding essay, Zane L. Miller uses the writings of Walter Prescott Webb and Chicago School Sociology to explore the various ways Americans have handled regional and/or racial and ethnic diversity since the late nineteenth century. Miller thus provides still another perspective for understanding today's interest in the Sunbelt.

The contributors to this volume are drawn from across the country —from the Pacific Northwest to the Southern Great Plains, the Midwest, and the Old South. Each is a recognized scholar in urban history. Raymond Mohl, former editor of the *Journal of Urban History*, heads the Department of History at Florida Atlantic University. He has edited *The Making of Urban America* and has authored several books, including *The New City: Urban America in the Industrial Age, 1860–1920* and *Poverty in New York: 1783–1825*.

Robert Fisher is associate professor of history at the University of Houston–Downtown and adjunct professor of social work at the Graduate School of Social Work, University of Houston–University Park. He has co-edited *Community Organization for Urban Social Change: A Historical Perspective* and is the author of *Let the People Decide: Neighborhood Organizing in America*.

Carl Abbott is professor and head of the Department of Urban Studies and Planning, Portland State University. Three of his recent publications are *The New Urban America: Growth and Politics in Sunbelt Cities; Portland: Planning, Politics and Growth in a Twentieth Century City;* and *Urban America in the Modern Age, 1920 to the Present*.

Roger W. Lotchin, professor of history, has taught at the University of North Carolina at Chapel Hill since 1966. Among his publications are *The Martial Metropolis: American Cities in War and Peace, 1900–1970* and *San Francisco, 1846–1856: From Hamlet to City*. He is currently completing *The City and the Sword: Urban California and the Rise of the Metropolitan-Military Complex, 1920–1953*.

Robert B. Fairbanks, associate professor of history at the University of Texas at Arlington is the author of *Making Better Citizens: Housing Reform and the Community Development Strategy in Cincinnati, 1890–1960,* and also has published articles in the *Journal of Urban History, Planning Perspectives,* and *Ohio History.*

Zane L. Miller is professor of history and co-director of the Center for Neighborhood and Community Studies at the University of Cincinnati. He has authored numerous books, including *The Urbanization of Modern America; Suburb: Neighborhood and Community in Forest Park, Ohio, 1935–1976;* and *Boss Cox's Cincinnati: Urban Politics in the Progressive Era.*

Kenneth T. Jackson is professor of history at Columbia University. Most recently he has authored *Crabgrass Frontier: The Suburbanization of the United States.* Other books include *The Ku Klux Klan in the City, 1915–1930* and *Cities in American History.*

Kathleen Underwood, co-editor of this volume with Robert B. Fairbanks, is associate professor of history at the University of Texas at Arlington. A social historian of the American West, she has authored *Town Building on the Colorado Frontier.*

Others also contributed to this volume in important ways. C. B. Smith, Sr., an Austin businessman and former student of Walter Prescott Webb, established the Endowment Fund that has made possible the publication of these lectures. This year's lecture series also benefited from the generosity of the Rudolf Hermanns' Endowment for Liberal Arts, for which the editors and the Webb Committee are most grateful. Stephen Maizlish, Webb Committee Chair, and Kenneth R. Philp, department head, provided helpful guidance in planning this year's lecture series. Sandra Myers and Stanley Palmer played important roles in the early development of the program, and continue to lend their support. The editors thank each of these contributors for their gifts of money, time, and encouragement to this forum on modern urban America.

We dedicate this volume to Wendell H. Nedderman, president of the University of Texas at Arlington. Dr. Nedderman has been a loyal patron of the Walter Prescott Webb Memorial Lectures for the past fifteen years. He has always provided enthusiastic support and generous funding for the lecture series, and in 1987 designated the Walter

Prescott Webb Memorial Lectures as a beneficiary of The Rudolf Hermanns' Endowment for Liberal Arts. Lastly, Dr. Nedderman and his wife, Mrs. Betty Nedderman, host a memorable party each year to climax the lectures series.

ROBERT B. FAIRBANKS
KATHLEEN UNDERWOOD

Essays on
Sunbelt Cities
and Recent Urban America

KENNETH T. JACKSON

Introduction: The Shape of Things to Come: Urban Growth in the South and West

THE THREE MOST IMPORTANT demographic trends in the United States in the twentieth century are the migration of southern blacks from farms to cities, the movement of urban Americans from older neighborhoods to developing suburbs, and the continued shift of the national population toward the South and West. None of these three continental phenomena has yet received the concentrated, consistent scholarship that they merit, but among them the history of the Sunbelt particularly deserves attention.

The most important research problem in dealing with the Sunbelt is that of definition. What do Oregon, New Mexico, and Virginia have in common other than the fact that all are political subdivisions of the same nation-state? Does membership in the "Sunbelt" depend upon the average number of sunny days or on the mean yearly temperature? Does it depend upon economic prosperity or rapid population growth? Is the Sunbelt characterized by a unique kind of cityscape, one that sprawls thinly over the suburbs and is unusually dependent upon the automobile?

As the essays in this book demonstrate, none of these definitions of the Sunbelt holds up under careful scrutiny. As anyone who has endured a North Texas winter can attest, the weather can be severe in many parts of the region. Nor do the South and West have a lock on economic growth and prosperity; portions of Arkansas and Mississippi, for example, have been completely bypassed by the post–World War II boom and seem permanently stuck in the Great Depression. Similarly, many of the areas that led the nation in population and business growth in the 1970s, such as Texas, New Mexico, Louisiana, and Oregon, went into a tailspin during the 1980s, while some of the states of the so-called Rustbelt, such as Massachusetts, New Hampshire, and New York, saw tax receipts soar and unemployment rates drop during the same years. Finally, southwestern cities are just about at the national average in population density, suburbanization, and automobile ownership.

Is there, then, a Sunbelt? The answer is yes, but the region stands in sharp relief from the rest of the country only when we examine it from the perspective of a half century, not a single decade. Between 1940 and 1989, for example, all ten of the most rapidly developing states in the nation were either west of the Mississippi River or south of the Mason-Dixon Line. When the Japanese attacked Pearl Harbor, the South and West were economically subservient to eastern financial centers. At that time, the North owned 80 to 90 percent of the wealth of the United States, and all major decisions affecting the continent were made either on Wall Street in New York City or in the Congress in Washington. As John Crowe Ransom complained just before World War II, "The North owns and operates the national economy; the South and West work under its direction."

The situation changed dramatically in the next half-century. Although most important decisions in this nation are still made either in Manhattan or in the District of Columbia, even casual observation reveals that the West and South are now economic pacesetters and are no longer weak and helpless colonies of eastern capitalists.

An important theme in understanding the growth of the Sunbelt is World War II as a catalyst for change. During those four years, 1941–1945, for example, approximately 40 percent of total military expenditures went to the South, and much of the remainder went to the West. More importantly, the federal government invested upwards of $100 billion in industrial facilities and permanent installations in the region. At least twelve million war workers and their families, in addition to eight million GI's in uniform, streamed into the area now known as the Sunbelt between 1941 and 1945. After four years of such federal pump-priming, great cities had risen where there had once been sleepy western towns, and industries of every description dotted the landscape. By the time the Germans and the Japanese called it quits in 1945, the South and West were economically strong and culturally mature, and they had visions of unlimited regional expansion.

World War II transformed Southern California, which was home port and home base for many millions of servicemen and women and which accounted for more than 10 percent of the nation's entire war production, in an especially spectacular way. Douglas, Lockheed, North American Aviation, Northrup, and Hughes Aircraft alone employed 250,000 workers in the manufacture of B-17 Flying Fortresses, Liberator bombers, and P-38 fighters. The Los Angeles area grew four times as fast as the United States as a whole, and the vast influx of population strained fire and police systems, tied up traffic, and caused the tightest housing market in the region's history.

The war also accelerated a regional shift in the nation's scientific research, as the Lawrence Radiation Laboratory in California, the Los Alamos testing center in New Mexico, and the atomic cities of Oak Ridge in Tennessee and Hanford in Washington helped win the war of brains. In addition, southern and western congressmen revised federal funding procedures for colleges and managed to throw off a part of their regional subservience to the prestigious universities of the Northeast. The war even transformed American popular culture, as ten thousand European refugees and intellectuals helped change Hollywood from a cultural backwater to an international center of creative achievement.

The broad patterns of disproportionate federal spending and unusually large and numerous military installations have continued to fuel western and southern growth in the four decades since the Japanese surrender. The Highway Trust Fund, for example, which funnels money into the Interstate Highway Program, has built many more roadways and many more miles of pavement per capita or per miles driven in the West and South than in other regions of the country. Similarly, the federal military connection continues to benefit assembly-line workers in Fort Worth and Los Angeles as well as merchants in San Antonio and Charleston.

The pervasive effects of World War II are not alone responsible for the southwestward tilt of the United States in recent decades. Deep structural changes in the American economy resulting from computer technology and communications innovations are also providing a new economic base for sunbelt urbanization. In essence, the information and service industries are less dependent upon the old central business districts and more able to take advantage of the cheaper land and labor costs in the South and West. Not surprisingly, Silicon Valley in California and Research Triangle Park in North Carolina are among the leaders in the new post-industrial and service economy of the United States.

In addition to governmental largess and structural economic shifts, two other developments have also dramatically transformed the region. The first is air conditioning, a technological development that has made life bearable in hot climates during the summer. Although there are no statistical data to confirm the impact of Willis H. Carrier's innovation upon southern life (other than the observation that the list of air-conditioning sales and repair firms in the Houston area runs to forty pages), "air-cooled" movie theaters in the 1930s created an American need for mechanically refrigerated offices, factories, shops, and homes. By the 1960s, three million such units were being produced annually, and even automobile air-conditioners were becoming standard equipment. For obvious reasons, the impact of this invention was particularly great on southerners, who began to expect it whenever they went out. Indeed, vast shopping centers, like Dallas's North Park Mall and Savannah's Oglethorpe Plaza were among the first to adopt completely climate-controlled environments. Appropriately, the Houston Sports Astrodome was completely air-conditioned when it was built in 1965. Such mechanically cooled environments enabled the Sunbelt to overcome its summer heat disadvantage and to capitalize on warmer air during the other seasons of the year.

A second major factor that has fueled Sunbelt population growth has been Hispanic migration. Although Dominicans, Puerto Ricans, and Colombians have recently pushed the Latin population of New York City above 27 percent of the total, and although sizable Hispanic communities now exist in many northern cities, it is in the South and West that Spanish-speaking newcomers have had their greatest impact. Cubans in Miami and Chicanos in San Antonio already make up as much as half of the population, and Mexican-Americans similarly represent the largest and fastest growing minority in a half-dozen major cities. These new groups give a cosmopolitan and international atmosphere to places that previously were more provincial and less sophisticated.

Essays on Sunbelt Cities and Recent Urban America is an important compendium of recent research on these pervasive phenomena. The six prominent historians represented in these pages — Carl Abbott, Robert B. Fairbanks, Robert Fisher, Roger W. Lotchin, Zane L. Miller, and Raymond A. Mohl — provide insights into broad regional patterns as well as specific case studies of such major cities as Dallas, Houston, and San Diego. More importantly, they provide evidence of the usefulness of history to contemporary public policy concerns. Although few Americans think of historians as having anything important to say about the future, I would argue that history in fact offers us the best approach we have for understanding the shape of things to come. This is not because history provides a road map to the unknown world ahead and not because a knowledge of history will keep us from repeating the mistakes of the past. Rather, history is the discipline that can best help us to deal with change, and at the same time help us to identify the deep continuities that link past and present. The South and West have experienced and will continue to experience enormous demographic, physical, and economic transformations. Because we are all on a moving train of history, the essays in this volume will be particularly useful not only in explaining how the South and West came to be as they are now, but also in suggesting possible new directions in the years to come.

RAYMOND A. MOHL

The Transformation of Urban America since the Second World War

DURING THE PAST fifty years, the United States has experienced dramatic social, economic, and political change. Nowhere is this pattern more evident than in the nation's big cities, the vast, sprawling metropolitan areas that dominate the landscape throughout the United States. By the mid-1980s, more than 75 percent of the American people lived in urbanized areas — in cities or their suburbs. In fact, old municipal boundaries had become blurred, as city and suburban populations pushed out the residential periphery far beyond anything imagined in the nineteenth century. The New York City metropolitan area, for instance, now contains more than sixteen million people spread over 3,600 square miles in three states. The Los Angeles urbanized area of about 2,200 square miles is home to almost twelve million people. In the 1980s, some twenty-nine urban centers in the United States each had more than one million residents; many of these "supercities" were created by suburban sprawl, as undeveloped land between existing cities and metropolitan areas was filled in by residential housing and shopping centers and linked to the central cities by the interstate highway system. According to one study, the urbanized northeastern seaboard of the United States will contain about eighty million people, or one-fourth of the nation's population, by the year 2000.[1]

These statistics might at first glance suggest a recent history of continuous and undiminished urban growth and development. The reality, of course, is much more complicated and not uniformly positive or beneficial. The nation's volatile demographic, economic, cultural, and political shifts during the past several decades have shaped the urbanization process and produced vastly different urban outcomes.

Since 1940 huge population shifts within metropolitan regions have become commonplace in the United States. The older central cities of the Northeast and Midwest that experienced the industrial revolution of the late nineteenth century have not only stopped growing, but have been losing population to suburban regions. The classic example is St. Louis, once the western anchor of the industrial heartland, which suffered a 50 percent population loss between 1950 and 1980. Incredible as it may seem, St. Louis's 1980 population of about 450,000 was the same as it had been in 1890.[2]

A similar pattern of population deconcentration could be demonstrated for virtually every major city in the northeastern-midwestern manufacturing belt. The rate of population loss varied, to be sure, but the trend has been evident throughout the so-called "snowbelt" or "rustbelt" region. By 1980, for instance, Detroit lost about one-third of its 1950 population of 1.8 million. Both Pittsburgh and Cleveland lost 37 percent of their population bases in the thirty years after 1950. Boston, Baltimore, Philadelphia, and New York City experienced population declines ranging from 10 to 30 percent by 1980. For smaller cities, the trend of central city population decline was much the same: Buffalo, Providence, Youngstown, Minneapolis, Rochester, Newark, and Jersey City — all old manufacturing cities — each lost between 25 and 37 percent of their 1950 populations.[3]

Several consequences flowed from these massive, central-city population shifts. Most of those fleeing the cities were middle-class and working-class whites, who found in the suburbs a more pleasant lifestyle and an opportunity to demonstrate their upward economic mobility. Thus, while central cities suffered the devastating consequences of a declining population base, the suburban rings surrounding the cities were expanding at an enormous rate, even as early as mid-century. Central city populations were on the downswing, but virtually every major industrial city witnessed large population increases in its metropolitan area between 1950 and 1970. The trend began reversing slightly in a few northeastern and midwestern metropolitan areas between 1970 and 1980. During that decade seven of the thirty-nine largest metropolitan areas contracted in population: New York, Philadelphia, St. Louis, Pittsburgh, Cleveland, Milwaukee, and Buffalo. But generally the metropolitan population trend was upward for the industrial cities during the entire 1950–1980 period, with increases ranging from 16.7 percent in Boston to 44.3 percent in Detroit and 62.6 percent in Baltimore.[4]

As the urban whites fled to the suburban frontier, the shrinking central cities came to be more heavily populated by poor and low-income blacks, Hispanics, and other new immigrant groups. The rapid turnover of urban population left the cities with a declining population base increasingly characterized by precarious economic circumstances. One recent study has demonstrated, for example, that almost two million middle-income people abandoned New York City between 1945 and 1980, while at least that many low-income people moved in. As a result, one writer has argued, New York "has developed a permanent underclass"— people unemployed, underemployed, or dependent on the city's huge welfare system. As the population turned over and the cities aged, housing stock and infrastructure deteriorated. To cite a notable example, between 1950 and 1980 St. Louis lost 25 percent of its housing stock through abandonment. In New York City's South Bronx, population dropped by 50 percent between 1970 and 1980 while tens of thousands of apartment buildings were abandoned, leaving a vast, burned-out, rubble-strewn wasteland where vibrant neighborhoods once stood. Not surprisingly, social problems, conflict, and crime intensified in the central cities affected by these changes. The combination of a declining tax base and higher welfare and service costs pushed some cities like New York and Cleveland to the brink of bankruptcy in the 1970s.[5]

Race is also centrally involved in the recent urban history of the United States. The core cities of the old manufacturing belt have become home to heavy concentrations of black Americans. A great migration of blacks from the rural and urban South to the urban North began during and after the First World War. This flow from the South slowed during the depression era of the 1930s, but surged forward again after 1940. About one and one-half million blacks migrated from the South to the North and West each decade between 1940 and 1970.[6] As whites were moving to the expanding suburbs after the Second World War, aided by favorable federal housing, mortgage, and highway programs, newly arriving blacks were settling in the aging, inner-city neighborhoods abandoned by the new suburbanites. In short, as whites moved out, blacks moved in, and in many places whites moved out because blacks were moving into their old urban neighborhoods. And the process continues. In the aggregate, U.S. central cities lost 7 percent of their white populations during the 1970s, while the black population of central cities gained 15 percent.[7]

This process of population displacement produced a long history of racial tension and conflict as existing neighborhoods turned over.[8] It has also dramatically altered the demographic character of the modern American city. In most of the large industrial cities black population at least doubled between 1950 and 1980; in Boston and Detroit it quadrupled during the same years. Black population majorities or near majorities now prevail in such northern cities as Detroit, Baltimore, Washington, Chicago, Cleveland, St. Louis, Philadelphia, Newark, and Gary. Blacks also became numerically dominant in many southern cities, including Atlanta, Birmingham, Richmond, and New Orleans. In 1890 about 90 percent of black Americans lived in the South, but by the 1970s less than half of the black population remained in the southern region. Similarly, early in the twentieth century blacks were heavily concentrated in rural areas, but by the 1980s they had become the most urbanized of all racial and ethnic groups in the United States.[9]

The post-war American city has other newcomers, too. An enormous Hispanic migration to the urban Southwest and to selected other cities has added to the ethnic, linguistic, and political complexity of urban America. By the mid-1980s, for instance, more than 800,000 Hispanics lived in the Miami metropolitan area, about 45 percent of the entire population. Massive influxes of Cuban exiles and refugees after Fidel Castro's rise to power in 1959 caused a virtual demographic revolution in south Florida.[10]

Miami was not the only destination of Hispanic immigrants. Hispanics made up about 20 percent of New York City's population of nearly seven million in 1980; Puerto Ricans began coming to New York in sizable numbers by mid-century and in more recent years they have been joined by hundreds of thousands of Colombians, Dominicans, and other Latin newcomers. In Los Angeles, Hispanics — largely Mexican and Mexican-American — represented 27.5 percent of the city's entire population in 1980. In Houston, San Antonio, Albuquerque, El Paso, and other southwestern cities the proportion of Hispanic residents is rising rapidly. Even in Chicago, in the center of the industrial snowbelt, Mexican, Cuban, and Puerto Rican newcomers have pushed the Hispanic population above 15 percent in the 1980s. The U.S. Census Bureau has reported, moreover, that the proportion of Hispanics to the total population is rising much more rapidly than are black and white proportions. Since 1980 the Hispanic population in the United States has increased by 16 percent; black population during the same period increased by 8 percent, while white population grew by only 3 percent. Most demographers agree that Hispanics will surpass blacks as the nation's largest minority group by the first decade of the next century.[11]

The modern American city, like its industrial-era counterpart, has also exercised a magnetic attraction for millions of new immigrants. European immigrants provided the labor to propel the industrial revolution in nineteenth-century America, but now the newcomers are arriving from all over the globe, and especially from Third World nations. This new immigration has been accelerated by 1965 legislation abandoning the national-origins quota system that had restricted immigration since the 1920s. From Central America, South America, and the Caribbean, and from Asia, the Middle East, and the Pacific region, the new immigrants have been pouring into the United States, driven by revolution, oppression, famine, or simple economic aspiration. During the 1970s, according to one careful study, net immigration to the United States — legal and illegal — totaled more than seven million people, a figure that surpassed the previous decennial record high of about 6.3 million between 1900 and 1910. As in the past, the city has provided the widest range of opportunities for social adjustment and economic advancement.[12]

In the short span of two decades, native-born Americans have been confronted with a bewildering variety of new ethnic peoples sharing their urban living space. Typically, the largest ethnic immigrant groups in Los Angeles, in addition to Mexicans, are now Iranians, Salvadorans, Japanese, Chinese, Filipinos, Koreans, Vietnamese, Arabs, Israelis, Colombians, Hondurans, Guatemalans, Cubans, Indians, Pakistanis, and Samoans and other Pacific Islanders. As one writer has suggested, Los Angeles is "a racial and cultural borderland" standing "on a frontier between Europe and Asia and between Anglo and Hispanic cultures."[13] In New York City, where one-fourth of the population is now foreign-born, its new immigrants have created "a city more diverse in race, language, and ethnicity than it was at the turn of the century when immigrants from Europe poured through Ellis Island."[14] Much of urban America now shares some of the ethnic and cultural complexity of New York and Los Angeles.

The central cities have become new melting pots — or perhaps boiling pots might be more accurate — and even some older, inner suburbs have received an infusion of black, Hispanic, and new immigrant population. But most of the suburban periphery continues to be overwhelmingly white and mostly middle class. The suburban phenomenon dates back to the middle years of the nineteenth century, when new mass transit technology permitted a more widespread spatial distribution of urban population. Simultaneously, changing conceptions of the role of family and home emphasized the salutary effects of domesticity and private residential space. Romanticized views of nature encouraged Americans to distance themselves from the congestion, commercialism, and other problems associated with urbanization. In addition, the introduction in the mid-nineteenth century of a cheap, new building technology — the so-called "balloon-frame" house — transformed home building into a profitable industry for land speculators and suburban developers.[15]

The suburban pattern intensified in the twentieth century, especially after the introduction of the automobile. The United States has come a long way since 1899, when the *Literary Digest* noted of this newfangled device: "The ordinary 'horseless carriage' is at present a luxury for the wealthy; and altho its price will probably fall in the future, it will never, of course, come into as common use as the bicycle."[16] But the automobile soon triumphed, eventually displacing not only the bicycle but urban mass-transit systems as well. The automobile has restructured the pattern of everyday life in metropolitan America, and it has, moreover, had a powerful and shaping impact upon the landscape of the American city. More than one-third of the land within the Los Angeles metropolitan area has been given over to streets and freeways, traffic interchanges and parking lots; auto-related space increases to two-thirds in the downtown Los Angeles area. And widespread automobile ownership has opened up distant fringe areas for suburban development, stimulating new commuting patterns from suburban homes to city jobs.[17]

Perhaps equally important in the twentieth-century development of suburbia, however, has been the shaping role of the federal government since the mid-1930s. A multibillion dollar federal investment in interstate highway construction encouraged this suburbanization process. Federal housing, mortgage, and tax policies placed a premium on home-owning rather than renting, thus promoting the dispersal of central-city population, particularly the white population. An affluent economy from 1945 through the early 1970s put suburban homeownership within the reach of even the urban working class, which by then had middle-class incomes. More than one hundred million Americans, or over 40 percent of the nation's population, resided in the suburbs by the 1980s — a larger proportion than those living in the central cities. The poor, blacks, and other minorities, of course, have been left behind in the deteriorating inner cities.[18]

Suburbia has grown tremendously since mid-century, but demographers have also noted the more recent growth of rural or non-metropolitan areas — not suburbia, but exurbia. In fact, during the 1970s rural and small-town America grew more rapidly than the urban and suburban regions of the nation, a process now labeled "counterurbanization." As a recent demographic analysis in the influential journal *Scientific American* suggested, in the 1970s the rate of urbanization began to slow for the first time since the depression decade of the 1930s. While metropolitan regions were still growing, the rate of growth had eased considerably, especially for the largest metropolitan areas.[19]

Much of this non-metropolitan growth stemmed from industrial relocation. In the thirty years after 1947, for instance, New York City and Chicago together lost some 900,000 blue-collar manufacturing jobs as a result of shifting American economic and business patterns. By contrast, between 1970 and 1978 about 700,000 new manufacturing jobs were created in non-metropolitan areas, especially in the small towns of the American south. This shift in economic location has speeded the population growth of non-metropolitan America — people follow jobs, a pattern that is likely to continue until rising population fills in empty spaces and these distant areas, too, are pulled into the metropolitan orbit. For the present, however, demographers see these new small-town, non-metropolitan clusters as "small centers of urban culture transplanted to the countryside and enabled to survive by recent advances in communications, transportation, and methods of industrial production."[20]

The rise of non-metropolitan America reflects the shifting character of the American urban and industrial economy. The manufactur-

ing cities of the industrial heartland have experienced dramatic transformation, even significant decline in many cases. Production shifted
to non-metropolitan areas, particularly in the American south. As a
1978 economic study noted: "Over the past three decades, Texas, Florida, the Carolinas, Georgia, Oklahoma, Arizona, and other Sunbelt
states have been transformed into major manufacturing centers." Industrial production has also moved to less developed nations around
the world. Multinational corporations have shut down factories in the
old industrial belt and transferred production to Mexico, South Korea,
Taiwan, Singapore, and Third World nations. High labor costs in the
United States, the competition of cheaper or better-made foreign im-
ports, higher energy costs in the 1970s and early 1980s, and numerous
corporate mergers all resulted in a massive reorganization of the American economy. A renewed drive for productivity and profit prompted
corporate decision-making that led to factory closings, heavy blue-collar
unemployment, and troubled times in such basic industries as textiles,
automobiles, and steel.[21]

The process of "deindustrialization"— the dismantling and abandonment of the industrial infrastructure — has been proceeding for several decades. Large cities with diverse economies such as Boston, Philadelphia, New York, and Chicago have adjusted to the post-industrial
economy, but single-industry cities such as steel-producing Gary and
Youngstown have withered economically. Declining fortunes in the steel
industry have produced 30 percent or more unemployment in Gary,
a formerly white-ethnic, blue-collar town that is now about 80 percent black. In Youngstown, three steel companies shut down their blast
furnaces and rolling mills, actually dynamiting them to the ground,
selling off the remains for scrap metal, and adding tens of thousands
of steel workers to the unemployment rolls in the process. Akron,
Ohio — once the rubber capital of the world — no longer produces automobile tires. The major rubber companies retain their corporate offices
in Akron, but tire manufacturing has been decentralized, primarily
to rural southern states where labor costs are lower. Meanwhile, some
40,000 rubber workers in Akron have lost their jobs. This is not an un-
typical story, and aging industrial cities like Gary, Akron, and Youngstown that have failed to adapt to the transformation of the American
economy face a difficult future. As one urban scholar has suggested,

"there is no reason to believe that aging industrial cities will be able to revitalize unless they are able to develop a post industrial high-technology or service activity base."[22]

As more traditional forms of manufacturing and production declined, a post-industrial and service-oriented economy rose to take its place. This process of economic transformation was well under way in the aftermath of the Second World War. In fact, as early as 1955 blue-collar manufacturing laborers were outnumbered by white-collar, professional, and service workers. By the 1980s, the service economy employed twice as many workers as the manufacturing and production sector. Basic manufacturing has deindustrialized over the past thirty to forty years, but the American economy has been powered by a tremendous expansion in the post-industrial service sector. Since the mid-1960s, over thirty-eight million new service jobs have been created in the United States. The service economy now employs over seventy-five million American workers, about 70 percent of the American workforce. Many of these service jobs are held by women who entered the labor force in large numbers in the post-war era. An enormous expansion in educational services, medical services and health care, information and data processing, a wide array of business services, communications, computers, and other forms of high technology have all been central to the rapidly growing service economy. The same is true of recreational, entertainment, and tourist activities, the travel and restaurant industries — especially the ubiquitous fast-food chains — and anything related to the vast consumer appetites of the American people. Governmental services have become a particularly important ingredient in the new American economy. By the 1980s, government at all levels in the United States employed more than sixteen million civilian workers.[23]

The fortunes of the modern American city have been bound up in the structural transformation of the American economy. One consequence of this economic change can be seen in the declining populations of the older, heavily industrial cities of the Northeast and Midwest. Central city employment has suffered, too, because newcomers — blacks, Hispanics, and other new immigrants — often lack the training or skills required for most high-tech jobs in the information-processing sector. The large number of low-skill, or "no-tech," service jobs created in the past two decades have also been low paying jobs, leaving the aging central cities with chronic problems of underemployment, unemployment, poverty, and social welfare. The older central cities have become, one study has asserted, the "wasteland of the bypassed economy." The modern American city, in short, has been unable to avoid the human and social consequences of the post-industrial economic transformation.[24]

Also linked to the shifting American economy is the remarkable rise of the sunbelt cities of the South and Southwest. In 1890, and again in 1920, nine of the ten largest U.S. cities were located in the Northeast and Midwest. The same was true in 1950. But forty years of shifting economic and demographic activity has brought enormous change to the American urban system. Between 1940 and 1980, for example, the sunbelt states grew in population at almost triple the pace of the old industrial-belt states. Cities like Miami, Tampa, Atlanta, Houston, Dallas, Phoenix, and San Diego all at least quadrupled in population during the same forty-year period. By 1980, five of the ten largest American cities were located in the Southwest: Los Angeles, Houston, Dallas, Phoenix, and San Diego.[25]

These sunbelt cities never experienced the nineteenth-century industrial revolution. They are twentieth-century automobile cities, less densely settled and more widely spread over the urban and suburban landscape. Aided by mid-twentieth-century highway building and almost universal automobile ownership, sunbelt city populations pushed out the urban and metropolitan periphery to an extent unimagined in the industrial era. Annexation of surrounding territory, which had virtually ceased for older cities by the early twentieth century, became a way of life in the urban Southwest. Between 1950 and 1980, for instance, Houston grew from 160 to 556 square miles, Oklahoma City from 51 to 603 square miles, and Phoenix from 17 to 324 square miles. By contrast, Philadelphia has remained stable at 130 square miles since the 1850s, St. Louis has not added to its 62 square miles since 1876, and New York City's 299-square-mile territory has remained unchanged since 1898.[26] In one way, however, the newer southwestern cities are similar to the older northern cities: despite massive annexations, the peripheral suburban regions of the metropolitan Sunbelt are still growing more rapidly than the central city areas.

The explosive urban development of the sunbelt South and Southwest has stemmed from several decisive factors. Recent historical research has identified the crucially important role of federal government military and defense spending in the promotion of sunbelt urban expansion, as Roger W. Lotchin's essay in this volume describes. Urban and military interests converged as early as 1919, when the main U.S. naval fleet was shifted to the Pacific Ocean. Political and business leaders in San Francisco, Los Angeles, and San Diego leaped at this new opportunity, for vast military expenditures and big military payrolls boosted local economies and spurred urban development. During the 1920s and 1930s, California's largest cities developed important symbiotic alliances with the federal military establishment.[27]

Urban growth in the sunshine regions began in earnest during the Second World War, when the federal government built dozens of new air bases, naval bases, and military training facilities in the southern and western states. Almost 40 percent of total wartime expenditures for military facilities went to the South, with much of the rest going to the West and Southwest. The federal government invested an additional four to five billion dollars in southern war-production plants and factories, substantially increasing the region's traditionally weak industrial capacity. This vast federal investment persisted into the cold war era. Heavy military and defense spending has continued to sustain prosperity and urban growth in the sunbelt region. From San Francisco, Los Angeles, and San Diego in California to Pensacola, Tampa, Miami, and Jacksonville in Florida, the sunbelt cities have profited enormously from the federal military connection. Military airfields surrounded San Antonio, aircraft production boosted Seattle and Los Angeles, big U.S. Navy facilities fueled growth and prosperity in San Diego and Jacksonville, and the aerospace industry propelled economic and urban expansion in California, Texas, and Florida. Through vast military and defense spending over fifty or more years, urban historian Carl Abbott has written, the federal government "massively redistributed resources among the nation's regions and cities."[28]

It should also be clear that the emerging sunbelt cities were benefiting from the deep structural changes taking place in the American economy. With little inherited from the industrial era, the sunbelt cities have grown in tandem with the new post-industrial and service economy. Major business firms have shifted their corporate headquarters from northern to southern or western cities. Such high-technology industries as computers and communications equipment, electronic components, and aerospace manufacturing provided an important new economic base for sunbelt urbanization, as did energy development in the southwestern "oil patch." The information and service economy that surged in the 1960s and after no longer relied on a few major northeastern centers. Like the railroad in the nineteenth century, the computer has become the technological catalyst for a new era. Modern computer technology and communications equipment now link the regions of the nation in a web of instantaneous transmissions of data and decision-making. As the urban geographer Brian J. L. Berry noted: "The time-eliminating properties of long-distance communication and the space-spanning capacities of the new communication technologies are combining to concoct a solvent that has dissolved the agglomeration advantages of the industrial metropolis." In the industrial age, the railroad liberated the city from locations with access to water transportation; now the computer and other new communication technologies have encouraged urban development in the once distant or isolated regions of the nation.[29]

Shifting cultural patterns also were at work in the surge to the Sunbelt. As post-war prosperity roared ahead after 1950, the amenities factor increasingly came into play. As early as 1954, scholars began to recognize the emergence of a "frontier of comfort" in the rapidly growing states of California, Florida, and Arizona. Americans with more leisure time and higher disposable incomes avidly pursued outdoor recreational interests such as golf, tennis, boating and water sports, camping, and hiking, all of which could be enjoyed year round in the sunny climes of Florida or California. Moreover, as the commercialization of amusement swept the nation in the 1960s and 1970s, every American child and many adults wanted a trip to Disneyland in California or Disney World in Florida. The completion of the federal interstate highway system permitted even working-class Americans to become winter vacationers in the distant sunshine regions of the country. And like the hundreds of thousands of wartime servicemen who returned to settle in the Sunbelt, vacationers and visitors increasingly became permanent residents. The rapid spread of home air-conditioning in the 1950s made permanent residence in hot and humid climates acceptable. Finally, as Americans lived longer and retired earlier, the elderly began a migration of their own to Florida, Arizona, southern

California, Hawaii, and other retirement havens in the urban and suburban Sunbelt.[30]

For whatever reason, five and one-half million Americans migrated from the Northeast and Midwest to the sunbelt regions during the 1970s. The Florida story is especially dramatic. In the late 1980s, more than one thousand people move to the state of Florida every day of the year. With about twelve million people in 1987 and growing more than twice as fast as the national population, Florida is already 85 percent urban and continues to urbanize more rapidly than any other large state. Five of the nation's ten fastest-growing metropolitan areas are now located in Florida. Demographers have projected Florida's population at over twenty-two million by the time the post-war baby-boomers reach retirement age early in the twenty-first century. Florida has become the quintessential urban state of the post-industrial age.[31]

The impetus for sunbelt urbanization, then, has come from federal military spending, the transformation of the American economy, and shifting cultural patterns of the American people. The regional redistribution of population and economic activities seems well entrenched, if not irreversible. In the post-industrial era, the looming and almost interchangeable glass and steel skyscrapers of Atlanta, Miami, Houston, Dallas, and Los Angeles suggest the power and persistence of the information age. There have been some setbacks in some places, to be sure, as reflected in the impact of recent oil price declines upon the economic vitality of the Houston area. Nor have all parts of the Sunbelt shared equally in prosperity and growth: much of the rural and small-town South, for example, is mired in economic stagnation and has been left behind.

Most analysts, nevertheless, expect prevailing regional growth patterns to persist at least into the near future. According to many economic and demographic projections, urban areas in Florida, Arizona, California, and possibly Texas will grow more rapidly than any others over the rest of the twentieth century and probably beyond. The older, generally uncompetitive "smokestack" industries will decline further, and many more factories and mills will close down. Newer "clean" industries and service businesses will continue to concentrate in the sunshine states, which generally have low taxes, cheap labor, weakly developed labor unions, more amenities, and political climates favorable to economic growth and corporate activity. As one scholarly sur-

vey put it, "all indications are that for the rest of the century the factors that fashioned the Sunbelt phenomenon after World War II will
continue to give the region relative advantages over the Frostbelt."[32]

Some of the older northern cities with diverse economies have adjusted to the new economic transformations. Boston, Chicago, and New
York, for instance, remain vibrant economic and business centers even
as their peripheral areas, now known as the "outer city," surge ahead
as well. But as in the past, people have been moving in response to
economic opportunity and job openings, and the process is likely to
continue into the future. As urban historian James F. Richardson has
suggested, "now, and for the forseeable future, it looks as if those cities
that people want to live in will be those that generate the greatest
employment opportunities."[33] Regional and urban growth of the Sunbelt, it seems clear, reflects some long-term economic and migration
patterns.

Urban demographic and economic changes have been paralleled
by important transformations in the political life of the nation, both
at the federal and the municipal levels. One of the big changes in
twentieth-century America has been the tremendous expansion of federal government power and influence. Beginning in the New Deal era
of the 1930s, the federal government initiated for the first time a political partnership with the cities. President Franklin D. Roosevelt built
a new Democratic Party coalition, relying heavily on the urban elec-
torate for his political success. During the Great Depression, federal
initiative, intervention, and activism became the order of the day. New
welfare and public works programs along with a river of social legislation flowed out of New Deal Washington, much of it aimed at city
people and urban problems.[34]

From the age of Roosevelt to the beginning of the Reagan era, the
cities sought out and became reliant on the federal connection. Public
housing, urban renewal, new mass transit facilities, highway and public works construction, expanded public welfare programs — all were
funded with massive infusions of federal dollars. In the 1960s, President Lyndon B. Johnson revived the New Deal spirit with his Great
Society initiatives. The war on poverty, the model cities program, and
a vast array of new social agencies and community development efforts all had their roots in the cities. About the same time, however,
television and the print media discovered an "urban crisis," especially

when explosions of racial violence rocked cities across the nation from Harlem to Watts, from Chicago and Detroit to Newark and Washington, D.C.[35]

The burned-out black ghettos of the late 1960s suggested to many the failure of federal urban policy. In fact, the federal programs that shaped urban America after the mid-1930s did not always have positive effects. A national transportation policy emphasizing interstate highways and the automobile, rather than urban mass transit, ultimately siphoned population and economic activities away from the central city and toward the urban periphery. Urban expressways tore through existing neighborhoods, demolishing still good housing and leaving huge, useless empty spaces in the urban cores. Moreover, extensive urban renewal programs since the 1950s have destroyed inner-city housing, but did not always deliver on promised new low-rent housing units for displaced families. In some quarters, urban renewal became nothing more than black removal.[36]

Federal housing policies had particularly devastating consequences. Huge public housing facilities such as the Pruitt-Igoe project in St. Louis, for instance, turned into large scale disasters as new high-rise ghettos became virtually unlivable. Twenty years after its construction in the 1950s, this enormous public housing project of thirty-three eleven-story apartment buildings was dynamited to the ground.[37]

Some federal housing programs, such as those of the Home Owners Loan Corporation and the Federal Housing Administration, utilized a residential appraisal system that led to "redlining," the practice by banks and other lending institutions of refusing to grant mortgages or other loans in older, poorer, and black neighborhoods. The Federal Housing Administration, according to housing scholar Charles Abrams, "set itself up as the protector of the all-white neighborhood" and "became the vanguard of white supremacy and racial purity — in the North as well as the South." The combined impact of these federal housing and mortgage policies was to encourage white residential flight from the central city, while hastening the racial segregation and physical decay of inner-city neighborhoods.[38] Thus, a new era of federal-city cooperation emerged by the mid-twentieth century, but unanticipated and often negative consequences flowed from the implementation of the new federal programs.

In recent years the frustrations of urban policy-making, along with a changing national political climate, have brought a dramatic reversal of public policy and federal activism in the urban arena. In the late 1970s the Carter administration moved haltingly toward the establishment of a national urban policy based on "self-help" rather than extensive federal financial support. The Carter program was never fully implemented, however, and many critics perceived this policy-making effort as an attempt to write off the aging industrial cities, with their devastated economies and serious social problems. The Reagan era witnessed massive federal cutbacks in the public works and social programs that cities had come to rely on from the 1930s. Turning back the governmental involvement that marked the New Deal, the Reagan administration sought to restore social policy to the marketplace. With fewer financial resources and greater responsibilities, the cities are once more approaching crisis stage, especially in the provision of human and social services and in the maintenance of an aging and deteriorating infrastructure.[39]

These changes have come at a time when the municipal political pattern is experiencing major transformations. The shifting demography of the cities has now been reflected in the political structure. As the black and Hispanic populations of the central cities have surged, so have representatives of these groups come to dominate urban politics in many cities. Beginning in 1967, when black mayors were first elected in Cleveland and Gary, blacks have succeeded to the mayoralty in Detroit, Philadelphia, Chicago, Newark, New Orleans, Los Angeles, Atlanta, Richmond, Charlotte, Birmingham, and Washington, D.C., to name only a few major cities. By the mid-1980s, Hispanic mayors had been elected in Miami, Tampa, San Antonio, and Denver.[40]

The old political machines that dominated such cities as Chicago and Detroit have fallen into disarray, as their white working-class and ethnic constituencies moved to the suburbs. The machines had traditionally provided jobs and services to the urban poor, but post-war prosperity and suburban migration transformed the political game. As historian Arnold R. Hirsch has suggested, "urban machines died in the twentieth century, in large part, not because the poor disappeared, but because they became increasingly non-white." Meanwhile, black political leaders have built new coalitions with Hispanic voters and white liberals and anti-machine reformers. The old Chicago Democratic machine, for instance, kept Mayor Richard J. Daley in power for twenty years; now the Chicago party machine is moribund, internally divided, and bitterly racist in its political outlook. Mayor Harold Washington's sudden death in November of 1987 cut short a promising interracial and anti-machine political movement, but Chicago politics will never be the same as a result of his reformist administration.[41]

Sweeping political transformations have affected sunbelt cities, too. Traditionally lacking powerful ethnic blocs and a pattern of machine politics, the sunbelt cities most often were controlled politically by local business and professional elites. Motivated by booster mentality, the urban elites sought to govern in the interests of the downtown business community, at least until the 1950s. The rapid post-war growth of suburbia, however, resulted in newer forms of urban political conflict in which city and suburb struggled for dominance and control. Many of the political issues of the time were spatial, or territorial, such as where highways or public housing would be located, or what areas would be annexed or remain independent, or which schools were to be integrated by busing. Some urban regions resolved these conflicts with experiments in new governmental structure, as in the creation of metropolitan government of Miami–Dade County in 1957, and city-county consolidations in Nashville in 1962 and Jacksonville in 1967. But most metropolitan areas simply muddled along without ever fully resolving the city-suburban political controversies.[42]

The vast demographic changes within the cities since the 1960s have now pushed urban politics into a new and more participatory phase, one in which city-suburban battles have been supplanted by issues revolving around race, ethnicity, and neighborhood. As Carl Abbott has observed, neighborhoods and local communities have now "become focal points for political action."[43] In Miami, for instance, with its "tri-ethnic" population of whites, blacks, and Hispanics, virtually every local political issue is perceived in terms of race and ethnicity.

Typically, a bitter struggle over bilingualism has wracked Miami since 1980, when a white citizens' group successfully advanced an anti-bilingualism ordinance by a petition and referendum process. The key section of the ordinance stated that "the expenditure of county funds for the purpose of utilizing any language other than English, or promoting any culture other than that of the United States" would be prohibited; it also stipulated that only the English language could be

used in official meetings, hearings, and publications. The language issue is especially controversial in Miami because the Cubans and other
Hispanic newcomers have given no indication of giving up their native
Spanish, even in the second or later generations. The non-Hispanic
whites — or Anglos as they generally are called in Miami — are worried, both about language and about growing Cuban political power
in the city. Many Anglos back drives for constitutional amendments
to make English the official language of the United States and of the
state of Florida. Ironically, the anti-bilingualism movement in Miami
was led by a multilingual Jewish immigrant from the Ukraine, who
complained that she no longer felt like an American in Dade County.[44]

Dozens of other local political issues in Miami and elsewhere are
loaded with this sort of ethnic tension and community conflict. In cities
as diverse as Chicago and Miami, ethnic and racial emotions have
boiled over into the political arena. As the newcomers to the cities
from Asia, Latin America, the Caribbean and the Pacific Basin become citizens and voters, this new pattern of pluralistic urban politics
will almost certainly intensify.

The modern American city has been dramatically altered and re-
shaped during the past forty years. In many ways, American urbanites
are much better off than their counterparts of 1900. Contemporary
city people generally are healthier, better housed, better educated, and
more effectively served by urban government. Most are better off finan-
cially, enjoy more creature comforts, and have more leisure time than
in the past. But as this discussion has suggested, serious and unresolved
problems continue to plague the contemporary American city. Issues
of race and ethnicity have fragmented the city socially and politically.
Blacks, in particular, have never fully shared in the promise of American life. Millions of immigrants from the Third World pose new challenges to the American ideal of assimilation. Divisions between city
and suburb have prevented unified attacks on the governmental and
other problems that commonly affect entire urban or metropolitan regions. The idea of planning of any sort at any level of government con-
fronts a long and powerful tradition of individual ownership and private action. The economic dislocations associated with the shift from
an industrial to an information and service economy have been left
to the workings of the free market to resolve. Health, housing, education, and social welfare policies generally have been shamefully ne-

glected. An effective public policy—a national urban policy—is urgently needed to address these serious issues.[45]

History deals with the ways things change over time and with the causes and consequences of change. Modern urban history brings us an understanding of the contemporary American city and of how we have arrived at our current state of urban affairs. As a guide to the future it is less useful. But it seems safe to assert that the city will remain at the frontier of dynamic social, economic, and political change in the United States.

NOTES

1. Larry Long and Diana DeAre, "The Slowing of Urbanization in the U.S.," *Scientific American* 249 (July, 1983): 37.

2. U.S. Census, 1950 and 1980; Ira S. Lowry, "The Dismal Future of Central Cities," in Arthur P. Solomon, ed., *The Prospective City: Economic, Population, Energy, and Environmental Developments* (Cambridge: MIT Press, 1980), pp. 161–203.

3. U.S. Census, 1950 and 1980; George Sternlieb and James W. Hughes, "The Changing Demography of the Central City," *Scientific American* 243 (August, 1980): 40–45.

4. U.S. Census, 1950, 1970, and 1980; Bruce M. Stave, ed., *Modern Industrial Cities: History, Policy, and Survival* (Beverly Hills, Calif.: Sage Publications, 1981), p. 183. On metropolitan/suburban expansion, see also Peter O. Muller, *Contemporary Suburban America* (Englewood Cliffs, N.J.: Prentice Hall, 1981); Kenneth T. Jackson, *Crabgrass Frontier: The Suburbanization of the United States* (New York: Oxford University Press, 1985).

5. Ken Auletta, *The Streets Were Paved with Gold* (New York: Random House, 1979), p. 17; Gary Ross Mormino, *Immigrants on the Hill: Italian-Americans in St. Louis, 1882–1982* (Urbana: University of Illinois Press, 1986), p. 11; William K. Tabb, *The Long Default: New York City and the Urban Fiscal Crisis* (New York: Monthly Review Press, 1982), pp. 102–103. See also Solomon, ed., *The Prospective City*, and for New York City's well-publicized troubles, Charles R. Morris, *The Cost of Good Intentions: New York City and the Liberal Experiment, 1960–1975* (New York: W. W. Norton, 1980).

6. For the black migration, see Reynolds Farley, "The Urbanization of Negroes in the United States," *Journal of Social History* 1 (Spring, 1968): 241–58; and Daniel M. Johnson and Rex R. Campbell, *Black Migration in America: A Social Demographic History* (Durham, N.C.: Duke University Press, 1981).

7. Eric E. Lampard, "The Nature of Urbanization," in William Sharpe and Leonard Wallock, eds., *Visions of the Modern City: Essays in History, Art, and Literature* (New York: Heyman Center for the Humanities, Columbia University, 1983), p. 94.

8. Recent studies exploring the tensions created by the racial turnover of urban neighborhoods include Thomas L. Philpott, *The Slum and the Ghetto: Neighborhood Deterioration and Middle-Class Reform, Chicago, 1880–1930* (New York: Oxford University Press, 1978); Arnold R. Hirsch, *Making the Second Ghetto: Race and Housing*

in Chicago, 1940–1960 (Cambridge: Cambridge University Press, 1983); and Dominic J. Capeci, Jr., *Race Relations in Wartime Detroit: The Sojourner Truth Housing Controversy, 1937–1942* (Philadelphia: Temple University Press, 1984).

9. U.S. Census, 1980. For historiographical analyses of black urbanization and its consequences, see Zane L. Miller, "The Black Experience in the Modern American City," in Raymond A. Mohl and James F. Richardson, eds., *The Urban Experience: Themes in American History* (Belmont, Calif.: Wadsworth Publishing Co., 1973), pp. 44–60; Kenneth L. Kusmer, "The Black Urban Experience in American History," in Darlene Hine, ed., *The State of Afro-American History: Past, Present, and Future* (Baton Rouge: Louisiana State University Press, 1986), pp. 91–122.

10. Thomas D. Boswell and James R. Curtis, *The Cuban-American Experience: Culture, Images, and Perspectives* (Totowa, N.J.: Rowman and Allanheld, 1983); Raymond A. Mohl, "Miami: The Ethnic Cauldron," in Richard M. Bernard and Bradley R. Rice, eds., *Sunbelt Cities: Politics and Growth since World War II* (Austin: University of Texas Press, 1983), pp. 58–99; Mohl, "Miami: American Gateway," in Gail F. Stern, ed., *Freedom's Doors: Immigrant Ports of Entry to the United States* (Philadelphia: Balch Institute for Ethnic Studies, 1986), pp. 69–80.

11. U.S. Census, 1980; *Wall Street Journal*, May 21, 1987, p. 7. For general information on the Hispanic population, see Joan Moore and Harry Pachon, *Hispanics in the United States* (Englewood Cliffs, N.J.: Prentice Hall, 1985); A. J. Jaffe, et al., *The Changing Demography of Spanish Americans* (New York: Academic Press, 1980).

12. Douglas S. Massey, "Dimensions of the New Immigration to the United States and the Prospects for Assimilation," *Annual Review of Sociology* 7 (1981): 57–85; David M. Reimers, *Still the Golden Door: The Third World Comes to America* (New York: Columbia University Press, 1985); Thomas Kessner and Betty Boyd Caroli, *Today's Immigrants, Their Stories: A New Look at the Newest Americans* (New York: Oxford University Press, 1981).

13. Kurt Andersen, "The New Ellis Island," *Time*, June 13, 1983, pp. 18–25; Elliott R. Barkan, "Los Angeles: A New Ellis Island," in Stern, ed., *Freedom's Doors*, pp. 81–90; David L. Clark, "Improbable Los Angeles," in Bernard and Rice, eds., *Sunbelt Cities*, p. 269.

14. Quoted in *Miami News*, May 7, 1981. See also Elliott R. Barkan, "New York City: Immigrant Depot, Immigrant City," in Stern, ed., *Freedom's Doors*, pp. 1–12.

15. Jackson, *Crabgrass Frontier*, pp. 20–137; Sam Bass Warner, Jr., *Streetcar Suburbs: The Process of Growth in Boston, 1870–1900* (Cambridge: MIT Press and Harvard University Press, 1962); David Schuyler, *The New Urban Landscape: The Redefinition of City Form in Nineteenth-Century America* (Baltimore: Johns Hopkins University Press, 1986), pp. 24–36. See also Michael H. Ebner, "Re-Reading Suburban America: Urban Population Deconcentration, 1810–1980," *American Quarterly* 37 (1985): 366–81.

16. *Literary Digest*, October 14, 1899, quoted in Jackson, *Crabgrass Frontier*, p. 157.

17. Stanley Malloch, "The Origins of the Decline of Urban Mass Transportation in the United States, 1890–1930," *Urbanism Past and Present* 8 (Summer 1979): 1–17; Jackson, *Crabgrass Frontier*, pp. 157–71, 246–71. For the growing literature on the automobile and its impact, begin with the following: Mark S. Foster, *From Streetcar to Superhighway: American City Planners and Urban Transportation, 1900–1940* (Philadelphia: Temple University Press, 1981); Howard L. Preston, *Automobile Age Atlanta: The Making of a Southern Metropolis, 1900–1935* (Athens: University of Georgia Press, 1979); Paul Barrett, *The Automobile and Urban Transit: The Formation of Public Pol-*

icy in Chicago, 1900–1930 (Philadelphia: Temple University Press, 1983); David J. St. Clair, *The Motorization of American Cities* (New York: Praeger, 1986). For the inter- state highway system, see Mark H. Rose, *Interstate: Express Highway Politics, 1941– 1956* (Lawrence: University Press of Kansas, 1979); and Bruce E. Seely, *Building the American Highway System: Engineers as Policy Makers* (Philadelphia: Temple Uni- versity Press, 1987).

18. Mark I. Gelfand, "Cities, Suburbs, and Government Policy," in Robert H. Bremner and Gary W. Reichard, eds., *Reshaping America: Society and Institutions, 1945–1960* (Columbus: Ohio State University Press, 1982), pp. 261–81; Zane L. Miller and Patricia M. Melvin, *The Urbanization of Modern America*, 2nd ed. (San Diego: Harcourt Brace Jovanovich, 1987), pp. 162–72.

19. Long and DeAre, "The Slowing of Urbanization in the U.S.," pp. 31–39. See also Brian J. L. Berry, "The Counter-Urbanization Process: Urban America since 1970," in Berry, ed., *Urbanization and Counter-Urbanization* (Beverly Hills, Calif.: Sage Pub- lications, 1976), pp. 7–30; Amos H. Hawley and Sara Mills Mazie, eds., *Nonmetropoli- tan America in Transition* (Chapel Hill: University of North Carolina Press, 1981).

20. John D. Kasarda, "Caught in the Web of Change," *Society* 21 (November– December, 1983): 43–44; Long and DeAre, "The Slowing of Urbanization in the U.S.," p. 36.

21. Bernard L. Weinstein and Robert E. Firestine, *Regional Growth and Decline in the United States: The Rise of the Sunbelt and the Decline of the Northeast* (New York: Praeger, 1978), p. 19. On the structural transformation of the American economy, see also Ira C. Magaziner and Robert B. Reich, *Minding America's Business: The De- cline and Rise of the American Economy* (New York: Harcourt Brace Jovanovich, 1982); Robert B. Reich, *The Next American Frontier* (New York: Times Books, 1983); Michael J. Piore and Charles F. Sabel, *The Second Industrial Divide: Possibilities for Prosperity* (New York: Basic Books, 1984).

22. Brian J. L. Berry, "Inner-City Futures: An American Dilemma Revisited," in Stave, ed., *Modern Industrial Cities*, p. 218. On deindustrialization, see Barry Blue- stone and Bennett Harrison, *The Deindustrialization of America: Plant Closings, Com- munity Abandonment, and the Dismantling of Basic Industry* (New York: Basic Books, 1982). On Gary, see Raymond A. Mohl and Neil Betten, *Steel City: Urban and Ethnic Patterns in Gary, Indiana, 1906–1950* (New York: Holmes and Meier, 1986). For Youngs- town's special problems, consult Staughton Lynd, *The Fight Against Shutdowns: Youngs- town's Steel Mill Closings* (San Pedro, Calif.: Singlejack Books, 1982). On the rubber tire industry in Akron, see Charles A. Jeszeck, "Plant Dispersion and Collective Bar- gaining in the Rubber Tire Industry," Ph.D. dissertation, University of California, Berkeley, 1982.

23. Anatole Kaletsky and Guy de Jonquieres, "Why a Service Economy Is No Panacea," *Financial Times* (London), May 22, 1987, p. 12. On the post-industrial so- ciety generally, see Daniel Bell, *The Coming of Post-Industrial Society* (New York: Basic Books, 1973); Marvin Harris, *America Now: The Anthropology of a Changing Culture* (New York: Simon and Schuster, 1981).

24. President's Commission for a National Agenda for the Eighties, *Urban Amer- ica in the Eighties: Perspectives and Prospects* (Washington, D.C.: U.S. Government Printing Office, 1980); Kasarda, "Caught in the Web of Change," pp. 41–47; Sternlieb and Hughes, "The Changing Demography of the Central City," pp. 43, 45; Kaletsky and Jonquieres, "Why a Service Economy Is No Panacea," p. 12; "Service Area in a Fog," *The Economist* 303 (May 23, 1987): 75.

25. U.S. Census, 1950 and 1980. On sunbelt urban growth generally, see Bernard and Rice, eds., *Sunbelt Cities;* David C. Perry and Alfred J. Watkins, eds., *The Rise of the Sunbelt Cities* (Beverly Hills, Calif.: Sage Publications, 1977); Carl Abbott, *The New Urban America: Growth and Politics in Sunbelt Cities* (Chapel Hill: University of North Carolina Press, 1981); David R. Goldfield, *Cotton Fields and Skyscrapers: Southern City and Region, 1607–1980* (Baton Rouge: Louisiana State University Press, 1982); and Bradford Luckingham, *The Urban Southwest: A Profile History of Albuquerque, El Paso, Phoenix, and Tucson* (El Paso: Texas Western Press, 1982).

26. For statistics on city size in square miles, see U.S. Bureau of the Census, *County and City Data Book* (Washington, D.C.: U.S. Government Printing Office, 1983). For a historical analysis of the politics of annexation, see Jon C. Teaford, *City and Suburb: The Political Fragmentation of Metropolitan America, 1850–1970* (Baltimore: Johns Hopkins University Press, 1979), and Jackson, *Crabgrass Frontier*, pp. 138–56.

27. Roger W. Lotchin, "The Metropolitan-Military Complex in Comparative Perspective," *Journal of the West* 18 (July, 1979): 19–30; Lotchin, "The City and the Sword: San Francisco and the Rise of the Metropolitan-Military Complex," *Journal of American History* 65 (March, 1979): 996–1020.

28. James C. Cobb, *Industrialization and Southern Society, 1877–1984* (Lexington: University Press of Kentucky, 1984), pp. 51–52; Carl Abbott, *Urban America in the Modern Age: 1920 to the Present* (Arlington Heights, Ill.: Harlan Davidson, 1987), p. 103. On the links between military/defense spending and urban development, see also Roger W. Lotchin, ed., *The Martial Metropolis: U.S. Cities in War and Peace* (New York: Praeger, 1984); Philip J. Funigiello, *The Challenge to Urban Liberalism: Federal-City Relations during World War II* (Knoxville: University of Tennessee Press, 1978); and Gerald D. Nash, *The American West Transformed: The Impact of the Second World War* (Bloomington: Indiana University Press, 1985).

29. Berry, "Inner-City Futures," p. 207; Abbott, *Urban America in the Modern Age*, pp. 99–105; Weinstein and Firestine, *Regional Growth and Decline in the United States*, p. 130. For the shifting economic pattern in one sunbelt city, see Raymond A. Mohl, "Changing Economic Patterns in the Miami Metropolitan Area, 1940–1980," *Tequesta: The Journal of the Historical Association of Southern Florida* 42 (1982): 63–73. On the general pattern of economic change, see also George Sternlieb and James W. Hughes, *Post-Industrial America: Metropolitan Decline and Inter-Regional Job Shifts* (New Brunswick, N.J.: Center for Urban Policy Research, 1975). For a historiographical analysis, see Charles P. Roland, "Sun Belt Prosperity and Urban Growth," in John B. Boles and Evelyn Thomas Nolen, eds., *Interpreting Southern History* (Baton Rouge: Louisiana State University Press, 1987), pp. 434–53.

30. Edward Ullman, "Amenities as a Factor in Regional Growth," *Geographical Review* 44 (1954): 119–32; James E. Vance, Jr., "California and the Search for the Ideal," *Annals of the Association of American Geographers* 62 (June, 1972): 185–210; Raymond Arsenault, "The End of the Long Hot Summer: The Air Conditioner and Southern Culture," *Journal of Southern History* 50 (November, 1984): 597–628; Jeanne C. Biggar, "The Sunning of America: Migration to the Sunbelt," *Population Bulletin* 24 (March 1979): 1–42. On one retirement community in Florida, see Frances FitzGerald, *Cities on a Hill: A Journey through Contemporary American Cultures* (New York: Simon and Schuster, 1986), pp. 203–45.

31. Raymond A. Mohl, "The Urbanization of Florida," in Paul S. George, ed., *A Guide to the History of Florida* (Westport, Conn.: Greenwood Press, 1989); T. D. Allman, *Miami: City of the Future* (New York: Atlantic Monthly Press, 1987), p. 363.

32. Bradley R. Rice and Richard M. Bernard, "Introduction," in Bernard and Rice, eds., *Sunbelt Cities*, p. 20. On industrial shifts to the sunshine regions, see also James C. Cobb, *The Selling of the South: The Southern Crusade for Industrial Development, 1936–1980* (Baton Rouge: Louisiana State University Press, 1982).

33. Peter O. Muller, *The Outer City: Geographical Consequences of the Urbanization of the Suburbs* (Washington, D.C.: Association of American Geographers, 1976); James F. Richardson, "The Evolving Dynamics of American Urban Development," in Gary Gappert and Richard V. Knight, eds., *Cities in the 21st Century* (Beverly Hills, Calif.: Sage Publications, 1982), p. 44.

34. On federal interventionism and the urban, pro-growth coalition since the 1930s, see John Mollenkopf, *The Contested City* (Princeton, N.J.: Princeton University Press, 1983).

35. Mark I. Gelfand, *A Nation of Cities: The Federal Government and Urban America, 1933–1965* (New York: Oxford University Press, 1975); Kenneth Fox, *Metropolitan America: Urban Life and Urban Policy in the United States, 1940–1980* (London: Macmillan, 1985); Carl Abbott, *Urban America in the Modern Age*, pp. 117–25; Miller and Melvin, *The Urbanization of Modern America*, pp. 185–227.

36. For critiques of federal highway and housing programs, see Jane Jacobs, *The Death and Life of Great American Cities* (New York: Vintage Books, 1961); Martin Anderson, *The Federal Bulldozer* (Cambridge: MIT Press, 1964); Scott Greer, *Urban Renewal and American Cities: The Dilemma of Democratic Intervention* (Indianapolis: Bobbs-Merrill, 1965); and Delbert A. Taebel and James V. Cornehls, *The Political Economy of Urban Transportation* (Port Washington, N.Y.: Kennikat Press, 1977).

37. Jon C. Teaford, *The Twentieth-Century American City: Problem, Promise, and Reality* (Baltimore: Johns Hopkins University Press, 1986), p. 125.

38. Charles Abrams, *Forbidden Neighbors: A Study of Prejudice in Housing* (New York: Harper, 1955), pp. 229–30; Kenneth T. Jackson, "Race, Ethnicity, and Real Estate Appraisal: The Home Owners Loan Corporation and the Federal Housing Administration," *Journal of Urban History* 6 (August, 1980): 419–52; Raymond A. Mohl, "Trouble in Paradise: Race and Housing in Miami during the New Deal Era," *Prologue: The Journal of the National Archives* 19 (Spring, 1987): 7–21.

39. On Carter's urban policy, see U.S. Department of Housing and Urban Development, *The President's 1978 National Urban Policy Report* (Washington, D.C.: U.S. Government Printing Office, 1978); President's Commission, *Urban America in the Eighties;* Peter K. Eisinger, "The Search for a National Urban Policy 1968–1980," *Journal of Urban History* 12 (November, 1985): 3–24; and, for a critique, Thomas Bender, "A Nation of Immigrants to the Sun Belt," *The Nation*, March 28, 1981, pp. 359–61. On Reagan's urban policy, see Robert Benenson, "Reagan and the Cities," *Editorial Research Reports* II (July 23, 1982): 531–48; and Neal M. Cohen, "The Reagan Administration's Urban Policy," *Town Planning Review* 54 (July, 1983): 304–15.

40. On blacks in urban politics, see Jeffrey K. Hadden, et al., "The Making of the Negro Mayors, 1967," *Trans-action* (January–February, 1968): 21–30; Martin Kilson, "Black Politics: A New Power," in Irving Howe and Michael Harrington, eds., *The Seventies: Problems and Proposals* (New York: Harper and Row, 1972), pp. 297–317; William E. Nelson, Jr., and Philip J. Meranto, *Electing Black Mayors: Political Action in the Black Community* (Columbus: Ohio State University Press, 1977). For the rise of Hispanic urban politics, see David R. Johnson, et al., *The Politics of San Antonio: Community, Progress, and Power* (Lincoln: University of Nebraska Press, 1983); Alejandro Portes, "The Rise of Ethnicity: Determinants of Ethnic Perceptions among Cuban

Exiles in Miami," *American Sociological Review* 49 (June, 1984): 383–97; Raymond A. Mohl, "Ethnic Politics in Miami, 1960–1986," in Randall M. Miller and George E. Pozzetta, eds., *Shades of the Sunbelt: Essays on Ethnicity, Race, and the Urban South* (Westport, Conn.: Greenwood Press, 1988): 143–60.

41. Richard C. Wade, "An Agenda for Urban History," in Herbert J. Bass, ed., *The State of American History* (Chicago: Quadrangle Books, 1970), pp. 63–64; Arnold R. Hirsch, "The Last 'Last Hurrah,'" *Journal of Urban History* 13 (November, 1986): 108. For the changing political pattern in Chicago, see Paul Kleppner, *Chicago Divided: The Making of a Black Mayor* (DeKalb, Ill.: Northern Illinois University Press, 1985); and Melvin G. Holli and Paul M. Green, eds., *The Making of the Mayor: Chicago, 1983* (Grand Rapids, Mich.: William B. Eerdmans Publishing Co., 1984).

42. Abbott, *The New Urban America*, pp. 120–210; Scott Greer, *Metropolitics: A Study of Political Culture* (New York: Wiley, 1963); James F. Horan and G. Thomas Taylor, Jr., *Experiments in Metropolitan Government* (New York: Praeger, 1977); Raymond A. Mohl, "Miami's Metropolitan Government: Retrospect and Prospect," *Florida Historical Quarterly* 63 (July, 1984), pp. 24–50.

43. Abbott, *The New Urban America*, p. 211. For an early study that anticipated this new political pattern, see Nathan Glazer and Daniel Patrick Moynihan, *Beyond the Melting Pot: The Negroes, Puerto Ricans, Jews, Italians, and Irish of New York City* (Cambridge: MIT Press and Harvard University Press, 1963).

44. On bilingualism and other ethnic political battles in Miami, see Raymond A. Mohl, "Race, Ethnicity, and Urban Politics in the Miami Metropolitan Area," *Florida Environmental and Urban Issues* 9 (April, 1982): 1–6, 23–25; Mohl, "The Politics of Ethnicity in Contemporary Miami," *Migration World* 14, no. 3 (1986): 7–11; Christopher L. Warren and John F. Stack, Jr., "Immigration and the Politics of Ethnicity and Class in Metropolitan Miami," in John F. Stack, Jr., ed., *The Primordial Challenge: Ethnicity in the Contemporary World* (Westport, Conn.: Greenwood Press, 1986), pp. 61–79.

45. On these points, see Richard C. Wade, "America's Cities Are (Mostly) Better Than Ever," *American Heritage* 30, no. 2 (1979): 4–13; Wade, "Housing: A Comparative View," in Paula Dubeck and Zane L. Miller, eds., *Urban Professionals and the Future of the Metropolis* (Port Washington, N.Y.: Kennikat Press, 1980), pp. 69–78; Michael P. Conzen, "American Cities in Profound Transition: The New City Geography of the 1980s," *Journal of Geography* 82 (May–June, 1983): 94–102.

46. For introductions to the evolving historiography of modern American urban history, consult the following: Blake McKelvey, "American Urban History Today," *American Historical Review* 57 (July, 1952): 919–29; Charles N. Glaab, "The Historian and the American City: A Bibliographic Survey," in Philip M. Hauser and Leo F. Schnore, eds., *The Study of Urbanization* (New York: Wiley, 1965), pp. 53–80; Dwight W. Hoover, "The Diverging Paths of American Urban History," *American Quarterly* 20 (Summer, 1968): 296–317; Dana F. White, "The Underdeveloped Discipline: Interdisciplinary Directions in American Urban History," *American Studies: An International Newsletter* 9 (Spring, 1971): 3–16; Raymond A. Mohl, "The History of the American City," in William H. Cartwright and Richard L. Watson, Jr., eds., *The Reinterpretation of American History and Culture* (Washington, D.C.: National Council for the Social Studies, 1973), pp. 165–205; Michael Frisch, "American Urban History as an Example of Recent Historiography," *History and Theory* 18 (1979): 350–77; Kathleen Neils Conzen, "Community Studies, Urban History, and American Local History," in Michael Kammen, ed., *The Past before Us: Contemporary Historical Writing in the United States*

(Ithaca, N.Y.: Cornell University Press, 1980), pp. 270–91; Michael H. Ebner, "Urban History: Retrospect and Prospect," *Journal of American History* 68 (June, 1981): 69–84; Bradford Luckingham, "The Urban Dimension of Western History," in Michael Malone, ed., *Historians and the American West* (Lincoln: University of Nebraska Press, 1983), pp. 323–43; and Mohl, "New Perspectives on American Urban History," *International Journal of Social Education* 1 (Spring, 1986): 69–97. For a fascinating and informative collection of interviews with leading urban historians originally published in the *Journal of Urban History*, see Bruce M. Stave, ed., *The Making of Urban History: Historiography through Oral History* (Beverly Hills, Calif.: Sage Publications, 1977), which might be read in conjunction with Stave's, "In Pursuit of Urban History: Conversations with Myself and Others — A View from the United States," in Derek Fraser and Anthony Sutcliffe, eds., *The Pursuit of Urban History* (London: Edward Arnold, 1983), pp. 407–27.

ROBERT FISHER

The Urban Sunbelt in Comparative Perspective: Houston in Context

SINCE KEVIN PHILLIPS coined the term in 1969, the urban "Sunbelt" has achieved, at least among scholars, more consensus as to its nature than its parameters. Carl Abbott, for example, extends the urban Sunbelt from the upper Northwest (Portland, Oregon) to the Southeast (Norfolk, Virginia). Most others are more exclusive.[1] While its extremities are fuzzy, the core of the Sunbelt is clear — the urban Southwest — and no city better symbolizes the Sunbelt than Houston, Texas. As Richard M. Bernard and Bradley R. Rice put it: "Every mythical belt — cotton or corn, Bible or borscht — must have a 'buckle.' Atlanta, Phoenix, Dallas, and Research Triangle Park, North Carolina, have vied for the title, but Houston usually wins."[2] And it "wins" primarily because it best represents what distinguishes the urban Sunbelt: boomtown growth since World War II in a consciously conservative local context.[3] As such the Sunbelt is as much a phenomenon of political economy as it is a geographic region.[4]

In 1978 *U.S. News and World Report* saw Houston just that way. More than a city, it declared, Houston is

> a phenomenon — an explosive, roaring urban juggernaut that's shattering traditions as it expands outward and upward with an energy that surprises even its residents. . . . Absorbing capital, people and new corporations like a sponge, Houston is constantly being reshaped — physically by the wrecking ball and new construction and culturally by newcomers with fresh ideas and philosophies.[5]

While no sunbelt city prospered in the 1960s and 1970s to Houston's extent, all shared in the economic boom that accompanied the shift of capital out of the old industrial corridor.[6] But the sunbelt phenomenon is not simply one of economic growth, not simply one of being the beneficiaries in the 1960s and 1970s of the dramatically uneven

development characteristic of capitalist economies.[7] Equally significant is the consciously conservative political economy of the sunbelt
cities. "More than on any other dimension," John Mollenkopf has
concluded,

> the southwestern metropolitan areas can be distinguished from those of the
> Northeast by the small size of their governments, their private sector ori-
> entation, the lack of political conflict, and by the relatively great social
> stratification which underlies their conservative political cultures.[8]

In almost all of the sunbelt cities a "local business elite" has "dominated nonpartisan, at-large city elections"[9] and "the business community has a virtual monopoly in deliberation on solutions to civic problems."[10] The Sunbelt became the site of capital accumulation in the
generation after World War II not only because of the disincentives
to investment in the North but also because of the Sunbelt's pro-business,
anti-regulation, anti-government politics. In addition, in these relatively new cities there was little need for government intervention to
assure a politically stable resident population.

It is this distinctive political economy of the Sunbelt — conservative
politics amid rapid economic growth — that is most worthy of comparison over time and across space. There is, of course, no single city
which captures all of the diversity of the Sunbelt. Houston may be
an example extreme both in the extent of its growth and the extent
of its conservative political economy. Nevertheless, it is a vivid illus-
tration of the sunbelt phenomenon and therefore an excellent subject
for viewing the urban Sunbelt in comparative perspective.

AMERICAN CITY

It is easy when traveling across space and time in the United States
to see vast differences in our urban centers. Across space, northern,
midwestern, southern, and Pacific Coast cities are distinctive. People
who come to Houston from Boston or New York or San Francisco or
from small cities in Texas, Arkansas, or Louisiana find it foreign ter-
rain, not exactly a "real" city, at least as they know it. Over time,
differences are more obvious. Colonial Boston, industrial Chicago, contemporary Miami seem to bear little in common with each other. In

Houston, "the magnolia city," "the bayou city," "space city," and "the golden buckle of the Sunbelt" were not only public relations concepts but descriptions of a changing city. But in context, there is something characteristically American about all cities in the United States, across time as well as space, and the sunbelt cities are no exception. It is especially instructive therefore to extend the comparative perspective of sunbelt cities beyond the American urban experience.

Cities in the United States, like the nation, are young and filled with opportunity, cities of plenty with an ideology and socio-spatial pattern distinctly different from their western European counterparts. To begin, American cities are fundamentally the creations of seventeenth-century land law which, in response to the oppressiveness of feudal society, defined land as a civil liberty and created "the freest land system anywhere in the world."[11] As Sam Bass Warner, Jr. suggests,

> the faith of farmers and townsmen in land as a civil liberty meant not only freedom from the meddling of feudal lords or town officials, at least as important, it meant freedom for even the poorest farm family to win autonomy, freedom to profit from rising values in a country teeming with new settlers, and freedom to achieve the dignities and prerogatives that went with the possession of even the smallest holding.[12]

Private property reflected one's free status. It was seen as a personal ticket to economic and political freedom. Land was not intended to be a public social resource, and neither was the city.

In the eighteenth and nineteenth centuries the freest land law in the world produced the most intense and competitive speculation in land yet seen, and the founding, marketing, and building of cities displayed the pioneering spirit with a zeal equal to any on the frontier. "The famed entrepreneurial spirit of American capitalism," Todd Swanstrom notes, "was expressed as much in founding cities as it was in founding fortunes (although, in truth, it was often hard to separate the two)."[13] The speculator in America became the "central figure in the allocation of physical resources."[14] The city building process, largely anarchic, rested in the hands of land speculators and boosters who were forced to compete with thousands of others seeking to turn their own speculations into a New Athens, New London, or New Philadelphia.

Houston's founding fits the above model perfectly. The Allen brothers, two speculators from New York City, were like other would-be founding fathers. They were interested, as one commentator in 1818 summed up the American urban experience, in "Gain! Gain! Gain! [It] is the beginning, the middle and the end, the *alpha* and *omega* of the founders of the American towns."[15] The key to this gain was economic growth, and American cities have almost always followed a single-minded devotion to it. To be sure, the "capitalist city" is not an American invention or one that is limited to the United States. But as one commentator put it, American cities developed "in ways quite unlike the traditional city that had characterized the Western urban world for at least 2000 years."[16] In the United States the emphasis on profits and economic growth took a largely unbridled form — free of feudal conventions and traditional responsibilities — and when combined with an abundant supply of land yielded not only a distinctive urban political economy but a unique pattern of urban physical growth, a peculiarly American urban ecology.

First a brief look at the ecology. The traditional western European city was compact and centered, exhibiting a well-defined central business district surrounded by dense residential areas. "In most traditional cities," Amos Rapoport points out, "central location indicates higher status than does peripheral location."[17] The affluent live in what is now termed the inner city, preferring its convenience, its urbanity, and its safety. Living on the periphery is less desirable. In America, on the other hand, the opposite is true. The trend has been toward deconcentration rather than concentration, to low-density, suburban, segregated, sprawling, multi-nodal cities. The more American cities sprawled, the more suburban they became, the lower the density of settlement, the better they fulfilled, as individualistic, privatistic enclaves, the heritage of post-feudal cities.[18]

This suburban American city "reached its classic form west of the Mississippi, in the cities that had developed in the twentieth century under the influence of the automobile."[19] Houston and its fellow sunbelt cities are perfect examples.[20] To be sure, not all American cities are as suburban as Houston; many are more dense, more concentrated, and more dependent on their central business districts. The inner city of Boston, for example, looks more traditional, seems more European; but this is only true of the older areas of older American cities, parts of cities developed before the late nineteenth century. Almost everything built in the last century reflects a thoroughly deconcentrated American form, in the old industrial belt as well as sunbelt cities.

German critic Guenter Kunert sees older cities in America as "relics" of a prior age. "Contrary to European locales," he writes,

> whose original form can be recognized . . . and which — at least in local districts — invite one to look them over and get to know them on foot, American cities were from the beginning conceived only for people who came driving or riding. . . . Wandering, sauntering, strolling [are] foreign words in these cities. . . . If you use the sidewalks that are still around, you notice that they are European relics . . . frequented only as bridges between car door and shop anyway, and probably they will disappear one day to make way for another traffic lane.[21]

European critics are fond of exaggerating how horrible things are in the United States. But Kunert's critique of the sprawling American city as compared with its concentrated European counterpart, with differences as significant (or minimal) as whether people experience their environment on foot or in a car, does reflect a widely held perception that the American and western European city are two distinct spatial environments — and that younger cities or new parts of older cities, whether sunbelt cities or northern suburbs, are the culmination of this difference.

LAISSEZ-FAIRE CITY

Spatial form is but one element that identifies Houston and the sunbelt cities as thoroughly American. What is equally significant is the heritage of privatism, the legacy of seventeenth-century land law which persists throughout the United States but takes a unique form in Houston in particular and other sunbelt cities in general. When seen over time and across space, it is the political economy of the sunbelt cities — their ideology of unbridled free enterprise fueling boomtown growth — that distinguishes them markedly from other American and western European cities. As William Leuchtenberg noted in his 1986 presidential address to the Organization of American Historians, the growth of the public sector — the state — is the critical development in twentieth-century history.[22] The lesson of the twentieth century, according to Alan Brinkley, is that "no individual, no community in modern America, can live an isolated, unbroken life, insulated from the behavior of the state or national economic institutions."[23] But while Houston exists, and, until recently, thrives in a world economy, its attitude toward the state and toward its responsibility to address social as well as economic issues in an expanded public sector, is much more akin to a nineteenth-century, laissez-faire mentality, more like its founding principles, than the dominant impulse of the twentieth century.

A study of European cities reveals that indeed the expansion of the state is the dominant feature of the twentieth century. The social welfare state developed in Western Europe in the late nineteenth and early twentieth centuries in response to vigorous class struggle and debate over how to resolve the massive problems of industrial capitalism, over what was the proper role of the public sector in promoting the general welfare, and over who would control and benefit from an expanded state.[24] This conflict resulted in a large role for a centralized social welfare state to maintain economic as well as social order: to provide services more equitably, to ensure that essentials such as adequate housing and health care were a right of all citizens and not a privilege of only those who could afford them, and to seek a more equitable redistribution of income and resources through direct and progressive taxation schemes. These cities were not socialist utopias. The urban reforms won by the working class and implemented by socialists did significantly improve the lot of many citizens, but serious problems and inequities remained. Nevertheless, a significant change in thought and politics as to the relationship of the state to the city and its residents occurred. A shift in the political economy had taken place, moving from a laissez-faire conception that the individual bore sole responsibility for his or her welfare to a democratic socialist vision that a centralized state, as the representative body of the public, assumed responsibility for and greater control of the economic and social well-being of its citizens.

Vienna, for example, with its wide array of social welfare programs begun under socialist administrations in the 1920s, developed a reputation as the "mecca of social welfare."[25] The largest and most noteworthy project of the centralized state in Vienna was the communal residential building projects, the *Gemeindebauten*, which between 1923 and 1933 provided for 63,000 improved residential units, residence for some 220,000 people on the basis of need, at rents of less than 4 percent of an average worker's monthly wage.[26] By almost any standard, this public housing program was a great success for the time, testimony to the potential of public sector planning in addressing a widespread urban problem. As Peter Marcuse put it:

> Housing [in Vienna] was not seen, by any of the parties involved, as purely shelter, but rather as part of an overall reconstruction of life around goals of human dignity and public responsibility. The private housing market, in this context, was seen as, at best, useless and, at worst, the source of ills needing to be addressed.[27]

The serious hardships faced by the Viennese, especially the Viennese working class, after World War I were met head on by the development of the social democratic state in Austria when "the socialist administration of Vienna became an internationally recognized model for health, welfare, and housing programmes."[28] While Vienna was the model social democratic city, it was only the best example of a system of political economy replicated, in varying degree, over the next generation in most of Western Europe.

The experience of Houston *vis-à-vis* the public sector has been quite the opposite. Local boosters attribute Houston's extraordinary history of almost continuous economic growth since its founding, but especially in the twentieth century, not only to local resources (oil and gas) and new technologies (the automobile and air-conditioner) but to the climate of unbridled free enterprise that allows entrepreneurs with a vision and a willingness to gamble to put their ideas into practice without controls or intervention from the state. Like the "social welfare mecca" of Vienna it is an ideological city, but Houston touts the virtues of classical laissez-faire capitalism. According to this version of capitalism, one historian wrote, "the private sector is the driving force in the city. In this atmosphere, the government provides a minimum of basic services and assists business growth."[29] The Houston police force in 1981, for example, was one-third the size of that in Philadelphia and half that of most other big cities, although it had one of the highest murder rates in the country.[30] The per capita tax burden of Houstonians ($175) is very light when compared, for example, with that in Boston ($695) and New York City ($841).[31] As one report concluded, the laissez-faire attitude "has restricted the growth of city government and has kept Houston essentially a low-service city."[32] The classic expression of this anti-government attitude is Houston's lack of a zoning ordinance; it is the only major city in the nation without one. This does not mean, of course, that Houston lacks all land-use controls or planning, but rather that Houston is without signifi- cant *public sector* controls and planning.[33]

The idea of Houston as the bastion of laissez-faire capitalism, however, is as much myth as reality. "Free enterprise" has never meant no government intervention, no public sector activity. Rather, it has meant public sector intervention when it served the objective of economic growth and when it corresponded with the interests and needs of economic elites. The major stimuli to Houston's economy have come as much from federal programs lobbied for by local interests as they have from the unbridled marketplace. Whether it was the dredging of the ship channel in the second decade of the twentieth century, critical social programs during the Great Depression, major oil pipelines and military contracts during and since World War II, or NASA development funds more recently, federal projects have played a critical role in the growth of the Houston economy.[34] Nevertheless, the ideological thrust in Houston in the twentieth century has been anti-government, anti-regulation, anti-planning, anti-taxes, anti-anything that seemed to represent, in fact or fantasy, an expansion of the public sector or limitation of the economic prerogatives and activities of the city's business community.

Europeans see the "private" city with a diminutive public sector, limited services, impoverished neighborhoods, and glaring class inequities as an American phenomenon. They are partially right. All "successful" American cities tend to be characterized by what John Galbraith calls "public squalor amidst private opulence."[35] American cities have never been enthusiastic about public planning or the positive role to be played by the state in addressing citywide and quality of life concerns. Olaf Palme, the late prime minister of Sweden, once said that the objective of social democracy was to make relations between people more gentle. American cities have often seemed to Europeans to be the opposite — winner-take-all centers of social Darwinism — where the affluent prosper, the poor suffer, and collective social problems mount.

Not all American cities, however, pursue the same laissez-faire urban policy. It is much more common in the Southwest, where, as noted earlier, cities are characterized by "the small size of their governments" and "their private sector orientation."[36] Other cities, most commonly but not exclusively older cities of the North, pursue liberal growth strategies instead. As Swanstrom puts the dichotomy,

> Liberal growth politics emphasizes a central role for government, both in guiding private sector expansion and in creating an expanded welfare state to help those left behind by growth. Conservative growth politics advocates a passive role for government — with taxes kept to a minimum and planning left entirely to the private sector.[37]

Mollenkopf sees the shift from laissez-faire to liberal growth strategies as synonymous with the transition from the nineteenth- to the twentieth-century city. The nineteenth-century idea of cities as essentially private, profit-oriented, growth machines "produced tremendous wealth," but, he adds, "it also created new miseries and intense new forms of political conflict."[38] Accordingly, beginning with social engineering efforts during the Progressive era, continuing with federal intervention programs during the New Deal, and expanding during the 1960s, an active, enlarged public sector able to shape and affect urban development patterns gained increasing legitimacy and acceptance. Examples in American urban history of this process abound. Roy Lubove's *Twentieth Century Pittsburgh* details the evolution of urban policy in Pittsburgh from a conservative to a liberal growth ideology as the social and physical problems of industrial Pittsburgh mounted from the early twentieth century through the 1960s. In Pittsburgh, Lubove emphasizes, there was a "nearly universal rejection of the kind of city which rapid, haphazard, and rapacious growth of industrial capitalism produced between 1850 and 1930."[39]

Houston had a comparable, though brief, episode. The 1890s and early years of the twentieth century were characterized by intense struggle over whether the city would be oriented primarily to economic growth or neighborhood services. Municipal control of utilities provided one arena of hot debate. Joseph Jay Pastoriza, city tax commissioner between 1911 and 1917 and mayor-elect in 1917, went so far as to suggest that people should not be allowed to individually profit from land speculation. In Houston economic elites professing a conservative growth ideology won this struggle, partly by disenfranchising much of their opposition.[40] Since the 1920s, or at least until very recently, this nineteenth-century laissez-faire ideology has dominated urban policy in Houston.

Why did this ideology remain dominant in Houston while Europe and much of the United States moved in a different direction? In European and American cities one of the reasons for the expansion of the public sector in the twentieth century was the magnitude of serious urban problems resulting from the industrial revolution, the Depression, and, in Europe, from two world wars. In contrast, Houston did not adopt a more state-oriented strategy to meet urban problems because the city never encountered problems sufficiently great and never experienced a crisis that might have produced comprehensive alternatives initiated by either elites or grassroots insurgents. Houston came of age after the traumas of late nineteenth-century industrialization. The First and Second World Wars, which occasioned a massive infusion of federal funds, helped Houston. The ship channel, for example, which connected Houston to the Gulf of Mexico and made it one of the major deep water ports in the United States, was begun during World War I as a defense project. During and after World War II Houston continued to benefit from defense contracts with its petrochemical and space industries. Moreover, the Great Depression in Houston was mild. No banks failed in the 1930s, as the city remained on the periphery of the international capitalist economy and as Houston leaders like Jesse Jones, who chaired the Reconstruction Finance Corporation and later served as Federal Loan Administrator and Secretary of Commerce in the Roosevelt administration, channeled funds to Houston to ease what were modest burdens of the decade.

When Houston did come of age—beginning in the 1920s and, much more significantly, after World War II—it did so in a local context of economic prosperity, a national context of conservative ideology during the 1920s and 1950s, and a regional context of a South opposed to social change and government interference. The combination of business elites determining urban policy in an economic climate of perpetual boomtown growth and in a national and regional context which actively discouraged statist solutions helped sustain the laissez-faire strategy in Houston. There seemed to most people little need for an alternative.

CONSENSUS CITY

Whereas the distinctiveness of the political economy of Houston and other sunbelt cities took root before the 1960s, the decades of the 1960s and 1970s dramatized what was truly different about the Sunbelt. Most obvious was the extraordinary economic, spatial, and demographic growth of the sunbelt cities. The litany of Houston's claim to international urban fame during the 1960s and 1970s needs no detailed retelling. By 1980 Houston was the national leader in population growth, growth in retail sales, per capita income, and employment. "It was first among the nation's cities in residential construction, and in the latter part of the 1970s in overall construction," boasted a twenty-page advertisement in *Fortune* in 1980.[41] Magnificent office towers sprang up all over the city, not just downtown but ten miles or more to the north, south, and west. From 1970 to 1983 alone 205 large office buildings (each more than 100,000 square feet) were built, representing three-fourths of all the large office buildings in the city.[42] Even with a population growth of half a million people in the 1970s, even with, at its peak, almost one thousand new residents arriving weekly, jobs abounded and unemployment at the end of the decade hovered around 2.6 percent when the national rate was three times greater.

Sunbelt cities, especially the ones in Texas, were distinctive worldwide in the 1960s and 1970s as much for what they were not as for what they were. They were not cities experiencing an urban crisis. Citizen unrest in response to mounting urban problems, opposition to elite leadership, challenges to economic growth strategies were unknown in most of these cities; when they did arise, they were relatively mild in comparison to those occurring at the same time throughout the "contested cities" of the northern United States and Western Europe.[43]

In the United States in the 1960s northern cities primarily but not exclusively were burdened with serious urban problems, mounting public sector costs, and political instability in the form of insurrection and social movement challenges. Almost every major American city with a sizable black population erupted in the late 1960s, especially in the northern metropolises. There, urban policy makers had built successful liberal pro-growth coalitions, with elite and mass support and heavy dependence on public sector and especially federal programs. But the liberal growth strategy did not adequately address the mounting and very serious problems of the poor, primarily blacks. At the same time social protest movements of the 1960s, specifically the civil rights and black power movements, raised levels of citizen political self-confidence and militance. Unable to harness sufficient funds to deliver jobs and services, these cities in the late 1960s faced the wrath of decades of unattended problems and decades of frustration and discontent.[44]

The phenomenon, however, was not limited to cities in the United States. "Cities everywhere in the developed Western countries appear[ed] to be in 'crisis,'" concluded a multi-national investigation of cities conducted between 1974 and 1976.

> The urban crisis is neither isolated nor symptomatically limited to a few unlucky administrations. In all the advanced countries, cities appear to be suffering similar strains of this disease. In the United States, not only New York City, but Detroit and San Francisco — to pick only two examples — are echoing with the reverberations of crisis. In Italy, not only Naples and Rome in the South but also Milan and Venice in the North, are feeling the effects. In Germany, cities as distinct as Munich and Hamburg seem equally afflicted. And the list goes on. If there are social problems which are "common" to the advanced Western countries, the "urban crisis" certainly seems to be one of the most dramatic.[45]

To be sure, the urban crisis of the 1970s took a different form than its counterpart in the 1960s, but both were part of a much larger economic and political transformation. The "urban crisis" of the 1960s was based on the demand in cities in the United States and in Western Europe for a resolution of serious, long-term social problems and for greater equity in the distribution of benefits and opportunities pouring into these cities. The "fiscal crisis" of the 1970s resulted from a decade of city spending exceeding city revenues, a political reaction against demands for equity, and, most important, a dramatically diminished economic context.[46] New York City and Cleveland, for example, bordered on bankruptcy. The federal government — the funding source of the 1960s — turned a deaf ear. Corporate elites demanded a retrenched welfare state and "fiscal conservatism." Citizen groups in the United States mounted actions to protect what they had won in the 1960s and prevent the dismantling of what was by European standards already scanty social services and public resources.[47]

The unifying feature of the urban crises of these decades was the mobilization of urban social movements. In the 1960s in response to housing, transportation, health care, and racial problems, and then in the 1970s in response to welfare cuts, hospital shutdowns, and red-lining of neighborhoods by banks, citizens mobilized in extra-political organizations to pressure the system for benefits, for services, and for social change. Such citizen action seemed sufficiently widespread in most major cities in the United States to lead more than one commentator to declare a "backyard revolution" of community-based activism in American cities born in the 1960s and expanding in the 1970s.[48]

Citizen action was also widespread in Western Europe.[49] By the mid-1980s, Joyce Marie Mushaben estimates, some 38,000 *Buerger-initiativen* existed in the Federal Republic of Germany, with a membership numbering between two and three million. Over the years, these citizen initiatives developed "a systematic political critique directed against unrestricted economic growth and technological destruction of the environment."[50] Stuart Lowe describes "an upsurge of social movement activity in Britain over the last two decades."[51] From tenant and squatter movements to efforts opposing public spending cuts and highway destruction of stable communities, urban social movements of the lower middle class as well as the poor proliferated. "What happened in Britain," Lowe concludes, "was but a small part of a much wider post-war escalation of urban protest throughout the world, with an intensification in the 1960s and 1970s."[52]

The climate of urban crisis in the 1960s and 1970s in cities in the United States and in Western Europe resulted as much from the citizen challenges to these problems as from the actual existence of urban problems. Serious problems are part and parcel of the urban experience. Every city, colonial Boston with its garbage dumped in the streets to be devoured by pigs, nineteenth-century New York with its corrupt politicians arrogant with power, modern-day (name most any large city) with its violence, traffic problems, pollution, class and race inequities, etc., every city — conservative, liberal, or socialist — has had serious urban concerns which needed to be addressed.

Houston, too, has had its share of major social problems. The city faces serious quality-of-life concerns, such as water and air pollution, toxic waste dumping, crime, and inadequate transportation problems, to note but a few "social costs of boomtown growth" that affect all residents. But the condition of the poor in Houston starkly illustrates the liabilities of laissez-faire boomtown growth. Ex-mayor Louie Welch declared in 1980, after he had "stepped-up" to head the Houston Chamber of Commerce, that "no city is without poor people but the opportunity not to be poor is greater [in Houston] than in most cities. . . . The free market has functioned in Houston like no other place in America. It has a method of purging itself of slums."[53] The duplicity of such boosterism, however, is quickly realized by traveling across the Gulf Freeway to some of the city's poor black and Hispanic neighborhoods. The nature and extent of problems facing the poor, blacks, and Hispanics — past and present — are serious and long-standing: poverty, racism, residential segregation, neighborhood decay and destruction, inadequate housing, insufficient health care and social services, and meager public services. These are also the legacies of a laissez-faire city. A few examples must suffice.

U.S. News and World Report described the situation graphically in 1978:

> Left behind in Houston's headlong flight toward growth and economic success are an estimated 400,000 people who live in a 73 square mile slum that, says a college professor, has an infant mortality rate "that would have embarrassed the Belgian Congo.[54]

In the mid-1960s Houston had four hundred miles of unpaved streets, almost all in the impoverished sectors of the inner city.[55] In 1969, in the midst of the economic boom, Houston's poor neighborhoods had an unemployment rate higher than many comparable urban neighborhoods throughout the nation.[56] Significant social problems are not limited to the inner city. Wolde-Michael Akalou contends that as late as 1983 there were eighty-three black and Hispanic neighborhoods, annexed between 1949 and 1972, that remained without such basic public services as sewer systems and indoor plumbing.[57]

Urban problems alone are not sufficient to bring about social change or to create a crisis that forces those in power to act. Historically, a state of crisis developed in cities when (1) elites saw the problem as threatening either economic growth or their very safety, or

(2) when a sufficient level of insurgency in the form of social disorder, social movements, or electoral challenges occurred to force the problem onto the political agenda and to demand that what had been ignored now must be addressed.[58] In the 1960s in most major cities of the United States and Western Europe it was this second form, citizen insurgency and rebellion, which created an atmosphere of crisis. In the 1970s a sense of crisis resulted from elites seeking to prevent economic decline and, simultaneously, to curb costly demands from the grassroots.[59] It was not only boomtown growth in an era of general metropolitan decline which sets the Sunbelt apart; it was also the consensus atmosphere, the limited extent of citizen challenges which distinguishes Houston and the sunbelt cities during these decades.

Like citizens throughout the nation, Houstonians have banded together in grassroots associations to advance their interests. But in the conservative political economy of Houston the dominant form of community organization has mirrored and reinforced the laissez-faire, business orientation of the city. In Houston there are more than six hundred neighborhood civic clubs that, in the absence of a public zoning ordinance, serve the primary function of enforcing deed restrictions to control land use and protect property investments.[60] Where private individuals or organizations must shoulder such responsibility, civic clubs are a vivid expression of the ideology of laissez-faire capitalism at the community level. The laissez-faire consensus demands that community groups form to protect their own interests. Citizens can expect little assistance from the public sector or from public urban planning. In response, an elaborate system of deed restrictions and widely proliferated, essentially conservative civic clubs have developed.[61] Instead of challenging the laissez-faire status quo, these neighborhood civic clubs serve as one of the many means of maintaining it.

There has, of course, been a long history of struggle by minority groups and the poor in Houston. There have been numerous struggles fought and challenging organizations formed to redress grievances and address problems since the early twentieth century. The C.I.O. organized locals in the 1930s among the white working class, especially among oil workers. In the black and Hispanic communities a wide array of social change efforts arose in response to social problems faced by the poor and minorities, from chapters of the NAACP and LULAC to dozens of less prominent but nevertheless important neighborhood-based social change organizations.[62] But this social history reveals few challenges and very limited success in Houston when compared to the number and gains of comparable efforts in other large American cities. The absence of success is not because Houston's challenging groups have lacked a critical mass. Since 1900 Houston's black population has constituted approximately 25 percent of the citizenry. Yet Houston was, remarkably, one of the only major cities in the United States with a large black population that did not experience extended racial conflict in the 1960s.[63]

The consensus atmosphere created by boomtown growth and economic prosperity constructed a giant obstacle to social change efforts from the grassroots. When prosperity was mixed with the laissez-faire ideology, the opportunity for grassroots groups to turn to the public sector, either as an arena to discuss problems or as a target to organize against, was removed.[64] In a laissez-faire city it was not the proper role of the limited public sector to intervene in the free enterprise economy to promote a more equitable mix of benefits and resources. Government was not responsible for the public welfare; if citizens were not millionaires, it was their own fault. Disaffected Houstonians continued to organize, but as long as economic growth reinforced laissez-faire ideology, they were able, in the best of times, to achieve only modest reforms.

The case of the Clinton Park area, on the east side of the city near the Ship Channel, is especially instructive. In the early 1950s residents of this primarily black working-class neighborhood organized a civic club, as had their counterparts in affluent white areas, to unite neighborhood residents and lobby city hall for basic services. The primary objective of the Fidelity Civic Club was to pave the major artery in the neighborhood, Fidelity Street. Members paid their poll taxes and voted in city elections. They wrote letters and occasionally met with city officials, but in general politicians turned a deaf ear to the neighborhood's problems. Not until federal funds were provided in the 1970s were the streets completely paved. The limited public sector in Houston had to choose where to spend limited funds, and poor black neighborhoods were never high on the list.

A severely limited public sector posed other dilemmas for citizens seeking services. Members of the Fidelity Civic Club were fearful that blacktopping would cost them too much money, for residents were expected to pay for this benefit, and they were afraid the city would put liens on their houses if they could not afford the service. The problem was not only to persuade a limited public sector to provide a service but then, because it was a laissez-faire city, citizens had to pay for the service as well. Accordingly, the affluent areas of Houston had paved streets, street lighting, trees, even extra police protection, most of which they paid for themselves and some of which they were able to secure by exerting sufficient pressure on the city. In the poor sections, people had no significant public sector from which to seek assistance or toward which to direct grassroots insurgency. Problems were perceived as personal and not public, and the poor had few personal resources for addressing them.[65]

There is a great deal to be said for social stability and consensus in a society, urban or otherwise. Houston's economy during these decades made social movement challenges unnecessary for most; and structural constraints made social movement formation extremely difficult for those who advocated change. Nevertheless, efforts like the civil rights, black power, and more recent urban social movements illustrate the power such challenges have in forcing urban policy to represent a wider constituency and in moving it beyond nineteenth-century conceptions of laissez-faire and social Darwinism. Without conflict and challenges, in the street or at the ballot box, social and political change on behalf of the poor and powerless rarely occurs. The status quo is maintained. In the 1960s and 1970s, it was the maintenance of that status quo in Houston that markedly distinguishes it from most major cities outside the Sunbelt in the United States and Western Europe, and even sets it and other southwestern cities apart from sunbelt cities like Atlanta and Los Angeles, which experienced large-scale social movement challenges.

CONVERGING CITY

What is most striking in the 1980s in Houston, in the rest of the urban Sunbelt, and in Western Europe (perhaps Eastern Europe too) is a convergence of urban form and strategies. Spatially, this convergence is evident in a growing similarity of physical form in cities. Deconcentration remains dominant in the United States. Low-density suburbs, single-family detached housing, shopping malls, and auto-mobiles are what American consumers seem to prefer. But there is a smaller, countertendency of recentralization — referred to as downtown "reconversion" and residential "gentrification"— that is much more akin to the old spatial pattern in Western Europe of focusing on and pre-ferring central city location. The revival of interest in Houston's inner city as a residential area of choice, not to mention the extraordinary downtown building explosion and recent efforts to make the down-town attractive to tourists and citizens after work hours, stand as tes-timony to this tendency.

An even more distinctive trend of spatial convergence is the "Ameri-canization," or the suburbanization, of western European centers. From the top of Notre Dame, Paris looks as though it is surrounded by Hous-ton or its equivalent. The old city of Paris is ringed by modern sky-scrapers and suburban neighborhoods. The area surrounding Inns-bruck, Austria, is a mini-boomtown, with an abundance of suburban housing projects throughout the Inn valley climbing the steep sides of the Alps. In Innsbruck those with enough money choose not to re-side in the central city (the Altstadt, which has been sacrificed to tourism) or surrounding inner-city neighborhoods, but instead move to suburbs which offer fresher air, spectacular views, and greater dis-tance from the tourists.[66]

There is also an ideological convergence in the 1980s, apparent throughout the United States and Western Europe. It is the product of shifting demands in the international economy, the impact of uni-form technologies, and the growing acceptance among elites and part of the citizenry that "hard decisions" must be made to remain com-petitive in the high-tech, post-industrial era of global cities. Through-out Western Europe and the United States old industrial centers and the centralized social welfare state endure unrelenting attack. In the last decade the very concept of the welfare state and public interven-tion has been shaken. Under attack, the welfare state has yielded in some key western countries to neo-liberal and neo-conservative posi-tions which seek to strengthen the dominance of market forces.[67] Prime Minister Margaret Thatcher's transformation of the British welfare state and urban policies, Chancellor Helmut Kohl's efforts at privatiza-tion throughout West Germany, and Mayor Ed Koch's New York City are the three most significant examples. This tendency is pushing all agendas and policy discussions — national and urban — away from liberal and socialist conceptualizations. The social welfare state will not wither away by the turn of the next century, but if current trends continue, the dominant political development of the twentieth century will certainly arrive into the next in a dramatically altered form.

Convergence also cuts the other way. It is not as though the urban world is shifting to replicate "free enterprise" cities like Houston and Houston is standing still, waiting to be heralded as the urban model of the twenty-first century. Of course, it would if it could, but the vicissitudes of the world economy are not kind forever. Sunbelt cities like Houston, free of urban and fiscal crisis in the 1960s and 1970s, are experiencing in the 1980s serious fiscal and quality-of-life problems of crisis proportion. The immediate cause of Houston's crisis has been the dramatic decline in world oil prices beginning in 1982, but the crisis is compounded by the shifting of capital to other investment sites and by the social costs of prior boomtown growth left unattended by the laissez-faire urban strategy.

In response to the current economic crisis in Houston, segments of the political and economic elite see the need to expand government and to use it as a means of financing, planning, and coordinating large scale economic and social projects. They seek the cooperation and support of an expanded public sector to address such quality-of-life concerns as the need for improved public transportation and other public services. "The bare bones approach of local government" may have "at long last outlived its usefulness," warned a planning group for the Houston Chamber of Commerce just before the economic collapse.[68] Discussions in Houston now range widely about the need to improve public services, about the declining quality of life in the city, and even about the importance of increasing taxes to address city problems. These are topics that were heretofore political suicide. Since the early 1980s, however, the city has passed a variety of measures, from regulating road signs to sex shops, from improving mass transit to beautifying the bayou that runs through downtown.[69] Increasingly it is acceptable to note how, not whether, the public sector needs to be expanded to address specific urban problems and more general quality of life concerns. There is even some discussion of how the current crisis may be a blessing in disguise, because it stopped boomtown growth and gave the city an opportunity to address its mounting problems and because it has taught Houston that a laissez-faire approach is not in the best interests of a city and all its citizens.[70]

In addition, in the last decade citizen action movements have begun to mount in Houston. This grassroots activism was assisted, first, by federal programs of the late 1960s and 1970s in Houston which legitimized public sector responsibility for urban problems and, second, by the current economic crisis, which makes difficult the maintenance of such programs on which people have come to depend. As Susan MacManus suggests, the attack on federal social service programs in the 1970s and 1980s, and the inability of the City of Houston to fund such programs locally, has spawned "a public demand for new [social] programs."[71] Recent victories by citizen action groups are obvious. Black voters in Houston now hold the balance in city-wide elections, at least to the extent they remain unified. This is a long way from the era of the white primary and poll tax which effectively disenfranchised black Houstonians from the early twentieth century through the 1960s. Blacks and Mexican Americans now sit on the city council and increasingly hold highly visible key positions in the small but growing city bureaucracy. The women's movement is responsible in large measure for the development and for the election to political office as city controller in 1977 of current Mayor Kathy Whitmire. Gay rights supporters have organized a sizable grassroots movement and form an important voting bloc in the city. Alinsky-style community efforts such as The Metropolitan Organization (TMO) have recently developed neighborhood organizations in non-affluent communities throughout the city to fight for improved services and political responsiveness, and they are willing to use protest as well as negotiations with city officials to achieve their objectives.[72]

One of the common ingredients of the recent social movements in Houston is a willingness to focus attention on city government as the target for activism. From the successful federal lawsuit that replaced the at-large electoral system for city council with one that includes district representation from "minority" neighborhoods to the mayor's meeting regularly with neighborhood leaders and organizers from organizations such as TMO, challenging groups since the late 1970s have demanded greater responsiveness from government at all levels and have demanded that the government assume responsibility for addressing the claims of city residents heretofore ignored.[73] Of

course, the ability of the city to address demands for a more responsive and expanded public sector, not to mention its ability to resolve
quality of life as well as social problems, is seriously complicated by
its current economic decline. But the economic crisis has stimulated,
not diminished, calls for a rethinking of and a shift in urban policy.

It is ironic that at the historical moment when social welfare systems are being "restructured" toward privatization, from the top down
by conservative elites, that Houston and other sunbelt cities find themselves moving in the opposite direction, from laissez-faire to an expansion of state activity and to more, not less, debate over urban policy.[74]
Perhaps there is a middle meeting ground, a political economy for the
twenty-first century — decentralized democratic socialism or neo-
liberalism, to name two competing visions — near to which all successful "post-industrial" cities will find themselves eventually. As Evers and
Wollmann argue, in response to these demands

> the local level and local government should not be seen in [a] mere "stop
> gap" and crisis management role, but should be interpreted as an arena
> and an agent that might help to gain the conceptual and practical poten-
> tial for redefining and redesigning a welfare state more adequate and re-
> sponsive to the new challenges.[75]

For the present the Sunbelt remains a valid symbol, a means of
distinguishing the urban experience of cities in the South and Southwest from that of other cities throughout the United States and Western Europe. But the nature of sunbelt distinctiveness has changed. As
a symbol of boomtown growth and conservative politics, the "golden
buckle" of Houston is increasingly inappropriate, and so are most of
the other sunbelt cities. Often the new boomtowns in the United States
are in the North and along the two coasts; many, like Portland, Maine,
were once dubbed decaying cities of the Frostbelt. For Houston and
much of the Sunbelt, the 1980s brought decline or slowed growth rather
than boomtown growth. Serious social problems mount and demand
attention. Urban citizen action efforts, as Abbott emphasizes, are widespread, from Portland and Seattle to Denver, San Antonio, and Atlanta.[76] The Sunbelt is a different place now. The shining years were
the 1960s and 1970s, when capital and people flowed into the South
and Southwest and when other cities throughout the United States and
Western Europe were in the midst of a serious economic and political

transformation. That transformation in the older industrial cities is certainly not over; the push to privatization may only be another stage in a long struggle over how these cities will survive and who in these cities will benefit most and sacrifice least in the post-industrial transformation. In the relatively young cities of the Southwest, the questions are the same but the shift in urban policy is to the "left" rather than "right." The shift is toward legitimizing and expanding the role of the state, toward opening the themes of public debate, and toward acknowledging the existence of serious urban problems.[77] The sunbelt cities remain distinctive in the late 1980s but in a markedly different manner than before.

NOTES

The author would like to acknowledge the assistance of Marty Melosi for helping to initiate this project, Bruce Palmer for his always careful reading, and the Fulbright Commissions in Europe, especially the Austrian Fulbright Commission, for making this research possible.

1. Carl Abbott, *The New Urban America: Growth and Politics in Sunbelt Cities* (Chapel Hill: University of North Carolina Press, 1987); David C. Perry and Alfred J. Watkins, eds., *The Rise of the Sunbelt Cities* (Beverly Hills, Calif.: Sage Publications, 1977); Richard M. Bernard and Bradley R. Rice, eds., *Sunbelt Cities: Politics and Growth Since World War II* (Austin: University of Texas Press, 1983); Barry Bluestone and Bennett Harrison, *The Deindustrialization of America: Plant Closings, Community Abandonment, and the Dismantling of Basic Industry* (New York: Basic Books, 1982).

2. Bernard and Rice, *Sunbelt Cities*, p. 6. Perry and Watkins, *Rise of the Sunbelt Cities*, p. 105, asserted in 1977 that "there appears to be little dispute that Houston is now the 'shining buckle' of the Sunbelt."

3. The Bernard and Rice collection is subtitled "Politics and Growth since World War II." Abbott's monograph is subtitled "Growth and Politics in Sunbelt Cities." The points about growth and conservative politics were stated earlier in Kevin Phillips, *The Emerging Republican Majority* (New Rochelle, N.Y.: Arlington House Press, 1969); Kirkpatrick Sale, *Power Shift: The Rise of the Southern Rim and Its Challenge to the Eastern Establishment* (New York: Random House, 1975).

4. Political economy, as used here, indicates the interrelation of political policies and economic developments and their influence on social institutions.

5. Paul Recer, "The Texas City That's Bursting Out All Over," *U.S. News and World Report*, November 27, 1978, p. 47.

6. Richard Murray, "Houston: Politics of a Boomtown," *Dissent* 27 (1980): 500, notes that sunbelt cities, such as Los Angeles, Memphis, and New Orleans, had no-growth or slow-growth patterns in the 1970s, and that even some boomtowns of the 1960s, like Atlanta and Dallas, experienced slower rates of growth a decade later. Nevertheless, the sunbelt phenomenon is closely associated with dramatic economic growth since World War II and Houston's growth is unique only in its magnitude and persistence.

7. Bluestone and Harrison, *Deindustrialization of America*, p. 202. See also Norman I. Fainstein and Susan S. Fainstein, eds., *Urban Policy under Capitalism* (Beverly Hills, Calif.: Sage Publications, 1982).

8. John Mollenkopf, *The Contested City* (Princeton, N.J.: Princeton University Press, 1983), p. 242.

9. Ibid., p. 246.

10. Leonard Goodall, cited in Mollenkopf, *The Contested City*, p. 48.

11. Sam Bass Warner, Jr., *The Urban Wilderness: A History of the American City* (New York: Harper and Row, 1972), p. 18.

12. Ibid., p. 16.

13. Todd Swanstrom, *The Crisis of Growth Politics: Cleveland, Kucinich, and the Challenge of Urban Populism* (Philadelphia: Temple University Press, 1985), p. 34.

14. Warner, *Urban Wilderness*, p. 19.

15. Morris Birkbeck, *Notes on a Journey in America from the Coast of Virginia to the Territory of Illinois* (1818), quoted in Swanstrom, *The Crisis of Growth Politics*, p. 34.

16. Peter Hall, "The Urban Culture and the Suburban Culture: A New Look at an Old Paper," in John Agnew, John Mercer, and David Sopher, eds., *The City in Cultural Context* (London: Allen and Unwin, 1984), p. 120.

17. Amos Rapoport, "Culture and the Urban Order," in Agnew, Mercer, and Sopher, *The City in Cultural Context*, p. 59.

18. Agnew, Mercer, and Sopher, *The City in Cultural Context*, p. 286.

19. Hall, "Urban Culture and Suburban Culture," p. 120.

20. This is well stated in Martin V. Melosi, "Suburbanization in the South: The Case of Houston," paper presented at "Houston: In Search of a Vision" conference, October, 1987.

21. Guenter Kunert, "Das Amerikanische," translated by A. Leslie Wilson in *Dimension: Contemporary German Arts and Letters* (special issue, 1983), pp. 321–23.

22. William Leuchtenberg, "The Pertinence of Political History: Reflections on the Significance of the State in America," *Journal of American History* 73 (December, 1986): 585–600.

23. Alan Brinkley, "Writing the History of Contemporary America: Dilemmas and Challenges," *Daedalus* 113 (Summer, 1984): 124–25, cited in ibid., p. 592.

24. See, for example, Ian Gough, *The Political Economy of the Welfare State* (London: Macmillan, 1979).

25. Inge Lehne and Lonnie Johnson, *Vienna: The Past in the Present* (Vienna: Oesterreichischer Bundesverlag, 1985), p. 128.

26. Ibid. The U.S. figure in 1929 was 26.1 percent. See Peter Marcuse, "Red Vienna: Lessons and Warnings for the Housing Movement," *Shelterforce* 9 (July, 1985): 10.

27. Marcuse, "Red Vienna," p. 10.

28. Lehne and Johnson, *Vienna*, p. 124.

29. Barry Kaplan, "Houston: The Golden Buckle of the Sunbelt," in Bernard and Rice, *Sunbelt Cities*, p. 199.

30. Bluestone and Harrison, *Deindustrialization of America*, pp. 87–88.

31. Ibid., p. 84.

32. George Antunes and John P. Plumlee, "The Distribution of an Urban Public Service: Ethnicity, Socioeconomic Status, and Bureaucracy as Determinants of the Quality of Neighborhood Streets," *Urban Affairs Quarterly* 12 (March, 1977): 321.

33. Barry J. Kaplan, "Urban Development, Economic Growth, and Personal Lib-

erty: The Rhetoric of the Houston Anti-Zoning Movements, 1947–1962," *Southwestern Historical Quarterly* 84 (October, 1980): 133–68. Zoning is said to be replaced in Houston by deed restrictions, implemented and maintained by private citizens.

34. Joe R. Feagin, "The Role of the State in Urban Development: the Case of Houston, Texas," *Environment and Planning* 2 (1984): 447–60.

35. Galbraith cited in Blair Badcock, *Unfairly Structured Cities* (London: Basil Blackwell, 1984), p. 240.

36. Mollenkopf, *Contested City*, p. 242.

37. Swanstrom, *Crisis of Growth Politics*, p. 35.

38. Mollenkopf, *Contested City*, p. 14.

39. Roy Lubove, *Twentieth Century Pittsburgh: Government, Business, and Environmental Change* (New York: Random House, 1969).

40. Harold Platt, *City Building in the New South: The Growth of Public Services in Houston, Texas, 1830–1915* (Philadelphia: Temple University Press, 1983); Stephen Davis, "Joseph Jay Pastoriza and the Single Tax in Houston, 1911–1917," *Houston Review* 8 (1986): 57–78. Pastoriza died shortly after his mayoral victory.

41. Bluestone and Harrison, *Deindustrialization of America*, p. 83.

42. Joe Feagin, "Global Context of Metropolitan Growth: Houston and the Oil Industry," *American Journal of Sociology* 90 (May, 1985): 1204–1230.

43. These are the arguments developed in Roger Friedland, *Power and Crisis in the City* (New York: Macmillan, 1982); and Mollenkopf, *Contested City*.

44. See, for example, Friedland, *Power and Crisis in the City;* and Joe R. Feagin and Harlan Hahn, *Ghetto Revolts* (New York: Macmillan, 1973).

45. Research Planning Group on Urban Social Services, "The Political Management of the Urban Fiscal Crisis," in *European Studies Newsletter* 6 (November, 1976): 1.

46. Roger Alcaly and Helen Bodian, "New York's Fiscal Crisis and the Economy," in Roger Alcaly and David Mermelstein, eds., *The Fiscal Crisis of American Cities: Essays on the Political Economy of Urban America with Special Reference to New York* (New York: Vintage, 1977), p. 30.

47. Robert Zevin, "New York City Crisis: First Act in a New Age of Reaction," in Alcaly and Mermelstein, *Fiscal Crisis*, pp. 11–29.

48. Harry C. Boyte, *The Backyard Revolution: Understanding the New Citizen Movement* (Philadelphia: Temple University Press, 1980); Robert Fisher, *Let the People Decide: Neighborhood Organizing in America* (Boston: Twayne, 1984), pp. 121–52.

49. On Europe see Donald Appleyard, "Introduction," in Donald Appleyard, ed., *The Conservation of European Cities* (Cambridge: MIT Press, 1979), p. 18. He offers four structural reasons for the emergence of urban citizen protest in the 1970s in Britain, ones appropriate for much of Western Europe. First, there was a growing sense of social rootlessness generated by a "faceless industrialism" and the "break-up of traditional community life." Second, the welfare state failed to deliver benefits to many groups. Third, urban physical development projects generated problems, specifically the destruction or threatened destruction of lower income housing, already in short supply. Fourth, young radicals, coming out of the 1960s movements, disillusioned with established party politics and interested in decentralized, participatory forms, turned to urban citizen action projects.

50. Joyce Marie Mushaben, "Cycles of Peace Protest in West Germany: Experiences from Three Decades," *West European Politics* 8 (January, 1985): 31. A participant profile of Buergerinitiativen members emphasizes their affluent status, high de-

gree of education, confidence in their own political skills, and roots in movements of the 1960s.

51. Stuart Lowe, *Urban Social Movements* (London: Macmillan, 1986), p. 4.

52. Ibid.

53. Louie Welch cited in Joe R. Feagin, "Tallying the Social Costs of Urban Growth under Capitalism: The Case of Houston," in Scott Cummings, ed., *State, Class, and Urban Revolution* (Albany: State University of New York Press, 1987).

54. Recer, "The Texas City That's Bursting Out All Over," p. 47.

55. Chandler Davidson, *Biracial Politics: Conflict and Coalition in the Metropolitan South* (Baton Rouge: Louisiana State University Press, 1972), p. 134.

56. Roberta Burroughs, "The History of Social Planning in Houston," unpublished paper (1972).

57. Wolde-Michael Akalou, "The Impact of Annexation on Black Communities in Houston," unpublished paper presented to the Southwest Social Science Association (March, 1983), p. 9.

58. The threat to economic growth is more common than the concern for safety in the twentieth century, but in the nineteenth century and before, whether the threat was outside invaders, the plague, or a cholera epidemic, the issue of safety was often the cause of an urban crisis.

59. See, for example, Boyte, *Backyard Revolution* and Fisher, *Let the People Decide.*

60. Fisher, *Let the People Decide*, pp. 61–89.

61. Ibid. Also see Robert Fisher, "Be on the Lookout: Neighborhood Civic Clubs in Houston," *Houston Review* 6 (Winter, 1984): 105–16.

62. For additional information on social movement challenges in Houston see Robert Fisher, "Where Seldom Is Heard a Discouraging Word: Social Movement Formation in Houston, Texas," *Amerikastudien/American Studies* 33 (1988): 73–91.

63. Robert Bullard, *Invisible Houston: The Black Experience in Boom and Bust* (College Station: Texas A&M University Press, 1987).

64. The relationship between laissez-faire ideology and social movement challenges is discussed in Frances Fox Piven and Richard Cloward, *The New Class War: Reagan's Attack on the Welfare State and Its Consequences* (New York: Pantheon Books, 1985).

65. Perry Family Manuscript Collection, Box 1, Houston Metropolitan Research Center.

66. Adalbert Evers and Hellmut Wollmann suggest, however, that the problem of "deep socio-spatial segmentation," which they see as characteristic of American cities, has recently appeared in Europe, a negative consequence of deconcentration. See Adalbert Evers and Hellmut Wollmann, "Big City Politics – New Patterns and Orientations on the Local Level of the Welfare State," *Eurosocial Research Paper* (Vienna, 1986), p. 23.

67. On the other hand, there are others who call for the greater expansion of the state, viewing the current problems as the result of too much market control and too little public intervention. See, for example, Peter B. Evans, Dietrich Rueschemeyer, and Theda Skocpol, eds., *Bringing the State Back In* (Cambridge: Cambridge University Press, 1985).

68. Deborah Meeks, "Houston, Texas: Image of A City," M.A. thesis, American University, 1981), pp. 61–62.

69. "City Moves to Curb Bad Effects of Growth," *Houston Post*, March 24, 1985, p. 4D.

70. George Greanias, Houston City Council, lecture at "Houston: In Search of a Vision" conference, October, 1987.

71. Susan MacManus, *Federal Aid to Houston* (Washington, D.C.: Brookings Institution, 1983), p. 6.

72. Chandler Davidson, "Houston: Where the Business of Government Is Business," in Wendell M. Bedichek and Neal Tannahill, eds., *Public Policy in Texas* (Glenview, Ill.: Scott Foresman, 1982), pp. 277, 281–84; Robert Fisher, "Community Organizing in Historical Perspective: A Typology," in Fred Cox et al., eds., *Strategies of Community Organization*, 4th ed. (Itasca, Ill.: F. E. Peacock, 1987), pp. 387–97; Bullard, *Invisible Houston*, chap. 10.

73. For additional information and sources related to recent developments in Houston see Fisher, "Where Seldom Is Heard a Discouraging Word," esp. n. 72.

74. Norman I. Fainstein and Susan S. Fainstein, "Restructuring the American City: A Comparative Perspective," in Fainstein and Fainstein, eds., *Urban Policy under Capitalism*, pp. 161–89.

75. Evers and Wollmann, "Big City Politics," p. 2.

76. Abbott, *New Urban America*, chap. 9. Also see "Neighborhood Militants," *Southern Exposure* 15 (Spring, 1987): 58–60; Gary Delgado, *Organizing the Movement: The Roots and Growth of "Acorn"* (Philadelphia: Temple University Press, 1986).

77. Juergen Habermas sees the opposite tendencies in neo-conservative efforts in the United States and Western Europe. See Peter Dews, ed., *Autonomy and Solidarity: Interviews with Juergen Habermas* (London: Verso, 1986), p. 137.

CARL ABBOTT

Southwestern Cityscapes:
Approaches to an American Urban Environment

MY POINT of departure for understanding the southwestern cityscape is a startling comment by John Brinkerhoff Jackson, the founding editor of *Landscape* magazine and one of the most creative thinkers about the ways in which Americans have adapted their natural environment to everyday use. Writing in the mid-1980s, he commented that "almost all up-to-date American cities west of the Mississippi are variations on a basic prototype, and that prototype is Lubbock, Texas. . . . There is a new kind of city evolving in America, chiefly in the Sunbelt, and on a small scale Lubbock tells us what those new cities look like."[1]

The suggestion that Americans look to Lubbock for the typical city is more than a rhetorical device that plays on our national prejudice about things Texan. It is also a concealed argument for a major redirection of our approach to American urban development. For more than a century and a half, Americans have been accustomed to study the nation's northeastern cities in detail while glancing hazily and occasionally to the south and west. Jackson wants us to jump two thousand miles and pivot 180 degrees—to stand in the clear air of Lubbock, Albuquerque, Amarillo, and El Paso and take a look around from a very different vantage point.

There is an implicit challenge in the idea of learning from Lubbock. As with all efforts to understand social phenomena, the first step is to clarify the central interpretive idea, its origins, and its important statements. The second step is to measure the idea and its implications against the evidence—in this case to ask what's really different about the new cities of the Southwest in appearance, form, or function.

LEARNING FROM SOUTHWESTERN CITIES

The idea that we can learn about current patterns of urban development from the cities of West Texas and the wider Southwest is new to the closing decades of the twentieth century. In the nineteenth century, in contrast, Americans' first impulse was to learn from Philadelphia, the country's largest and most sophisticated city at the start of the national era. New cities throughout the Mississippi Valley copied Philadelphia's layout, building types, cultural institutions, and even street names. Travelers in Cincinnati, Pittsburgh, Lexington, Nashville, Zanesville, St. Louis, and other new cities repeatedly noted the Philadelphia connection. "So dazzling was this plain and staid metropolis to the eyes of Western members and merchants," commented James Parton, "that, in laying out the cities of the West, they could not but copy Philadelphia, even in the minutest particulars."[2] More generally, new cities copied their public services and improvements from the big three of Philadelphia, New York, and Boston. These largest cities were the first to face problems of growth and demands for new services from police protection to pure water supply. Their experiments simultaneously spread westward across the continent and down the urban hierarchy to smaller and smaller cities.[3]

When nineteenth-century Americans looked at cities in the trans-Mississippi West, in contrast, they believed that they learned a great deal about American national growth but little about the character of American urbanism. In a simple equation, many commentators viewed urban development as the key to western growth and the West as the key to the American future, putting Denver, San Francisco, and their counterparts in the forefront of national progress. Mid-century writers like Jesup Scott of Toledo and William Gilpin of Kansas City and Denver extrapolated statistical trends and created geopolitical theories to link western urbanization and national growth. The center of population and wealth, they argued, was moving into what Gilpin called the Great Central Plain. Eastern states and seaboard cities would soon be appendages to the heartland. The westward course of empire would create great cities in the erstwhile wilderness where "the great minds and wealth of the nation would concentrate."[4]

Journalists repeated the same theme at the end of the century. The always quotable James Bryce visited Portland and Tacoma, Seattle and San Francisco, Bismarck and Walla Walla during the 1880s. He found in this "most American part of America" an intense excitement about national growth and the creation of new societies. William Thayer's thick compendium of *The Marvels of the New West* gave prominent place to the "populous and wealthy cities that have grown into power and beauty as if by magic." In another hundred years, he predicted, western cities would surpass those of the East and usher in "a national growth and consummation without parallel in human history."[5]

As residential communities, however, western cities continued to imitate the East. A city that adapted national models of architecture, public services, and social institutions was a respectable city — a "finished" city in contemporary terminology. The process can be seen at work in Denver, whose residents by the turn of the century could boast that they had successfully negotiated the transition from frontier town to mature city. The local economy had diversified, public services had improved, and socially distinct neighborhoods had appeared. The census of 1900 reported for the first time that women outnumbered men, and citizens of both sexes could choose among scores of literary groups, fraternal organizations, charitable associations, churches, and clubs. Visitors looking for the wild west were disappointed to find another version of Rochester or Indianapolis.[6]

In the first half of the twentieth century, popular and practical understanding of cities was augmented by the new social sciences. As researchers tried to understand the country's urban and industrial growth, they added Chicago to the list of examples but otherwise left the eastern model of American urbanism intact. The interaction between social reform and social research at the University of Chicago produced a comprehensive theory of urban life and urban form that drew heavily on the city's experience. Other investigators during these formative years of urban social science centered their work on other northeastern cities from Boston to Pittsburgh to Muncie. Studies of New York complemented those on Chicago by emphasizing economic functions and governmental roles. The New York tenement code of 1901 and its comprehensive land use zoning ordinance of 1916 were quickly imitated in scores of cities across the country. The *Regional Plan of New York and Its Environs* (1929–31) offered ten volumes on land use, economic growth, transportation, and physical services, an approach replicated a generation later in the nine volumes of the New York Metropolitan Region Study.[7]

The urban scholars who focused their attention on the experience of Chicago, New York, and smaller northeastern urban centers largely ignored the cities of the American West during the years from 1900 to 1940. The decline of western resource frontiers slowed the growth of regional cities and allowed them to settle into an undemanding middle age. Towns like Portland and Tacoma, Denver and San Antonio earned descriptions such as "prematurely gray" and "spinster city."[8] The urban role in the heart of the desert Southwest was scarcely recognized at all. The national image of New Mexico and Arizona was formed by frontier historians, anthropologists, and novelists like Harvey Ferguson, Oliver LaFarge, Frank Waters, and Paul Horgan. They described a region whose small Anglo-American cities were far less interesting than its overpowering space and landscape and its multiethnic heritage.[9]

The great exception in the interwar decades was Los Angeles, whose explosive boom in the 1920s and continued growth during the 1930s demanded explanation. An articulate set of new residents, many associated with the movie industry, developed a strongly colored depiction of Los Angeles as a great and usually grotesque exception. It was a city of odd people, from retired Middle Westerners to movie moguls and evangelists. It was also a city whose often fantastic architecture supplied the metaphors for confusion and lies. In the novels of Nathanael West, Aldous Huxley, James Cain, Raymond Chandler, and Evelyn Waugh, garish, pretentious, and eclectic buildings masked a rootless society.[10]

Attention to an "unnatural" Los Angeles was the first step toward a fundamental redefinition of *southwestern* rather than northeastern cities as the American model. In the 1950s, national journalists increasingly looked to California as an exemplar of urban trends rather than an exception. Writing in *Fortune,* William S. Whyte offered Santa Clara and San Bernardino counties as epitomes of uncontrolled sprawl. Peter Blake used a photographic sequence on the construction of Lakewood, a new community in Los Angeles County, to illustrate the contribution of large-scale subdivisions to the growth of *God's Own Junkyard.* The Association of American Geographers devoted a special issue

of their scholarly journal in 1959 to the thesis that greater Los Angeles
"epitomizes the recent dominance of the city" in American society.[11]

The next step was to consider LA not just as an example of larger
trends but as a genuine "urban prototype." San Diego journalist Neil
Morgan in 1963 restated the nineteenth-century idea that exuberantly
growing western cities represented the national future, nominating
Los Angeles as "the center of gravity in the westward tilt." Two years
later, *Fortune* described Los Angeles as the "prototype of the supercity." Richard Austin Smith found "a scaled-down, speeded-up version of the process of urbanization" and concluded that Los Angeles
"may now be emerging as the forerunner of the urban world of to-
morrow." To other writers of the decade it was a "leading city" or even
the "ultimate city." Journalist Richard Elman traveled to the Los Angeles suburb of Compton "with the thought in mind that this was the
future . . . what lies in store for all the new suburbs of all the big cities
of America."[12]

The 1970s and 1980s extended the California image to the newly
discovered Sunbelt. Austin, Denver, Salt Lake City, Tucson, and other
southwestern cities began to appear on lists of "centers of power" or
"cities of great opportunity."[13] Houston was offered as "the last word
in American cities" and *"the* city of the second half of the twentieth
century." It was "the place that scholars flock to for the purpose of
seeing what modern civilization has wrought," said Ada Louise Huxtable.[14] So was Phoenix, "the quintessential Sun Belt boomtown." It
is "the nation's best example of the shape of the new recreation-oriented,
low-density settlement pattern beginning to emerge across the nation,"
says Richard Louv. It is "America's most super-American city," adds
geographer Pierce Lewis.[15]

At the same time, a group of urban specialists in southern California are consciously working to develop a Los Angeles-based equivalent
of the historic "Chicago School" theories of urban growth and change.
They point to the decentralization of the metropolis, its multiple independent centers, its international connections, and its shifting employment patterns as models of future urban development throughout
the United States. To quote Edward Soja and A. J. Scott, it is the "paradigmatic expression of late capitalist industrialization, urbanization,
and social life."[16]

Perhaps the key book for understanding complex interactions of appearance, form, and function in Los Angeles and its southwestern cousins is Rayner Banham's 1971 essay on *Los Angeles: The Architecture of Four Ecologies*.[17] A British architect and critic, Banham came to California with a fresh eye. His book mixes a traditional discussion of Los Angeles architects and buildings with an effort to define subareas ("ecologies") that are characterized by distinctive interactions between natural landscape, architectural choices, and prevailing lifestyles. The seventy miles of "surfurbia" make L.A. "the greatest City-on-the-Shore in the world." The region's foothills neighborhoods, its suburbanized valleys, and its "autopian" freeways constitute the other ecologies. The book has become a point of reference that is directly cited and unconsciously quoted by critics and journalists alike.[18]

Behind the several ecologies, Banham finds two essential characteristics for Los Angeles — movement and linearity. As many observers have noted, Los Angeles is structured around individual control over personal travel. It functions because its citizens are able to utilize its freeway system for access to all of its subareas. In turn, a city based on automobiles becomes a linear city, with Wilshire Boulevard as the first linear downtown. Freeways define the neighborhoods. Every parallel highway and every adjacent neighborhood carried equal weight in the city's design. Life in Los Angeles means choice and circulation within an open environment that is spatially and perhaps even socially egalitarian.[19]

Many traits of Los Angeles are drawn even more clearly in Las Vegas. At the same time that Banham was learning to drive the Southern California freeways, Robert Venturi, Denise Scott Brown, and Steven Izenour were leading a class of Yale architecture students through a seminar devoted to "Learning from Las Vegas."[20] The resulting book defines Las Vegas as a national model of emerging urban form, an exaggerated example of emerging patterns. For the second, Vegas is presented as the cultural expression of the sunbelt Southwest — a new Florence to the new Rome of Los Angeles. Its central component is the commercial strip, a new main street made up of separate nodes of activity that are separated by parking lots, announced by huge signs, and connected by automobiles. Like Los Angeles, it is a city designed around high speed, with spaces created by billboards and traffic signals rather than buildings.

The Sprawl City of Las Vegas, in turn, brings the discussion back to J. B. Jackson, for what we learn from the Strip is essentially what we can also learn from Lubbock. Throughout the Southwest, Jackson points out, highway strips are as old as the cities themselves. Residential areas fill in as repetitive, low-density units within the framework of the thoroughfares. Lubbock and its sister cities tell us "how the street, the road, the highway has taken the place of architecture as the basic visual element, the infrastructure of the city."[21]

Taken together, Lubbock, Las Vegas, and Los Angeles offer consistent lessons about the form and visual character of cities in the American Southwest. They are vernacular environments that have responded to the tastes and demands of middle Americans, with only sporadic and often *post facto* attention to consciously inclusive planning and urban design. These ordinary cities are linear rather than centered and hierarchical. The ideal model has no privileged locations comparable to the downtowns of turn-of-the-century American cities or the public centers of historic cities. With the automobile reducing the time and inconvenience of distance, each district has approximate equality of position along the axis or within the grid.[22]

The corollary of the uncentered city is the unbounded city. The archetypal southwestern city is capable of indefinite extension by adding easily reproducible units. The structure of the city itself presents no arguments against placing one more casino at the end of the strip or one more subdivision beyond the last. Indeed, the Southwest is often taken as the native ground of the new polycentric American metropolis. "Outer cities" or "outtowns" are loosely connected and substantially self-sufficient suburban realms in which hundreds of thousands of residents may focus on concentrations of employment, retailing, and services. Journalists consistently offer Los Angeles, Houston, Phoenix, and Denver as the pioneers of the new add-on metropolis. We can, if we want, continue the pattern that we've started with Lubbock and Las Vegas and call this new understanding "learning from Las Colinas and Costa Mesa."[23]

UNDERSTANDING SOUTHWESTERN CITYSCAPES

These writers and their rhetoric raise an implicit comparison. Los Angeles and Las Vegas are presumed to be worth our special attention because their internal structure and form are significantly different from those of other American cities. The assumption seems plausible at first glance, but a skeptic might well ask to be shown. It's well and good for architects and landscape critics to describe their essentially personal responses, but where is the evidence on which the rest of us can judge? To convince ourselves that these prairie and desert settlements have special lessons to teach, isn't it necessary to compare them systematically with cities in the rest of the country?[24]

The remainder of this essay explores some of the ways in which southwestern cities might constitute a distinct type. As any urban analyst would expect, measurement of two-dimensional structure can rely on straightforward quantitative data. Because the vertical dimension of human activity has seldom been subject to systematic data collection, in contrast, comparison of three-dimensional cityscapes requires eclectic data and more tentative conclusions. It is also the only way to test the core of the thesis of southwestern urban exceptionalism.

As soon as we move from consideration of representative instances to comparative analysis, it is necessary to define the full set of "southwestern cities." Most regional definitions emphasize either the Southwest's special ethnic heritage or its arid environment. Given a central concern with cityscape rather than social processes, I turned to Walter Prescott Webb's famous essay on "The American West: Perpetual Mirage" for an inclusive definition based on natural environment. His limit of desert influence runs from Canada to Mexico and from the margin of the Great Plains to southern California. On one side it includes San Antonio, Austin, Fort Worth, and Oklahoma City but excludes Houston, Tulsa, and Wichita. On the other it includes the Bay Area and central California but excludes Washington and Oregon. The region includes all of the communities discussed in Eugene Hollon's "Desert Cities on the March" in his Great American Desert, plus parts of Texas, Oklahoma, and California. It coincides closely with the sections of the country where annual runoff of rainfull averages less than five inches.[25]

This extensive Southwest contains twenty-six metropolitan areas with 1980 populations of 300,000 or more. I've matched them with twenty-five metropolitan areas located from the Mississippi River eastward, but excluding Florida and the North Atlantic seaboard. The southwestern metropolitan areas in 1980 ranged in size from 299,000 to 7,478,000, with a median population of 812,000 and a mean of 1,064,000 with the two extreme values dropped. The eastern metropolitan areas ranged from 362,000 to 4,488,000, with a median of 913,000 and a similarly modified mean of 1,039,000.[26]

The decennial census and other federal data sources allow comparisons of the two sets of cities on what are essentially two-dimensional measures of density (Table 1), decentralization of activities (Table 2), and use of transportation options that require compactness of settlement (Table 3). The results are clear. Southwestern cities are not markedly different from those of the nation's nineteenth-century heartland on these aggregated or comprehensive indicators of horizontality. They show virtually identical centralization of retail facilities and patterns of transportation availability and use. Hospital services remain more centralized in the East, presumably because of the inertia of heavy capital investment in older, centrally located hospitals. Residential patterns reverse our expectations, however, with southwestern cities showing higher population densities and a lower proportion of single-family houses. *On the whole,* there is no evidence that southwestern cities are spread more thinly over the landscape, depend more substantially on the automobile, or have extended the triumph of suburbs over central city.[27]

To discover the special character of southwestern cities, we have to look at three dimensions rather than two — at landscapes rather than

Table 1
Metropolitan Settlement Patterns

		26 Southwest Metro Areas	25 Eastern Metro Areas
Percentage of Dwelling Units in One-Unit Structures, 1980[a]	median	66.3%	69.5%
	mean*	65.9	68.8
Population Density per Square Mile for Urbanized Areas[b]	median	2703	2539
	mean	2691	2367

[a]*State and Metropolitan Area Data Book: 1986.*
[b]*U.S. Census of Population: 1980, Characteristics of the Population,* Part I, *U.S. Summary,* table 34.
*Means are calculated with omission of extreme values.

Table 2
Metropolitan Decentralization

		26 Southwest Metro Areas	25 Eastern Metro Areas
CBD Retail Sales as Percentage of SMSA, 1982[a]	median	3.2%	3.1%
	mean*	3.9	3.4
CBD Shopper Goods Stores as Percent of SMSA, 1982[a]	median	4.9%	5.3%
	mean	5.9	5.8
Hospital Beds per Capita: Ratio of Central City, 1980, to SMSA, 1979[b]	median	1.56	2.17
	mean	1.81	2.08

[a] Census of Retail Trade, 1982: Major Retail Center, table 1.
[b] For central cities, County and City Data Book: 1983; for metropolitan areas, State and Metropolitan Area Data Book: 1982.
*Means calculated with omission of extreme values.

Table 3
Metropolitan Transportation Options

		26 Southwest Metro Areas	25 Eastern Metro Areas
Public Transit Vehicle Revenue Miles per Capita, 1983[a]	median	7.4	7.3
	mean*	9.2	8.0
Percent of all Journeys to Work by Public Transit, 1980[b]	median	3.0	3.6
	mean	3.3	4.7
Percent of all Journeys to Work by Walking, 1980[c]	median	3.9	3.7
	mean	4.2	4.3

[a] U.S. Department of Transportation, Urban Mass Transit Administration, National Urban Mass Transportation Statistics 1983
[b] State and Metropolitan Area Data Book: 1986
[c] U.S. Census of Population: 1980, General Social and Economic Characteristics, table 118
*Means are calculated with the omission of extreme values.

maps. More than a Cincinnati or Atlanta, southwestern cities have held close to the ground and spread evenly across it. Denver, says one commentator, drapes over the Colorado plains and foothills like a "lumpy pancake." Los Angeles, agrees architecture critic Brendan Gill, has "hugged the ground on which it was built."[28]

The standard model of American cities assumes that the intensity with which land is used decreases steadily with distance from downtown. A high-rise central business district gives way first to a zone of multistory factories and warehouses left over from earlier generations, then to a ring of mid-rise and walkup apartments, then to multistory single-family residences, and finally to postwar tracts of split-level and single-level houses. The regular decline of population destiny as we move outward from the center allows us to define standard density gradients that describe straight lines or continuous curves.

In the greater Southwest, in contrast, land use does not taper gradually in intensity from the edge of the typical downtown. It plunges abruptly from a glimmering set of new high-rises into a low-rise and usually one-story city that stretches away to the horizon. In the 1840s, Frederick Engles described the *The Condition of the Working Class in England* by "walking" his readers through the neighborhoods of Manchester. The modern equivalent is to "drive" the reader from the airport to the central business district. Leaving Los Angeles International Airport for the center of LA we turn from Sepulveda onto La Tijera, La Cienaga, Stocker, Crenshaw, Coliseum, Rodeo, and Figeroa. There are one-floor commercial strips, one-story bungalows on tiny lots, blocks of two-story apartments, a failed first-generation shopping center, more one-story retailing, and a handful of multistory business buildings in a rudimentary light-manufacturing zone just south of downtown. The stranger's path into Los Angeles repeats the experience of a character in Alison Lurie's novel about *The Nowhere City*: "She gestured at Mar Vista laid out below the freeway: a random grid of service stations, two-story apartment buildings, drive-ins, palms, and factories; and block after block of stucco cottages."[29]

What some observers have taken to be a cityscape peculiar to Los Angeles is actually typical of the Southwest. The region's characteristic styles in residential architecture have had their roots outside the traditional sources of Great Britain, the North Sea littoral of Europe, or northeastern America. Spanish colonial styles and their derivatives, bungalows, and twentieth-century modern have not been confined to the Southwest, but they evolved and flourished in response to the region's particular physical and social environment. Their common traits have included low profiles; prominent horizontal lines established by flat or sweeping shallow-angle roofs; wide porches and patios for protection from the high sun in the days before air-conditioning; and openness to the outdoors through porches, wide windows, and open floor plans.

Even before the arrival of Anglo-Americans with their North Atlantic architectural heritage, Spanish colonists in the Southwest had established a one-story vernacular that adapted the urban courtyard design of Spain and Mexico to the circumstances of the frontier. Settlers filled a town like Tucson with "low-profile, flush-front rectangular cluster houses built on a single level."[30] Early sketches of San Antonio, Santa Fe, and Los Angeles show similar assortments of low-built strucures set in rows or arranged around courtyards. Agricultural settlers on the Hispanic frontier in New Mexico and Colorado adapted the same forms, starting with one-story houses around a plaza and later adding *correlleras*, or terraces of houses flanking the roads into the plaza. When migrants arrived in smaller groups they usually built a *placita*, using low adobe sheds, workshops, and houses with common walls to enclose a hollow square.[31]

Ranch houses of the nineteenth-century cattle frontier and ranch-style tract houses of the twentieth century have been the direct descendants of the Hispanic buildings. Ranchers usually started with a set of directly connecting rooms, sometimes wrapped around a courtyard or growing incrementally at the ends. In more elegant versions, ranch houses were separated from their auxiliary buildings and turned outward through wider windows and broad porches. In turn, the gentleman's ranch house inspired the suburban versions of the mid-twentieth century with their low profiles, flowing interior spaces, and orientation to the outdoors. A book on *Western Ranch Houses* published in 1945 by *Sunset* magazine, the great proponent of the California idyll, emphasized the Spanish origins of the newly popular style. Critic Brendan Gill has more recently stressed the regional character of a style brought into being by "a Pacific climate and a Pacific culture."[32]

Spanish colonial building also led more self-consciously to a pro-
liferation of Hispanic revival houses between 1910 and 1940. In several variants—"Mission," "Pueblo," "Mediterranean"—these buildings
were the particularly southwestern equivalents of the Georgian, Dutch
Colonial, Tudor, and European farmhouse styles that were simultaneously filling the new neighborhoods of northeastern cities. As advertisements liked to emphasize, they were adapted for sunny climates
and outdoor access.[33]

Contemporary with Spanish Revival architecture was the even
more popular bungalow. The style derived in part from British colonial buildings in India, where *bangla* meant a low house with gal-
leries or porches on all sides. Although one American adaptation was
sophisticated "rustic" country and recreational homes for the northeastern elite, the bungalow as a popular middle-class style found its
home ground in California. The term was scarcely known in 1900.
It was a vastly popular generic term by 1910, seen both on the west
coast and elsewhere as a southern California phenomenon. The typical
bungalow rose one or one and one-half stories, often disguising the
second floor with a long, projecting, low-pitched roof. Interior and
exterior space interpenetrated through large front porches and numerous windows. Interiors offered few barriers between the first floor
rooms.[34]

Bungalows matched the social and physical environments of the
Southwest. Informal interiors and emphasis on the outdoors seemed
appropriate to the new middle-class cities of the Pacific coast. Porches
and overhangs provided shelter from summer heat. As Clifford Clark
has commented, bungalows were "easily adapted to the low, sculptured
hills, and flat valley areas, helping to maintain the contour line of
the landscape. In such an environment, small, single-family houses
could be packed relatively closely together without creating a sense
of crowding or congestion." Bungalows spread quickly through the
greater Southwest. An architect who had recently relocated from California built Boise's first bungalow in 1904. The style caught on quickly
as the city boomed during the next few years. White-collar household-
ers in Salt Lake City filled the "Avenues" neighborhood to the northeast of Temple Square and the capitol with bungalows that reflected
the thrifty life-style of the Mormon middle class.[35] Denverites in the

1910s and 1920s built their own version, using brick rather than wood, and leaving daylight basements for partial protection from the extremes of the Great Plains climate.

The final characteristic style of Southwestern cities — the "modern" or "contemporary" house — has parallels to the bungalow. It is also an imported style, brought to the United States by members of the European avant-garde in the 1920s and 1930s. With horizontal lines, flat roofs, low profiles, open interiors, and large windows, modern houses seemed especially appropriate to California society and California light. European-born architects such as Richard Neutra and Rudolph Schindler helped to establish the style with a series of commissions for showplace houses that stretched close to the ground or cascaded over vertical sites. A study of the international style in 1940 found the largest number of examples in California, with increasing popularity elsewhere in the southern tier of states through Arizona, Texas, and Florida.[36] The California-based magazine *Arts and Architecture* helped to publicize the style after World War II by publishing a long series of "Case Study Houses."[37]

The southwestern preference for low-slung, horizontal styles has created neighborhoods very different from those of the Northeast and Middle West. The sprawling working-class neighborhoods on the west side of San Antonio, with their blocks of one-story houses, stand in sharp contrast to Milwaukee or Chicago, where successful immigrant families built two-story houses over raised basements beneath steeply pitched roofs.[38] They contrast even more sharply with the vertical row houses of Baltimore or Philadelphia that stacked two narrow floors, attic, and basement. For a more recent period, the Cape Cod houses of Levittown, New York, with their strong vertical emphasis, offer the same contrast to the contemporaneous hip-roofed ranch houses of Lakewood, California.

Impressionistic evidence is supported by a systematic comparison of popular housing choices in Ohio and California. Richard Fusch and Larry Ford counted single-family housing styles within corridors leading from the centers of Columbus and San Diego through their historic growth rings. The results are clear. Ohioans have preferred to live on two levels. Depending on the decade, they have built steep-roofed Queen Anne houses, two-story American basic and foursquare houses, European colonial revival houses, Cape Cods, and two-story "colonial moderns." San Diegans have built exactly what we would predict — low-set bungalows, Spanish Revival houses, and ranch houses.[39]

Multi-family housing shows the same contrast between vertical cities in the Northeast and horizontal cities in the Southwest. The apartment house was a European import to the United States after the Civil War.[40] Well into the twentieth century, high-rise housing for both the upper and lower classes remained largely a phenomenon of New York and other large northeastern cities. An apartment boom of the 1920s had much greater impact in the northern half of the country than in the southern. In eight northern tier cities in 1950, the proportion of dwelling units located in structures with ten or more units ranged from 9 to 43 percent, with a median of 14 percent. In nine southwestern cities, the same proportion ranged from 2 to 14 percent, with a median of 5 percent.[41] When southwesterners did build multi-family housing, moreover, they often used the distinctly regional style of the one-story U-shaped apartment court. Whether they are carefully designed examples from the 1910s and 1920s by Los Angeles architects Irving Gill and Rudolph Schindler or speculative units thrown up for low-income renters, the origins of the apartment court obviously lie in the Hispanic terraces and *placitas* of the previous century.[42]

The same low-rise preference was expressed in styles of public housing from the 1940s and 1950s. The high-rise public housing warehouses of New York, Chicago, or St. Louis have become notorious as architectural and social mistakes. Southwestern cities during the same decade commonly built public housing in one-story or two-story blocks.[43] As Richard Elman reported, the practical result could sometimes be confusion between East and West. In search of a motel, he found "a greenish low building of stripped-down cinder block with a sign in front on which only the word 'Gardens' was legible." He was looking for the rental office when a passing policeman pointed out in no uncertain terms that it was a *housing project* for *poor people*." "Never mind my embarrassment," Elman continues, "if that was a housing project I was now completely disoriented. There weren't more than eight tiny units with little boxy windows and a wooden stoop in front, no trees anywhere. It looked just the way motels used to look."[44]

A new apartment boom since the 1960s has brought the proportion of multi-family housing in southwestern cities even with national levels.[45] However, much of the new construction has been in garden apartments and two-story apartment blocks scattered through older districts.[46] We can establish the difference with the help of the Annual Housing Survey of the U.S. Department of Housing and Urban Development, which gathers data for selected cities on the percentage of housing units in buildings of four or more stories. Information is available for the years around 1980 for fifteen of the twenty-six southwestern cities used in previous comparisons and for thirteen of the eastern cities. In the East, the percentage of housing units in structures with at least four stories in these thirteen cities ranges from 0.7 to 9.1 percent with a median of 2.7 percent. In the Southwest they range from 0.2 to 19.0 percent with a median of 1.5 percent. If the unusual case of Honolulu is omitted, the southwestern range is 0.2 to 6.7 and the median is 1.35 percent.[47]

The architectural choices of southwestern city neighborhoods are responses to environments of high sun, sharp shadows, and warm, dry summers. The same aesthetic has recently found a confirming expression in public architecture through the design competition for the Phoenix Municipal Government Center. The goal of the competition was to create a central focus for an amorphous city and to define a "Phoenix style." Architects responded obviously with "desert" colors and references to Indian and Spanish pasts. The winning design by Barton Myers, however, goes several steps further. It breaks decisively from the European-influenced monumentality of most United States civic centers. Instead, it establishes a horizontal space that will generate flows of activity among a large number of visually accessible low-rise buildings.[48]

As the Phoenix example indicates, the openness of the natural environment in southwest cities underlies and accentuates the horizontality of their built environments. In the simplest terms, we can appreciate their special form because we can see it. We can take in smaller cities like Santa Fe or Cheyenne at a single glance. We can see enough of most larger cities to comprehend them as units in a way that is impossible in the East.

Southwestern cities are held together by the bright air of the American West. It is clarity of sight that makes a region special — not the brown earth, and not flowing water or its absence, but open horizons. It is changes in the air that we notice first as we travel eastward out of the greater Southwest and hit the summer humidity barrier in eastern Kansas or Texas. The horizon draws in and the sky thickens with haze. In the winter, travelers find that Gulf moisture often turns to thick fog as they drop toward the Mississippi. In contrast, one of the classic interpretations of the Southwest is titled *Sky Determines*. "The emotional and aesthetic effect of the sky is no less real than the practical one," Ross Calvin originally wrote in 1934. "Here one sees it all—180 glorious, colorful degrees of it. In any direction save downwards, it fills the larger part of the view and the eye cannot lift without being aware of its magnificence."[49]

Eight hundred miles westward, Alison Lurie took light as the symbol of the intrusive newness of Los Angeles. The California sun shines with "impartial brilliance" on the transplanted New Englanders in *The Nowhere City*, filters through the drawn drapes of their new house, floods them at the beach. The central character stands on his front walk and looks up at the "intense blue overhead, crossed by trails of jet vapor, dimming to a white haze at the horizon." His letters home talk about "the dry light, the white-walled houses with their orange and lemon trees, the Santa Monica Mountains rising smoky green and brown against the north edge of the sky."[50]

The environmental degradation that southwesterners lament most vigorously in their cities is smog. The contrast with the East is marked. Pittsburgh may be proud that it has freed its air of smoke and soot, but its defining ties to the natural environment are its hills and rivers. The measure of environmental damage and recovery for Cleveland has been Lake Erie. In Denver or Los Angeles, the essential link to nature has always been the air. Water has been a utility and a luxury, but air has made them special places to live—crisp air for TB sufferers, clear air for chamber of commerce pictures of a city set against its mountains. Atmospheric pollution that turns the high blue sky into a hovering yellow lens damages more than property and health. It undermines one of the key elements in the urban experience of the Southwest.

Clear air is dry air. Southwestern cities by our definition are desert cities whose natural vegetation is sparse and low. They are built in landscapes of bunchgrass and brush, where cottonwoods fringe the streams and scrub trees climb the foothills. Sometimes the nineteenth-century settlers planted them with irrigated trees, but the thin natural growth on the surrounding hills does nothing to block the view.

From a distance, the patch of summer green precisely identifies the old residential neighborhoods.

The contrast could not be more clear with the luxuriant landscape of the Atlantic coast, where exuberant vegetation turns vacant lots to thickets and returns unused fields to woodland. Altantic cities are carved into natural forests and embedded in a landscape of jumbled hills and small sheltered valleys. The successive new neighborhoods of Atlanta, Washington, Philadelphia, or Cleveland have hidden themselves in the woods. Southwest cities have grown across far more open landscapes of range land or waste land, prairie dog towns, mesquite fields, and desert.

Perhaps most obviously, southwestern cities are open to view because so many of them offer natural vantage points. Baltimore or Milwaukee can only be experienced as a series of neighborhoods and a succession of scenes unfolding at eye level. Los Angeles (or at least a substantial part) we can see all at once. "Once in the fall of '64," wrote Christopher Rand, "I got a fine view of the whole West Side [of Los Angeles] . . . I was walking southward in the Santa Monica Mountains, and suddenly I rounded a peak and saw the ocean. . . . Small waves were breaking on the beach, which ran off below me, in a graceful curve, to the dune-shaped, hazy height of Palos Verdes, twenty miles away. Inland from the beach, from all twenty miles of it, lay the sprawling city, stretching on to the interior and finally meeting the distant faint brown hills that rimmed the L.A. Basin. Most of their expanse, lying down below me, didn't look too urban; it was the old, familiar mosaic, rather, of white houses amid green."[51] Versions of this view of LA from its mountains have become a cliché in everything from *Fortune* magazine photospreads to advertisements for new Buicks, but it is a cliché because it forms and confirms our image of how we view and understand the urban complex of southern California.

Other southwestern cities are equally open to inspection. San Francisco, wrote Jean-Paul Sartre, is "a city of air, salt, and sea, built in the shape of an amphitheatre."[52] Santa Barbara and Oakland are built against coastal hills, Honolulu against the central peaks of Oahu, Tucson below the Santa Catalina Mountains, Albuquerque, Sante Fe and Colorado Springs at the base of the Rockies. Salt Lake City lies as Richard Burton saw it 130 years ago, occupying "the rolling brow of a slight decline at the western base of the Wasach . . . stretched before us as upon a map."[53] The mass of the Franklin Mountains thrusts at the center of El Paso. Other river cities—Denver, Cheyenne, Casper, Boise, Billings, Bismarck, Grand Junction—sweep up broad, shallow slopes from the stream at their center. When we find the proper vantage points on the ridges and escarpments that mark the margins of their valleys, we can see them as single metropolitan units.

Walter Van Tilburg Clark opens *The City of Trembling Leaves*, his 1945 novel about coming of age in Reno, with a summary of the special openness of the southwestern city. Built along the Truckee River as it pours out of the Sierra Nevada, Reno is defined by "the vigor of the sun and the height of the mountains." From the hills that line the north side of the city, "you look down across the whole billowing sea of the treetops of Reno [and] . . . see the tops of downtown places, the Medico-Dental Building, the roof sign of the Riverside Hotel." Beyond to the south the city slopes upward again from the river, "a high region of new homes, bungalows, ornamented brick structures of greater size, a number of which it would be difficult to describe fairly, and white, Spanish houses. This region seems to become steadily more open, windy and sunlit as you move out." To the east the city spills into the widening valley, where "the light spreads widely." Like the other cities of the Southwest, Reno is a city built to be seen.[54]

As often as not, critics have found that southwestern cities are incomprehensible. To a distinguished historian, Los Angeles is a nebulous entity that remains "the least 'legible' of the great settlements of the world." To an anonymous journalist it is "topless, bottomless, shapeless and endless . . . random, frenzied, rootless, and unplanned." Its suburbs are "formless"; it is a "nowhere city"; it is a "violently aggressive organism" with no focus and no pattern but "helter-skelter" growth.[55] Other southwest cities have inspired the same complaints. Phoenix is a "huge unplanned urban complex." Houston, like Los Angeles, is a "nowhere city" that seems randomly scattered over its landscape.[56]

The argument of this essay has been precisely the opposite. Southwesterners have in fact built our *most* comprehensible cities. We can apprehend them because of their physical and visual openness. We can comprehend them because they are simple. They cluster straightforwardly around their highways. Their cityscapes are constructed from common elements of natural environment and common choices of architecture and design.

What actually bothers the critics is not that southwestern cities are formless, but that they are unfamiliar. Most broadly, they lack the sense of closure that lies at the heart of the European tradition of urban design. Southwestern suburbs march outward without regard for the tidy and tightly organized plans of Frederick Law Olmsted, Ebenezer Howard, and other advocates of planned decentralization.[57] In the city centers we seldom find the time-tested sequence of well-defined public spaces linked by streets that lead from one carefully composed view to the next. The difference, said Jean-Paul Sartre, is that Europe's "slanting, winding streets run head on against walls and houses; once you are inside the city, you can no longer see beyond it. In America, these long, straight unobstructed streets carry one's glance, like canals, outside the city. You can always see mountains or fields or the sea at the end of them."[58]

At the more personal level, southwestern cities are unfamiliar to many critics because they lack the "old urban neighborhoods" that have become the touchstones of nostalgia for "lost" urban community and the valued targets of stylish gentrification.[59] For all its insightful iconoclasm, a book like Jane Jacobs' *Death and Life of Great American Cities* has reinforced the assumption that real urban neighborhoods have busy sidewalks lined with row houses, apartment buildings, and multistory commercial buildings that enclose the street.[60] Only in San Francisco do the southwestern cities offer anything resembling Brookline, Massachusetts or Brooklyn, New York, Georgetown in Washington or Hyde Park in Chicago.

One conclusion from this interpretation is the importance of examining particular circumstances of location and history to understand the ways in which southwest cities may be distinctive. What is different about the southwestern cityscapes is partly a product of their natural settings. It is also substantially the legacy of previous generations, especially those who built between 1900 and 1950. Their choices of neighborhood patterns, preferences about density, and tastes in architecture set these cities apart and created the spatial and aesthetic framework that has been extended during the Sunbelt era. It is as true for Albuquerque and San Diego as for Philadelphia that the urban present is built firmly on the past.[61]

If the disturbances of these cities is based on the unreproducible factors of environment and history, there is reason to doubt that references to a southwestern prototype should be taken at face value. Theory and evidence both suggest that the similarities between southwestern and eastern cities in easily measured aspects of land use structure are the result of convergence of established national patterns rather than a new southwestern type.[62] Aggregate comparisons are supported by more detailed information on Los Angeles, where social scientists trying to measure the uniqueness of transportation, land use, ethnicity, community patterns, and spatial structure have kept coming up short. On such factors, wrote geographers Howard Nelson and William Clark in 1976, Los Angeles is not "particularly different from Chicago, Denver, Detroit, Minneapolis, or a host of other American cities."[63]

Nevertheless, the thrust of this essay has been to point up the equal importance of visual images and impressions in understanding urban America. I started the essay in the world of architectural and landscape interpretation, took an inconclusive detour into the social sciences, and returned at the end to an attempt at cityscape appreciation, drawing on the work of novelists, journalists, and others presumably sensitive to the nuances of the social environment. To test their insights, I suggested that two-dimensional land use and demographic data be supplemented with information on the third dimension of the built environment. To urban specialists whose academic upbringing has revolved around the data in the U.S. Census, factors like architectural styles, building heights, and vegetation types seem like intangibles. In fact, they are perfectly tangible and measurable if we make the effort. As a case in point, Broad Street in Columbus and Colfax Avenue in Denver may both be commercial strips that formed parts of U.S. Route 40, but they are very different in appearance. A comparative analysis would almost surely help us understand why by finding a different mix of building styles and types, different business and institutional uses, and different ways of accommodating automobiles on-street and off-street. Local planning surveys and reports could be mined for comparative information. The U.S. Census of Housing and the Annual Housing Survey could easily supplement their data on costs and conditions with information on height and lot size.

To understand the cities of the Southwest, we need to think both in national and regional terms. Basic trends of metropolitan deconcentration are shared nationwide. Major patterns of economic growth and political responses — topics that have been set to the side in this essay — are shared by cities throughout a Sunbelt that curves from the South Atlantic coast to the Southwest and Pacific. Their characteristic cityscape, however, the cities of the Southwest share largely with themselves. A number of critics have invited our attention to particular aspects of this built environment — to freeways, to commercial strips, to California suburbia. If we put the pieces together, we have a different environment — a different look for southwestern cities that shapes the responses of locals and outsiders alike.

NOTES

1. J. B. Jackson, "The Vernacular City," *Center: A Journal for Architecture in America* 1 (1985): 27.

2. Richard C. Wade, *The Urban Frontier* (Chicago: University of Chicago Press, 1964), pp. 314–19; John Reps, *Town Planning in Frontier America* (Columbia: University of Missouri Press, 1980), pp. 153–54; James Parton, "City of St. Louis," *Atlantic Monthly* 19 (June, 1876): 655.

3. Bayrd Still, *Urban America: A History with Documents* (Boston: Little, Brown, 1974), pp. 174–94; Wade, *Urban Frontier*, pp. 316–17.

4. For examples, see William Gilpin, *The Central Gold Region* (Philadephia: Sower and Co., 1860), and *The Mission of the North American People: Geographical, Social, and Political* (Philadelphia: J. B. Lippincott, 1874); Jesup W. Scott, "Progress of the West," *Hunt's Merchants' Magazine* 14 (February, 1846): 163–65, "The Great West," *DeBow's Review* 15 (July, 1853): 50–53, and "Westward the Star of Empire," *DeBow's Review* 27 (August, 1859): 125–36. For discussions of mid-century boosterism, see Charles Glaab, "Visions of Metropolis: William Gilpin and Theories of City Growth in the West," *Wisconsin Magazine of History* 45 (Autumn, 1961): 21–31, and "Jesup W. Scott and a West of Cities," *Ohio History* 73 (Winter, 1964): 3–12; J. Christopher Schnell and Katherine B. Clinton, "The New West: Themes in Nineteenth Century Urban Promotion," *Bulletin of the Missouri Historical Society* 30 (January, 1974): 75–88; Carl Abbott, *Boosters and Businessmen: Popular Economic Thought and Urban Growth in the Antebellum Middle West* (Westport, Conn.: Greenwood Press, 1981).

5. William Thayer, *Marvels of the New West* (Norwich, Conn.: The Henry Bill Publishing Co., 1891), p. 404; James Bryce, *The American Commonwealth* new ed. (New York: Macmillan, 1912), pp. 891–901. Also see Charles Dudley Warner, "Studies of the Great West: A Far and Fair Country," *Harper's New Monthly Magazine* 76 (March, 1888): 556–69; Josiah Strong, *Our Country: Its Possible Future and Its Present Crisis*, edited by Jurgen Herbst (Cambridge: Harvard University Press, 1963), pp. 27–40, 182, 194, 198.

6. Gunther Barth, *Instant Cities: Urbanization and the Rise of San Francisco and Denver* (New York: Oxford University Press, 1976), pp. 208–28; Carl Abbott, "Boom State and Boom City: Stages in Denver's Growth," *The Colorado Magazine* 50 (Sum-

mer, 1973): 207–30. Also see Lawrence Larsen, *The Urban West at the End of the Frontier* (Lawrence: Regents Press of Kansas, 1978).

7. Good summaries of the growth of urban social science from different points of view can be found in Charles N. Glaab and A. Theodore Brown, *A History of Urban America* (New York: Macmillan, 1976), pp. 209–29 and William H. Wilson, *Coming of Age: Urban America, 1915–1945* (New York: John Wiley and Sons, 1974), pp. 92–119, 136–38. The Regional Plan of New York and Its Environs was summarized in R. L. Duffus, *Mastering a Metropolis: Planning the Future of the New York Region* (New York: Harper and Brothers, 1930). The New York Metropolitan Region Study included now classic volumes by Edgar Hoover and Raymond Vernon, *Anatomy of a Metropolis* (1959), Oscar Handlin, *The Newcomers* (1959), and Robert C. Wood, *1400 Governments* (1961), all published by Harvard University Press.

8. John Chapman, "San Antonio," *Southwest Review* 22 (Autumn, 1936): 39–40; Richard Neuberger, "The Cities of America: Portland, Oregon," *Saturday Evening Post* 219 (March 1, 1947): 23; Robert Perkin and Charles Graham, "Denver: Reluctant Capital," in Ray B. West, ed., *Rocky Mountain Cities* (New York: W. W. Norton, 1949), pp. 280–317; Texas Writers' Project, *San Antonio* (San Antonio: The Clegg Co., 1938), p. 41.

9. John R. Milton, *The Novel of the American West* (Lincoln: University of Nebraska Press, 1980), esp. pp. 316–19. The literature of the Pacific Northwest subregion has similarly focused on individual encounters with nature. William Everson, *Archetype West: The Pacific Coast as a Literary Region* (Berkeley, Calif.: Oyez, 1976) discusses writers such as John Muir, Jack London, Robinson Jeffers, and Ken Kesey.

10. David Fine, ed., *Los Angeles in Fiction* (Albuquerque: University of New Mexico Press, 1984).

11. William H. Whyte, "Urban Sprawl," *Fortune* 57 (January, 1958): 103–109, 194–200; Peter Blake, *God's Own Junkyard: The Planned Deterioration of America's Landscape* (New York: Holt, Rinehart and Winston, 1964); "Man, Time and Space in Southern California," special issue of *Annals of the Association of American Geographers* 49 (September, 1959).

12. Neil Morgan, *Westward Tilt: The American West Today* (New York: Random House, 1963, pp. 136–37; Richard Austin Smith, "Los Angeles: Prototype of Supercity," *Fortune* 71 (March, 1965): 99–100; Werner Hirsch, "Los Angeles: A Leading City?" in Werner Hirsch, ed., *Los Angeles: Viability and Prospects for Metropolitan Leadership* (New York: Praeger, 1971), pp. 237–41; Christopher Rand, *Los Angeles: The Ultimate City* (New York: Oxford University Press, 1967); Richard Elman, *Ill-at-Ease in Compton* (New York: Pantheon, 1967), p. 4.

13. Peter Wiley and Robert Gottlieb, *Empires in the Sun: The Rise of the New American West* (New York: Putnam, 1982); John Naisbitt, *Megatrends* (New York: Warner Books, 1984).

14. Lynn Ashby, "The Supercities: Houston," *Saturday Review* 3 n.s. (September 4, 1976): 16–19; Ada Louise Huxtable, "Deep in the Heart of Nowhere," *New York Times*, February 15, 1976.

15. Gottlieb and Wiley, *Empires*, p. 76; Richard Louv, *America II* (New York: Penguin Books, 1983), pp. 49–51; Pierce Lewis, "Axioms for Reading the Landscape," in Donald W. Meinig, ed., *The Interpretation of Ordinary Landscapes* (New York: Oxford University Press, 1979), p. 16.

16. Edward W. Soja and A. J. Scott, "Los Angeles: Capital of the Late Twentieth Century," *Environment and Planning D: Society and Space* 4 (September, 1986): 249–

54; Michael Dear, "Learning from Los Angeles," *Urban Resources* 4 (Winter, 1987): LA1-2.

17. Rayner Banham, *Los Angeles: The Architecture of Four Ecologies* (New York: Harper and Row, 1971).

18. For example, Paul Gapp, John McCarron, and Stanley Ziemba, *The American City* (Chicago: Chicago Tribune, 1981), 104–107; Michael Sorkin, "Explaining Los Angeles," in Kenneth Frampton and Silvia Kolbowski, ed., *California Counterpoint: New West Coast Architecture* (New York: Rizzoli, 1982), pp. 8–14.

19. Banham, *Los Angeles*, pp. 23, 141, 169, 174. Also see Sam Bass Warner, Jr., *The Urban Wilderness* (New York: Harper and Row, 1972), pp. 113–49 and David Brodsly, *L.A. Freeway: An Appreciative Essay* (Berkeley: University of California Press, 1981).

20. Robert Venturi, Denise Scott Brown, and Steven Izenour, *Learning from Las Vegas: The Forgotton Symbolism and Architectural Form* (Cambridge: MIT Press, 1972).

21. Jackson, "Vernacular City," p. 27. Also see J. B. Jackson, *The Southern Landscape Tradition in Texas* (Fort Worth: Amon Carter Museum, 1980), pp. 25–35.

22. Robert Fogelson, *Los Angeles: The Fragmented Metropolis* (Cambridge: Harvard University Press, 1967), pp. 137–63, 186–204; Warner, *Urban Wilderness*, 136–49. It is significant that the zonal and sectoral models of urban form, which depend on the defining and organizing power of a center, were developed in Chicago between 1910 and 1940. The technique known as Social Area Analysis, in contrast, was developed and tested in Los Angeles during the 1940s. The factors of race, family stage, and socioeconomic status are considered initially without inclusion of a spatial dimension. When the resulting clusters of abstracted social measures are mapped, the spatial distribution is essentially an accident of the data. Social Area Analysis itself offers no theoretical reason to predict any particular pattern of social geography and treats all subareas as potentially equal.

23. Christopher Leinberger and Charles Lockwood, "How Business is Reshaping America," *Atlantic Monthly* 258 (October, 1986): 43–52; Joel Garreau, "The Emerging Cities of Washington," *Washington Post*, March 8, 1987; Paul Goldberger, "Stamford's New Look: Sunbelt in Connecticut," *New York Times*, March 11, 1985, and "When Suburban Sprawl Meets Upward Mobility," *New York Times*, July 26, 1987.

24. Assessments of Los Angeles and other southwest cities have been unclear whether the presumed fact of difference also involves a direction of change. Writers who talk about ultimate cities, archetypes, exaggerated examples, and paradigms simply imply that the cities are new and different. Writers who talk about prototypes imply a model for future development. Since the idea is usually not elaborated, however, it may imply that older cities will retain their historic character while younger cities follow a new path. In this interpretation, differences between old and newer cities are likely to remain sharp. Alternatively, the idea of a prototype might imply that older cities will incrementally move toward the southwestern type. In this latter interpretation, differences could be expected to erode at some unspecified rate.

25. Walter Prescott Webb, "American West: Perpetual Mirage," *Harper's Magazine* 214 (May, 1957): 25–31; W. Eugene Hollon, *The Great American Desert* (New York: Oxford University Press, 1966), pp. 217–37; U.S. Geological Survey, *National Atlas of the United States* (Washington: U.S. Government Printing Office, 1970), pp. 118–19.

26. The southwestern metropolitan areas are Austin, Dallas–Fort Worth, San Antonio, El Paso, Oklahoma City, Denver, Colorado Springs, Albuquerque, Phoenix, Tucson, Salt Lake City, Las Vegas, Honolulu, San Diego, Anaheim, Riverside, Los An-

geles, Oxnard, Santa Barbara, Bakersfield, Fresno, Stockton, Sacramento, San Jose, San Francisco–Oakland, and Vallejo. The eastern metropolitan areas are Rochester, Syracuse, Pittsburgh, Cleveland, Akron, Toledo, Canton, Columbus, Cincinnati, Indianapolis, Peoria, Lansing, Detroit, Milwaukee, Madison, Minneapolis–St. Paul, Louisville, Nashville, Memphis, Jackson, Birmingham, Mobile, Atlanta, Columbia, and Charlotte.

27. Housing choices, transportation choices, and population density in southwestern metropolitan areas are also similar to those in a set of twenty metropolitan areas located within the northeastern megalopolis. The following figures for the twenty northeastern metro areas can be compared with Tables 1 and 3:

	median	mean omitting extremes
percent of dwelling units in one-unit structures	67.8	65.2
population per square mile for urbanized areas	2497	2688
percent of journeys to work by public transit	6.0	6.6

The metro areas whose 1980 populations ranged from 313,000 to 4,768,000, with a median of 821,000 and an adjusted mean of 1,206,000, are Richmond, Washington, Baltimore, Wilmington, York, Lancaster, Philadelphia, Allentown-Bethlehem, Trenton, Monmouth-Ocean (N.J.), Middlesex-Somerset-Huntington (N.J.), Nassau-Suffolk (N.Y.), Albany, Stamford-Bridgeport-Norwalk, New Haven–Waterbury, Hartford, Providence, Springfield, Worcester, and Boston.

28. *New York Times*, March 14, 1974; Brendan Gill, "Reflections: Los Angeles Architecture," *New Yorker* 56 (September 15, 1980): 109.

29. Alison Lurie, *The Nowhere City* (New York: Coward-McCann, 1965), p. 25.

30. Janet Ann Stewart, *Arizona Ranch Houses* (Tucson: Arizona Historical Society, 1974), p. 3.

31. John Reps, *Cities of the American West* (Princeton, N.J.: Princeton University Press, 1979), pp. 35–155; Alvar Ward Carlson, "Rural Settlement Patterns in the San Luis Valley," *Colorado Magazine* 44 (Spring, 1967): 111–28; Hugh and Evelyn Burnett, "Madrid Plaza," *Colorado Magazine* 42 (Summer, 1965): 224–37; Marc Simmons, "Settlement Patterns of Village Plans in Colonial New Mexico," *Journal of the West* 8 (January, 1969): 7–21.

32. *Sunset Western Ranch Houses* (San Francisco: Lane Publishing, 1946); Gill, "Los Angeles," p. 142; Stewart, *Arizona Ranch Houses*.

33. Alan Gowans, *The Comfortable House: North American Suburban Architecture, 1890–1930* (Cambridge: MIT Press, 1986), pp. 113–18; David Gebhard, "The Spanish Colonial Revival in Southern California," *Journal of the Society of Architectural Historians* 26 (May, 1967): 131–47.

34. For an introduction to a substantial literature on bungalows, see Clay Lancaster, *The American Bungalow, 1880–1930* (New York: Abbeville Press, 1985); Robert Winter, *The California Bungalow* (Los Angeles: Hennessey and Ingalls, 1980); Barbara Rubin, "A Chronology of Architecture in Los Angeles," *Annals of the Association of American Geographers* 67 (December, 1977): 521–37; Richard Mattson, "The Bungalow Style," *Journal of Cultural Geography* 2, (1981): 75–92; Clifford E. Clark, Jr., *The*

American Family Home, 1800–1960 (Chapel Hill: University of North Carolina Press, 1986), pp. 176–79.

35. Clark, *American Family Home*, pp. 185–91.

36. James Ford and Katherine Morrow Ford, *The Modern House in America* (New York: Architectural Book Publishing, 1940); Esther McCoy, *Five California Architects* (New York: Reinhold Publishing, 1960); David Gebhard, *Schindler* (New York: Viking Press, 1972); W. Boesinger, ed., *Richard Neutra, 1923–1950: Buildings and Projects* (Zurich: Verlag für Architektur, 1964).

37. Banham, *Los Angeles*, 223–33. Critics have found significant influences of the Spanish Revival movement on Southern California modern, particularly in the emphasis on horizontality and the role of courtyard or patio space. Irving Gill, a California architect who used the Spanish idiom for innovative houses in the 1920s, is an important transitional figure. See Thomas Hines, "Origins and Innovations," *Architectural Review* 182 (December, 1987): 73–79; Gowans, *Comfortable House*, p. 120; Gill, "Los Angeles," pp. 138–39.

38. Roger Simon, "The City-Building Process: Housing and Services in New Milwaukee Neighborhoods, 1880–1810," *Transactions of the American Philosophical Society* 68, pt. 5 (1978); Richard Wade and Harold Mayer, *Chicago: Growth of a Metropolis* (Chicago: University of Chicago Press, 1969).

39. Richard Fusch and Larry Ford, "Architecture and the Geography of the American City," *Geographical Review* 73 (July, 1983): 324–40.

40. Gunther Barth, *City People: The Rise of Modern City Culture in Nineteenth Century America* (New York: Oxford University Press, 1980): pp. 45–53; John Hancock, "The Apartment House in Urban America," in Anthony King, ed., *Building and Society: Essays on the Social Development of the Built Environment* (London: Routledge, 1980); J. C. Weaver, "The North-American Apartment Building as a Matter of Business and an Expression of Culture," *Planning Perspectives* 2 (January, 1987): 27–52.

41. The data are taken from Larry Ford, "Multiunit Housing in the American City," *Geographical Review* 76 (October, 1986): 390–407.

42. James Tice and Stefanos Polyzoides, "Los Angeles Courts," *Casabella* 412 (April, 1976): 17–23; Gebhard, *Schindler*, pp. 65–73.

43. Southwestern public housing designs drew on the same ideas that lay behind several large-scale projects from the end of the 1930s. Planner Clarence Stein consulted on the development of middle-class Baldwin Hills Village (1938) as well as the public housing projects of Ramona Village and Carmelitos (1939). Richard Neutra's Channel Heights (1942) accommodated six hundred war-worker households near San Pedro, California. The apartments were built in a mix of one- and two-story buildings with flat roofs, large windows, and open design to take advantage of unobstructed space on open slopes above the ocean.

44. Elman, *Compton*, pp. 34–35.

45. For the same subsets of cities cited in note 41, above, 1980 data for the percentage of housing units in structures of ten or more units ranges from 13 to 50 percent with a median of 20 percent for the northern cities; it ranges from 14 to 27 percent with a median of 20 for the southwestern cities. Also see Table 1.

46. Some architecture critics have adopted "L.A. dingbat" as the term for two-story block apartments with a wide variety of surface treatments (Banham, *Los Angeles*, pp. 175–77).

47. The Annual Housing Survey gathers information from a sample of cities on a five-year rotation. The available year closest to 1980 was used for each city.

48. Kenneth Frampton, "The Usonian Legacy," *Architectural Review* 182 (December, 1987): 26–31; Charles Jencks, "Phoenix Style and Free-Style Classicism, *Architectural Design* 57 (1987): 30–33.

49. Ross Calvin, *Sky Determines: An Interpretation of the Southwest*, rev. ed. (Albuquerque: University of New Mexico Press, 1965), p. 28.

50. Lurie, *Nowhere City*, pp. 4, 14.

51. Rand, *Ultimate City*, p. 95.

52. Jean-Paul Sartre, "American Cities," in *Literary and Philosophical Essays* (London: Rider and Co., 1955), p. 116.

53. Richard F. Burton, *The City of the Saints, and Across the Rocky Mountains to California*, ed. Fawn Brodie (New York: Alfred A. Knopf, 1963), p. 218.

54. Walter Van Tilburg Clark, *The City of Trembling Leaves* (New York: Random House, 1945), pp. 3–12.

55. Daniel Boorstin, *The Americans: The Democratic Experience* (New York: Random House, 1973), p. 269; "The Far West," *Better Homes and Gardens* 54 (November, 1976): 201; Blake, *Junkyard*, pp. 20–21; *New York Times*, December 18, 1955, and February 2, 1957.

56. Andrew Kopkind, "Modern Times in Phoenix," *New Republic* 153 (November 6, 1965): 14–16; Ada Louise Huxtable, "Deep in the Heart of Nowhere," *New York Times*, February 15, 1976; Larry King, "Bright Lights, Big Cities," *Atlantic* 235 (March, 1975): 84.

57. Lois Craig, "Suburbs," *Design Quarterly* 132 (1986): 3–31.

58. Sartre, "American Cities," pp. 116–17.

59. On nostalgia for the big city neighborhood, see Maurice Stein, *The Eclipse of Community* (Princeton, N.J.: Princeton University Press, 1960).

60. Jane Jacobs, *The Death and Life of Great American Cities* (New York: Random House, 1961).

61. The 1920s are identified as the formative years for the Los Angeles cityscape in both Scott Bottles, *Los Angeles and the Automobile* (Berkeley: University of California Press, 1987), and Donald W. Meinig, "Symbolic Landscapes: Models of American Community," in D. W. Meinig, ed., *The Interpretation of Ordinary Landscapes* (New York: Oxford University Press, 1979), pp. 169–71.

62. Leo Schnore, *Class and Race in Cities and Suburbs* (Chicago: Halstead, 1972); James Pinkerton, "City-Suburban Residential Patterns by Social Class: A Review of the Literature," *Urban Affairs Quarterly* 4 (1969): 499–519; Barry Edmonston, Michael Goldberg, and John Mercer, "Urban Form in Canada and the United States: An Examination of Density Gradients," *Urban Studies* 22 (June, 1985): 209–217; Carl Abbott, "The Suburban Sunbelt," *Journal of Urban History* 13 (May, 1987): 275–301; Kenneth T. Jackson, *Crabgrass Frontier: The Suburbanization of the United States* (New York: Oxford University Press, 1985).

63. Howard J. Nelson and William A. V. Clark, *The Los Angeles Metropolitan Experience: Uniqueness, Generality, and the Goal of the Good Life* (Cambridge, Mass.: Ballinger, 1976), p. 1. In addition, Stephen Thernstrom in 1971 found that the Los Angeles metropolis substantially matched national social and demographic patterns. Edward Soja has more recently emphasized the prominent manufacturing sector and diversified economic base that make Los Angeles the "paradigmatic industrial metropolis of the modern world." Kenneth Jackson has commented that Los Angeles now matches national norms in homeownership and commuting times. Stephen Thernstrom, "The Growth of Los Angeles in Historical Perspective: Myth and Reality," in Werner

Hirsch, ed., *Los Angeles: Viability and Prospects for Metropolitan Leadership* (New York: Praeger, 1971), pp. 3–19; Soja and Scott, "Los Angeles," p. 249; Edward Soja, Rebecca Morales, and Goetz Wolff, "Urban Restructuring: An Analysis of Social and Spatial Change in Los Angeles," *Economic Geography* 59 (April, 1983): 195–230; Gapp, McCarron and Ziemba, *American City*, pp. 94, 103.

ROGER W. LOTCHIN

The City and the Sword through the Ages and the Era of the Cold War

THE CITY and the sword have been partners for as long as there have been cities and war. Yet until recently, few have tried to narrate and analyze their essential relationship. Perhaps there is none. Given the magnitude of change over a span of five millennia, the association of the city and the sword may have been ad hoc, ephemeral, episodic, and incapable of codification. Possibly each era of warfare and urbanization-urbanism featured a different connection between the two. Perhaps not. In any case, it is high time that we attempt to find out whether any such relationship exists.

Urbanization and militarization have been central features of all civilized life in the Western world. Sometimes they have been more important and sometimes less, but both have always been significant. Many authors have written about one or the other, especially warfare. We have learned treatises on the principles of warfare; on land, sea, and air war; on military conflict in various epochs — ancient, medieval, Renaissance, Baroque, Enlightenment, and modern; about the essence of warfare; about civil-military relations; about militarism; about martial technology; about the great captains — Caesar, Marlborough, Vauban, Napoleon, Wellington, Rommel, Patton, and Zhukov; about the science of supply; about war and society; about war and the state; about war and the liberation of women; in short, about almost every conceivable aspect of armed conflict. The references to the subject take up many file drawers in any graduate library.

Although the literature of urban history is not as complete as that of war, it too covers many topics, eras, and nations. American urban history has been especially rich, and each edition of the bibliography in the *Urban History Review* reminds us of how completely we have encompassed the field. Urban history publications on different eras abound: on Western, Southern, Sunbelt, and other regional metropolises; on class, race, religion, and ethnicity; on mobility and persistence; on crime and collective violence; on such city services as fire, water, police, electricity, and transit; on childhood and womanhood; on politics; on sports and recreation; on work; on the family; on planning; and even on the dismal science of economics. Some of these studies treat military matters, but none makes the association of the city and the sword a central feature of its analysis. This is a curious omission, since wars have had such a dramatic impact on American cities. Whether one is looking at the racial and ethnic riots of the Civil and First World wars, the strategy of the American Revolution, the prosperity of the Second World War, or the polarization of the Vietnam War, the phenomenon of armed conflict has obviously influenced that of urbanization and urbanism.

The reverse has also been true. In the Second World War, for example, soldiers bombed Berlin in planes manufactured in Los Angeles, attacked the Pacific islands in landing craft curiously enough manufactured in Denver, fought Rommel in tanks produced in Detroit, and crossed the oceans in Liberty ships fabricated on San Francisco Bay. They loaded their ships from a Norfolk dock, threw their farewell parties in a Charleston bar, fought for housing in a San Diego neighborhood, and saw their first "exotic" person in San Francisco's Chinatown. Often, they slept in their cars on a Brooklyn street, sampled the night spots and sometimes the jails of Jacksonville, continually rumbled over the streets and on the trolleys, subways and pavements of scores of towns, kissed their wives and sweethearts good-bye from a New York City pier, and, when the conflict ended, rioted with the San Francisco police to celebrate their deliverance. The war touched the city at every turn, and the city touched the warriors back. It was the same during *most* American conflicts and during *every one* since the Civil War. Thus, there is a gap in the literature of both war and urbanization. At this point, it is impossible to explain the hiatus in two otherwise remarkably well researched fields, but it is not impossible to begin to fill it. It is the purpose of this essay to discuss this urban and military relationship.

For most of recorded human history, the partnership of armed conflict and urbanization has remained surprisingly static, despite the enormity of human change over that expanse of time. Until very recently, cities tended to force the expansion of war and wars have tended to restrict the development of urbanization and urbanism. In order to counter the city strongpoint, warfare had to become ever more complex and destructive, from the siege tower to the cannon to aerial bombing with chemical and ultimately, nuclear weapons. By the same token, until World War II, the activities of war retarded the growth and development of cities. Military conflict girdled the city with expensive and cramping defensive walls and works, disrupted the lines of urban commerce, and forced cities to shelter refugees from the countryside, thus inflicting both crowding and disease upon those unfortunate communities. Metropolitan areas also had to contribute heavily to the financing of wars and to endure the destruction and death they wrought. From the era of siege warfare to the epoch of strategic and terror bombing, cities have been roughly handled by martial conflict. The siege of Leningrad, the battle of Stalingrad, the blitz of London, and the aerial destruction of Hiroshima, Dresden, Nagasaki, Tokyo, and Berlin have been only the most recent and spectacular examples of the devastating impact of war upon cities.

However, with the advent of the megalopolis and nuclear and thermonuclear weapons, the relationship between cities and armed conflict has reversed itself. Since 1945, cities have restricted military activity, and war and defense have expanded cities. Modern high-powered weapons can seldom, if ever, be employed because of the devastation they would produce in urban centers, and as a result, they have lost much of their military significance. At the same time, they have been transformed from weapons of destruction into means of production. And just as cities have raised the cost of war to a prohibitive level, thereby contracting its realm, so they have taken the weapons of conflict and put them to the civilian purpose of city building; in effect, transforming warfare into welfare. California cities have led the way in this domestication of the art of war, and San Diego has led the way in California, using essentially military resources to make itself into a great American urban center. As a result, an out-of-the-way American place, located in a remote corner of the nation, has become one of its largest cities despite its lack of resources, centrality of location, or head start in the race for world-class urban status. Just as conflict formerly militarized cities, now cities have civilianized or domesticated war, and nowhere more so than in the martial city of San Diego. This process has been nearly as vivid in other California metropolitan areas and throughout the American South and West and has helped to encourage the shift of population and wealth to those regions.

"The Border City" traditionally likes to attribute its success to its natural advantages, namely climate and scenery, although San Diego has precious few of these assets, especially those that helped to create great cities before the twentieth century. It had no nearby deposits of coal or iron, little level land, little water, no adjacent river highways, no strategic location on the routes of trade or international migration, no proximity to the great markets of the United States or the world, and a very meager railroad network. It did not even possess a great harbor. San Diego Bay required successive dredging operations to make it useful in an era of steel ships, and so even the Harbor of the Sun as a strategic resource was nothing compared to San Francisco Bay or the harbor of New York City. San Diego did, however, have dedicated leadership determined to make it into a world-class city. They sometimes quarreled over whether the city should cater to industry or retirees because smokestacks might destroy the natural beauty of the place, but growth of some kind seemed eminently desirable.

Although social commentators and historians have accorded the Second World War a great influence in shaping the contemporary world, there were some things that war did not change at all. Or, perhaps the more they changed, the more they stayed the same. One such matter was the San Diego approach to the competitive process of urban development and the close connection to the military services that this association involved. San Diegans had long labored to create a tight interface between the services, especially the Navy, and the community after the war, and the Harbor of the Sun continued to look upon its relationship with the military as symbiotic. E. Robert Anderson, San Diego officer of the Navy League, captured the local sentiment vividly in a letter to Congressman Bob Wilson. "If, during my term of office, I can give muscle to the 'civilian arm' of our Navy, then I will have served San Diego," wrote the newly elected national vice-president. "And to serve San Diego is to serve our national defense because our city and the nation's security are like twins." The Navy Leaguer could not have summed up better the effort to use the presence of the Navy, and defense in general, as the cement of urban community and at the same time to elaborate further the already impressive community of interest between the city and the sword.[1]

In his farewell address to the nation in 1961, President Dwight Eisenhower called attention to the partnership between civilian, government, and military elements, which he termed the "military-industrial complex." This was not the first time the President had warned of this new economic force, but it was the one that stuck in the minds of press and public and the one that has come to characterize this civil-military relationship ever since. However happy the phrase might have been as a way to educate the public, it oversimplified the matter in several important ways. Ike described a monolith, whereas the nature of the military-industrial complex was much more pluralistic. He stressed the military partnership with industry, thus neglecting everything else. He conveyed a sense of "we" and "they," which has characterized discourse about the relationship from that point onward. And he gave the impression that the military-industrial complex was made up only of the rich and powerful, as opposed to common people. The President was correct that a relatively powerful alliance had grown up between the civil and military sectors in the United States, but the term military-industrial complex implied a number of very fundamental misapprehensions about the new powerhouse in American political and economic life.

None was more unfortunate than the idea that the military-industrial complex primarily served wealthy munitions makers, politicians, and government bureaucrats at the expense of everyone else. Neither the "we" and "they" aspect of his description nor the rich-poor dichotomy holds up under investigation. Historians have recently come to study nearly every imaginable social institution "from the bottom up," and that approach is a very useful corrective to Eisenhower's original conceptualization of the military-industrial complex. This perspective reveals the broad urban, social bases of the civil-military interface and the welfare dimension of twentieth-century warfare as well.

The "metropolitan-military" complex encompassed elites of all kinds — educators, business leaders, military officers and enlisted personnel, politicians, chamber of commerce activists, scientists, labor unionists. It also encompassed masses of non-elites, who often voted subsidies to the metropolitan-military complex, and who always clamored for ever more defense monies for their cities. Nowhere did this support of the "little people" reveal itself more dramatically than in San Diego.

Any threat of a reduction in force at one of the local bases, any threat to its missile or airplane programs, any demand to move a part of the fleet to Long Beach, or any whisper of a redistribution of ship-building contracts away from the Harbor of the Sun prompted a flurry of protests to the government. The language of these missives is both poignant and revealing. For example, the proprietor of a music company wrote to Congressman Wilson in early 1961 that his business had dropped off by 35 percent, that his work force was being laid off, and that two firms on his block would shutter their windows if conditions did not improve. "We have an idle aircraft industry that the Government should recognize in some positive manner," lamented Robert Mitchell. "I am writing to stress the urgent need for defense contracts," wrote James W. Bleford, bemoaning the "extent of unemployment," in San Diego. "Our industry consists, so very much more than most, predominantly of Military and Defense contracts." A union man added "If Convair is working strong then I will be working."[2]

Perhaps half of the correspondents were women. One stressed the advantages of living in San Diego and explained that her family had put down roots in the city. "We love San Diego . . . we have had a baby . . . my mother has joined us . . . we have built a new home here . . . we are college graduates. . . . However, our almost blissful existence here has been marred by the fear that my husband, along with thousands of others will lose his job" at Convair. "This is such a marvelous place to live, and we certainly hope we can continue here," concluded Mrs. Paul W. Bergstedt. The wife of a twenty-year veteran at Convair asked, "Will it come to giving up our home, our children's education which we happily sacrificed for, so they could be part of the future of our county?" It was not fair for a man to invest twenty years in job, "just to find yourself washed up and out in the cold," she observed. "Here's to a bigger and better Convair and more contracts from the Defense Dept."[3]

An Army veteran of twenty-three years already considered San Diego, a "Lost County." Democracy itself seemed to hang in the balance. "If it be in your representative's [Congressman Bob Wilson] power to give new birth to the unemployed in this county," concluded M. Sgt. W. W. Law, paraphrasing Abraham Lincoln, "it would long be remembered that, government of the people, by the people, for the people, shall not perish from this earth." Moving away from the Gettysburg battlefield to a closer one, the soldier added that "no county in the United States can offer the relaxation to our defense workers like San Diego County, with its many Parks, National Forest Camp Grounds, State Forestry Parks and Camp Grounds, and Seashores." Between amenity and democracy, the Harbor of the Sun seemed to have it all. Many of the pleaders believed that Convair had been cheated out of its fair share of contracts by sinister political influences, especially after the new Kennedy Administration took power in 1961. "I feel that the talents of a large engineering force, such as the one at Convair, should be utilized for the good of our country," wrote the wife of an engineer. Obviously, in her mind, the national well-being and that of her husband were closely linked.[4]

These letters document the widespread popular belief in the Harbor of the Sun that what was good for Convair was good for the U.S.A. They also emphasize the belief that political manipulation was used to deny the company its fair share of contracts. In reality, this discrimination was very unlikely. At the very moment of this urban "crisis of contracts" only 8 percent of the San Diego work force was unemployed and in early 1961 the company had a backlog of over one billion dollars' worth of military orders. While the mass backers of the Martial Metropolis complained that San Diego was becoming a ghost town and that "Convair had not received a contract in years," the *San Diego Tribune* reported that this firm had "spent a record $936 million with suppliers in 1960," mostly in San Diego. For those with short memories, the *Tribune* pointed out that the previous record had been set at $862.2 million—the year before.[5]

The letters also document the fact that most San Diegans understood quite clearly the close connection between the city and the sword and their heavy dependence upon military contracts. They were not manipulated by some greedy elite, but were rather willing participants in the creation of a fortress city or bastide. Finally, this view of the metropolitan-military complex from the bottom up reveals a thoroughly special-interest approach to national defense matters. Few judged the matter of local contracts within the context of overall defense spending policies. Although San Diego leaders often had a clear idea of defense strategy and tactics, their constituents had not the foggiest notion of what these were. They instinctively assumed that if Convair or San Diego did not get the contract, "politics" had cheated them

out of their "fair share," and that being the case, politics should restore it to them again. The mass of citizens of that place partook of
the defense feast as willingly as any of the other diners — military, industrial, bureaucratic, political, or scientific — and with the same in-
satiable appetite.

The mass adherence to the metropolitan-military complex can be
seen in an even more stark light in the ceremonial interface between
the city and the sword. Just as pre–World War II residents had involved
themselves heavily in putting on bomber shows over the World's Fair,
sham battle theater, and practice marine landings, so did their post-
war successors. None rallied the entire metropolitan area more fully
than Air Power Day, 1953. Other cities traditionally have staged their
own peculiar celebrations — A Taste of Chicago; A Taste of Peoria; the
Pekin, Illinois, Marigold Festival; the Newport and Covington, Kentucky, Octoberfest; the Pennsylvania National Pike Festival — during
which the downtown streets are blocked off and the citizens assemble
to sample the town cuisine, flowers, beer, and crafts, listen to the municipal band, and enjoy the sunshine of a summer's afternoon. In San
Diego, it was Air Power Day. This civil festival grew out of the fiftieth-
anniversary celebration of "Controlled Powered Flight" and the
seventieth-anniversary celebration of "Controlled Winged Flight."
Cities across the nation joined in this celebration, but California cities
joined in more than most. Of the forty-six events scheduled nationwide, California cities provided sixteen and co-sponsored a seventeenth,
staging dances, air shows, factory open houses, lectures, and public
school observances. Of the California total, San Diego put on more
than half.[6]

The crowning event, Air Power Day itself, took place at Miramar
Naval Air Station later that fall. To say that the event was a popular
success would be an understatement. The Jaycees expected a crowd
of some 125,000 people but instead found themselves mobbed by an
estimated 300,000. More Sea and Air Power observances followed over
the years, several of them attracting similar crowds. On a more pro-
saic level, the maritime museum, the offices of local clubs, the Historical Society, the Chamber of Commerce and other urban institutions displayed naval and military relics in order to keep the Navy story
before the community. Year after year, the boosters continued to join
the emotional, recreational, and vocational life of the urban masses

to the military in an ongoing series of pageants designed to bolster the city's fortunes in the Darwinian struggle for urban hegemony.[7]

Anyone who has spent any time in San Diego knows that no special pains are needed to "keep the Navy story before the community" because the Navy is an inescapable presence everywhere. Cruising the harbor, one passes a submarine base, a carrier anchorage, North Island Naval Air Station, hummock ammunition bunkers, docks and ships galore, barracks ships, shipbuilding firms, and drydocks. A drive down the boulevard bordering the harbor reveals an almost wall-to-wall presence of the Navy from just below Seaport Village to the San Diego–Coronado Bridge. In the bay, ships ply the waters and retired admirals cruise their sailing vessels; overhead, naval helicopters buzz and jets scream; and downtown, sailors throng the streets and crowd the beer joints close to the harbor. The inextricability of the Navy and the city is unavoidable in its everyday work life. But now its play life and its historic consciousness would be equally tied to that service as well. The "people" of San Diego would participate just as fully in the metropolitan-military complex as the elites, whether through their pleas for work, their attendance at the martial festivals, or by taking a harbor cruise or a trip to the Museum of Fine Arts in Balboa Park. They would be kept in touch with the Navy in their public schools, by visiting their congressional representative, or by walking past the display cases of the Fleet Reserve Association, the Military Order of the World Wars or the Navy League.[8]

Both the mass participation in the metropolitan-military complex and the transformation of military assets into civilian ones can be seen anew in the politics of military surplus. The requests for surplus government assets ranged across the spectrum — religious and secular, charitable and business, public and private. The military resources started out as weapons all right, but eventually were turned to economic, fraternal, and even genuinely benign purposes. Urban leaders traditionally complain of the adverse impact of the military on their communities, but that influence could quite often be rather helpful.

For example, Midway Motors needed several hundred trailers for a large engineering project, the Ramona Municipal Water District required some good government steel pipe, and the Gyrotor Helicopter Company (makers of military and civilian craft) wanted an HSL-1 helicopter. The tuna industry needed both air and naval power to pursue its catch, planes to spy out the fish, and tugboats to catch them. The American Legion wanted surplus uniforms to replace their own stock and horns for their youth drum and bugle corps; the San Diego Heart Association wanted a safe to store their donations securely; and the Fletcher Hills Elementary School urgently required a "surplus Navy aircraft" for playground equipment; so did the Community Methodist Chapel of the Hills in Descanso, preferably a P-40 or P-51. The South Bay Young Men's Christian Association begged for a surplus bus in order to serve its suburban district. Meanwhile, the San Diego Home for the Blind hoped for a former housing site on which to build a home, and the Boy Scouts angled for a ship. [9]

The American Association of University Women wished to know how to get in on the general phenomenon of surplus; the Clairemont High School hoped for some woodworking equipment; the City of San Diego hankered after a spare Navy tugboat. And James W. Turpin, M.D., desired to secure "as much surplus material as possible from the hospital ship, *Repose*, being decommissioned in San Diego, the materials to be used in treating Chinese refugees in Hong Kong." Perhaps the most unique request came from an enthusiast who wanted the military to stop destroying its surplus parachutes and make them available to sky divers like himself. He was firmly convinced that the parachutes would produce a distinct leveling influence on society, since "surplus parachutes give the low-budget sky diver a chance to compete with his richer neighbor," Milton Nodacker explained, adding that the move "would also make parachutes available at lower cost to private pilots for a greater margin of safety in cross-country flying, and local flying too." Of course the daredevil grounded his ultimate justification in the realm of military security: "Another case for the release of surplus parachutes for civilian use is the potential of trained parachutists for national defense, who would make a valuable . . . reserve. For this reason alone, the armed services should do all they can to promote, rather than hinder, sport parachuting." One does not note in these efforts a literal example of beating a genuine sword into an authentic plowshare, but the parachutes, buses, medical supplies, playground equipment, woodworking machines, tugboats, irrigation pipe, hospital supplies, land for the blind, and planes for the tuna dawn patrol at least come close. [10]

Nonetheless, popular participation and acquiescence in the metropolitan-military complex does not negate the fact of its domination by elite. In the immediate aftermath of the Second World War, San Diegans struggled to recover from the hurricane of urban development triggered by the war. After some low-grade complaining that the Navy had left their city in the lurch to deal with the problems that the *military* had caused, The Port of the Palms settled down to its normal routine of ingratiating itself with the Navy and monopolizing its property.

Although the Navy had poured millions into the infrastructure of the Harbor of the Sun by 1945, it would subsequently acquire many more crucial holdings. By 1954 the government investment in Marine and Navy installations in the Eleventh Naval District had risen to "about one billion" dollars, and it paid out annually another two hundred million plus to "uniformed and civilian personnel" in the district. And much more was on the way.

On April, 1, 1954, the government commissioned the United States Naval Repair Facility to "perform emergency and voyage repairs to any active fleet vessels" and "general repairs for all ships of the Pacific Reserve Fleet based at San Diego." This "facility" was a quintessential example of how San Diego parlayed one unassuming naval asset into a larger one and then a bigger one still. San Diego had begun in World War I with the usual land grant, originally ninety-eight acres, for use by the Emergency Fleet Corporation. The site then successively became an anchorage for servicing destroyers and other small vessels, and then in 1921 changed to a submarine and repair base. Finally, in 1954 it became a full-fledged repair base, a facility that could mend ships up to cruiser size. This installation represented an important consolation for the private industrial base that the city had not been able or willing to attract and a clean industry at that, one that would not disturb its geraniums. The auxiliary air station at Miramar Field began as Camp Kearny in World War I and reverted to the Navy before World War II. It then became a bona fide naval air station in 1952, to be used to provide an onshore home base for carrier planes when they were in port. Incidentally, without this base, the carriers would not have come to San Diego, a fact that the boosters well appreciated.

The Naval Electronics Laboratory, opened in 1949, provided another important element to the growing naval oligopoly in the Harbor of the Sun and at the same time gave it a piece of the electronics industry, then concentrated in rival Los Angeles County. Like Miramar and the fleet repair base, this institution grew out of previous Navy ones, in this case the Point Loma Radio Station, which was "the first radio station on the Pacific Coast to handle transcontinental traffic." In 1940 it became the Navy Radio and Sound Laboratory and was absorbed by the Electronics Laboratory in 1949.[11]

An important further addition to the growing integrated naval presence arrived through the attempt to modernize the naval base. The advent of nuclear-propelled submarines and aircraft carriers triggered two of the most significant modernizations of the port. The rise of nuclear propulsion forced a number of adjustments upon the military services and, in turn, opened up a series of opportunities for the martial metropolises. Nuclear power might propel submarines, aircraft carriers, and, until 1961 it was hoped, airplanes. Each of these technical innovations required new port or airport installations, and each generated scientific spinoffs that would benefit a city ever watchful of its opportunities. Of course, San Diego had always been vigilant and was again when Admiral Hyman Rickover's new nuclear-powered Navy grew big enough to raise the question of where and how to berth the ships in ports. That juncture provided the needed opportunity for San Diego, which moved expeditiously to exploit it.[12]

First the city needed to secure the status of home port for the atomic submarine fleet. When Admiral Arleigh Burke, Chief of Naval Operations, set in motion the plan to build the submarine piers necessary to handle atomic submarines at Ballast Point, San Diego stood ready to lend a hand. The president of the San Diego Navy League explained to Congressman Bob Wilson, "The continuation of San Diego as the home port for the Atomic Submarine Fleet should be assured by the building of these piers." As the fleet moved to an ever more nuclear basis, the home port issue loomed larger. The San Diego Union made clear exactly what was at stake: "San Diego is the home port for a fourth of all U.S. submarines, a third of the Navy's submarine tenders and more than two thirds of the subs in the Pacific Fleet." The city could and did argue that its current possession of the fleet sonar school and the Navy Electronics Laboratory strengthened its claim to the piers and the subs. It also championed the Navy's argument that the current sub tenders with their twenty to thirty submarines cluttered and clogged the harbor and that the piers would alleviate this congestion. As usual, the Navy expressed its interest forcefully. Captain Norvell G. Ward, commander of the Navy's first Polaris sub squadron, succinctly pointed out at a Military Order of the World Wars dinner that "if you want the nuclear submarines to call here, you'll need the pier at Balast Point." In seven to ten years, he continued, "nuclear subs will have replaced the conventional diesel undersea craft."[13]

By the time the captain spoke these words, San Diegans were already mobilizing behind the scenes to bring the piers to Ballast Point. In fact, Congressman Wilson had been at work for two years *before* Admiral Burke's request, and the Chamber of Commerce Military Affairs Steering Committee had been working for at least one. Others soon joined them. As the Chamber, the mayor, the Navy, and Wilson went public in support of building the piers, James S. Copley swung his powerful *San Diego Union* and *San Diego Evening Tribune* behind the effort. And the *San Diego Independent* argued that "surely the piers are important enough to San Diego's economy and the West Coast defense to have the piers put in the 1960 budget." Dr. Roger Revelle, Scripps Institution director, informed a congressional investigating committee that nuclear subs would "command the seas within 10 years." In what he must later have rued as an unfortunate prophecy, the good doctor went on to predict that "atomic submarines will achieve speeds approaching those of aircraft." The *Independent* explained the Scripps connection to the metropolitan-military complex. As "Scripps becomes more and more essential to our underseas warfare picture, the stronger our argument for the sub piers here will become."[14]

As so often in the past, Congressman Wilson could find a strategic theory to match the political and economic ambitions of the metropolitan area. "The present uneasy international situation, in my opinion, demands a speeding up of ASW [anti-submarine warfare] training," warned the modern William Kettner. Since the Pacific Fleet "ASW Forces which train in the San Diego area are to be trained with nuclear submarines," the city must have the piers. Otherwise the nuclear subs would be based in Hawaii, and they and the ASW forces would lose training time and "nuclear power core life" sailing to their rendezvous.[15]

With the Navy, the congressman, the Copley press, the *Independent*, the San Diego Chamber of Commerce and its journal, *San Diego*

Business, the American Legion, the Military Order of the Two World Wars, the mayor, the San Diego Council of the Navy League, and certain businesses and the like lined up in battle order behind the sub piers, the metropolitan-military complex had collected a formidable political coalition. Moreover, as so often seemed the case, it had attracted little local criticism. Some San Diegans worried that the piers would "conflict with residential areas," "interfere with harbor traffic," or provide atomic pollution, but the Navy and boosters deftly parried each of these half-hearted thrusts. Lest national security was not enough to carry the point, the *Union* added, "It's later than we think. Seattle and other West Coast cities are anxious to replace San Diego as the hub of Pacific naval activity." In fact, the ever pesky San Franciscans already *had* an atomic submarine pier.[16]

Congress intially torpedoed the sub base from the 1960 budget, but the San Diegans were not discouraged. "This is where the fine arts of public relations and political maneuvers will come into play," predicted the *Independent*, "with each national region putting forth its case in the strongest possible terms." San Diego's case must have been strong, for by July, 1960, the city had won. Acknowledging the political nature of the process, the Assistant Chief of Naval Operations thanked Wilson: "Without your fine help, I am sure we would have been in trouble." By 1963, Wilson and San Diego were well on the way to yet another sub pier. San Diego hoped to parlay these assets into a nuclear sub-building capacity, so that the city might "become the West Coast equivalent to New London, Connecticut." So the "fine arts of public relations and political maneuver" continued as 1961 came to an end.[17]

As early as 1957, the Chamber of Commerce made the acquisition of nuclear carrier wharves a high priority. The city and the Navy were soon hard at work trying to find ways to squeeze even bigger ships into an already crowded military harbor. As in the case of nuclear submarines, the carriers would add to the guaranteed annual income that the Navy provided and the carrier dock would assure the guarantee. Climate alone would not ensure the acquisition of the carriers, so the city must revamp its harbor, explained Ralph J. Phillips of the San Diego Chamber's Military Affairs Department (ironically abbreviated by the Chamber to MAD). Nor did the martial metropolis fail to meet these needs. In late October, 1958, Congress approved a $7 million appropriation to begin the carrier docks, and in 1960 a dredging appropriation followed. As usual, Darwinian competition spurred the city on, in this case the fear of Long Beach's acquiring the carriers. With the dredging and docks, that obscenity would not occur.[18]

Equally unthinkable ones threatened the city's shipbuilding industry. San Diego was not a great shipbuilding center after World War II, but it did aspire to proportionately more of this industry. Congressman Wilson helped spearhead these efforts, often in regional coalitions with other California cities. In 1953 the Martinolich Shipbuilding Company of San Diego thanked Wilson for the "contract for two A M Minesweeping Vessels," and in 1959 he received credit for the largest contract that the NASSCO (National Steel and Shipbuilding Company) firm had ever received. The shipbuilding interests soon turned their attention to bigger game in the form of a nuclear-powered supercarrier of the Forrestal Class. Coast cities and builders stood together in this battle, and by 1955 Wilson had made good headway with the Eisenhower administration. By 1959 San Diego shipbuilders had had enough success to lure the Convair firm into creating a hydro-dynamics department to bid on ship contracts.[19]

Besides the struggle for individual contracts, San Diego and its coast allies had to beat off the advances of other regional alliances. In order to develop a West Coast shipbuilding industry that would be available for defense, Congress in 1936 granted the area a 6 percent advantage in bidding upon government contracts. Arguing that the geographic cost factors that had justified the 6 percent differential had disappeared, a southern and eastern congressional coalition tried to repeal the law in 1960. Their attempt created a West Cost counter-alliance that included chambers of commerce, unions, and companies in each of the three leading California metropolitan areas.[20] Congressman Wilson prevented this law from coming to a vote, but as the period ended in 1961, the easterners and southerners were up to the same tricks.[21]

West Coast cities also competed for home porting the Navy's ships; and since San Diego had so many, it was the target of its neighbor's raids to acquire a few. Long Beach did so when San Diego was distracted and fat from the Korean War. The "Great Long Beach Ship Raid" did not permanently harm the Border City, but it did prompt it to take stock of its position and to improve its relations with the Navy.

Illustrative of the close ties between civilian and military society, the city chose retired Admiral Ray Tarbuck to report on its relationship with the Navy. In doing do, Tarbuck made one of the frankest admissions on record of the political nature of much of the Navy's business. The admiral explained that ships had home ports, operating bases, and home yards, or three basic ports per ship. In addition, no harbor except New York's could hold the entire fleet at once, so they had to be divided up between many cities. "Political and economic pressures have influenced the designation of home ports and yards in the past. They have even affected the strategic location of warships awaiting battle," explained the officer. "In lean years, Navy yards have been closed or reopened on a political basis, usually with the change of administration or congressman." On the other hand, noted Tarbuck, "from the local point of view there are times when an increase in naval activity at a port may look highly political, while it is the result of an impartial command decision." In that case, "before press release, it is not unusual to notify the local congressman in advance, so he might collect from his constituents any reflected glory." Regardless of party, "his amity is always welcome when the next naval appropriation bill comes up for approval." Tarbuck soothed San Diego's fears by assuring them that Long Beach could never capture the major portion of the Navy and urged cooperation: "By playing ball with them, and presenting a united front for Southern California, the San Diego–Long Beach position is strengthened with a view to keeping what we have in the south and acquiring more."[22]

Nonetheless, the Long Beach threat recurred later in the decade when it became known that the Commandant of the Eleventh Naval District lived in inadequate quarters on North Island, where his ears were continually jarred by the takeoff and landing of jets. Fearing that his discontent might lead to pressure to remove the headquarters to Long Beach where the commander's ears would not take such a beating, the city builders were soon moving to provide him with a better home. Surely this must be one of the most unique exercises in "public housing" on record in American cities.[23]

However, dredging, master planning, and port governmental reorganization were not unique, and these flowed just as inevitably from competition among cities as did the drive for shipbuilding contracts, the procurement of bases, or the home porting of ships. The vaunted

Harbor of the Sun required much dredging to enable it to accommodate the increasingly larger ships of the modern Navy. The urban threat to the city, together with the necessity of digging deeply enough to harbor supercarriers, led the city into another fight for dredging appropriations from Congress. The city recognized this need in the early fifties, but since congressional approval required action against other cites competing for the same funds, the appropriation was delayed until 1960, when the national legislature provided $5 million to do the work. The chair of the chamber's military affairs committee highlighted the welfare-warfare connection, maintaining that "one supercarrier will materially benefit the San Diego economy by providing a multimillion dollar payroll," and that it would also benefit the West Coast and American defense posture. Dredging would also help the city's tourist industry by creating soil that could be used to create new harborfront land for tourist facilities and would diversify the city's economy, both perennial local ambitions. Master planning grew apace. The Chamber of Commerce revived its Metropolitan Planning Committee, apparently at the insistence of its Harbor Committee; not surprisingly, it was headed by another retired admiral. In 1963, a plan of development was created.[24]

The establishment of a unified port authority came harder, but that too claimed major San Diego efforts from the Tarbuck Report onward. County representatives introduced legislation to create a unified harbor authority in 1955, but it was not passed and ratified in a referendum by voters until 1962. Although the often magisterial Richard Pourade *History of San Diego* makes no mention of the Navy as a critical stimulus to the creation of the port district, it is clear, as Bob Wilson's correspondence proves, that the Navy was indeed the principal reason for the creation of this new governmental entity. Both the city and the Navy needed a plan, but the Navy needed it worse.

By 1961 then, San Diego had literally provided a very comfortable berth for the Navy in its magnificent bay. Overall investment totals are not available, but the Navy supplied a startling summary of its growth and development in San Diego from 1953 to 1958. The Navy had sunk $144,000,000 into permanent investments at the various installations; it spent a cool $1.3 billion annually in Southern California; and it pumped in another $258,830,300 per annum in payrolls, "exclusive of pay to forces afloat, retirement benefits, and family allotments." It also attracted per month some seven thousand visitors who came to see servicemen stationed or inducted there. Yet even these mind-boggling figures greatly underestimate the Navy's full impact on the urban community. In 1957, the district commandant estimated that the Navy added 215,000 people to San Diego County, which equaled more than 20 percent of the county's population and 37 percent of the city's population. Nor did these figures count the large and growing military retirees' colony. Put another way, the 215,000 amounted to more people than lived in the contemporary Las Vegas metropolitan area; it was more than the combined total of all the California counties of 20,000 persons and under, and was very close to the median size of all American standard metropolitan statistical areas. The Navy also helped provide ordinary city services like health care, police in the form of the shore patrol, and water, not to mention its subsidization of urban purchasing power through the service exchanges and surplus disposal policies. The Navy entertained the city on many occasions. The manager of the chamber's Military Affairs Department (MAD) summed up the Navy's influence very well in 1958 when he observed that "when we take stock of assets providing impetus to our upward spiral which has made San Diego the fastest growing major city in the nation, we should not overlook the importance of the armed services." That was perhaps one of the most redundant suggestions in American history.[25]

Nor did the services overlook the influence of the city on their own "upward spiral," which made defense the fastest growing industry in the United States. Although historians have tended to emphasize the overweening importance of the nation-state on twentieth-century American life and especially on urban history, the reverse has also been very true. The national government owes much to the backing it has received from cities. The notion that cities are simply the victims or the beneficiaries of the actions of larger entities like class, demography, migration, international economics, the state, or central governments is not tenable. Certainly the powerful military establishments recognized the critical importance of its own urban constituencies. After thanking Congressman Wilson for his *Congressional Record* speech "stressing the importance of seapower and emphasizing the essentiality of the carrier forces and Marine Corps," Chief of Naval Operations

Arleigh Burke went on to state that "your outstanding ability to present the case for seapower to Congress is invaluable to our National
Security, and most gratifying to the whole of the Naval Establishment.
It was also obviously the quid pro quo for all the favors which that
service had bestowed on the ambitious Border City.[26]

Wilson aided the air arm of the country just as consistently and
efficiently, and that too did not go without notice. If anything, the
procurement practices of the Air Force and its contractors were even
more political than those of the Navy. Both the little people who staffed
the Convair, Ryan, Rohr, and Solar factories and clung desperately
to their houses, jobs, and hopes through the usual feast or famine of
defense contracting, and the corporate executives and scientists for
whom the feasts were greater and the famines shorter recognized the
political nature of the business in which they labored. Complaining
to Wilson of the "substitutions" made in Convair's Wizard anti-missile
program, J. W. Bond, Jr., chief of physics for the Convair Division of
General Dynamics, protested that "I believe the important point to
be made is the need to remove political considerations from defense
contracts." Nor was politics confined to the minor details of modifying
anti-missile systems. Less than two months before Bond's letter, one
of his bosses, W. H. Patterson, assistant to the division manager of
Convair-Astronautics, had also written to "Dear Bob." Far from dis-
avowing politics in the defense industry, this letter enclosed a two-
page draft of a speech on defense matters written by Convair, to be
delivered by President Eisenhower. "Bill" Patterson sent another copy
to Vice-President Richard Nixon. Although the proposed draft spoke
of the need for a military force balanced among the Army, Air Force,
and Navy and genuflected to the importance of truth, foreign aid, and
a strong economy in the struggle against communism, most of the
speech dealt with rockets, Polaris missiles, intermediate range ballistic missles, and intercontinental ballistic missiles. The talk called for
greater defense spending for such hardware in 1959 and, if necessary,
higher taxes in order to pay for them. "This as you well know is expensive and will require an even greater sacrifice by all of us in the
future," intoned the Convair executive, hopefully speaking through
the President. "I feel that it is you, the American public, who must
know and be kept advised of this state of affairs." Of course, in out-

lining "this state of affairs," Patterson did not refer to the fact that Convair manufactured most of those products that would "require an even greater sacrifice by all of us in the future."[27]

Wilson acknowledged the same overriding importance of influence in thanking Herb Kunzel, president of Solar Aircraft, and his executive team for "your very generous assistance during my campaign" for reelection in 1958. "It is support such as this which certainly will make me work even harder to bring more jobs and contracts to San Diego." And when those jobs did not roll in, his constituents did not hesitate to remind the congressman of the political process. Johnnie M. May of the final assembly section of one of the San Diego Convair plants and twenty-eight of his colleagues wrote Wilson in late 1961 to inform him that they supported the American government, paid taxes, had fought for the country, and would again. "We are proud of our company," said May, but he wondered why "every firm except the one we work for is getting contracts from the government." He went on to say that "we are like a bunch of rats on a sinking ship, we don't know whether to jump off and swim for shore, or stay with it and sink to the bottom." Their letter's stated intention was to gain "equality."[28]

Wilson responded that Convair had received a tremendous amount of government patronage over the years, which was very true; unfortunately, that truth did not exempt the representative from both popular and union criticism. The congressman had succeeded very well in mobilizing the resources of the nation-state on behalf of urban development, and as the International Association of Machinists let him know, he must do at least that well in the future.[29]

He and San Diego both did well in the era of jets and missiles. The government built the F-102 fighter there. This plane eventually evolved into the F-106, which the company continued to manufacture until the Kennedy Administration. By then, it had become one of the largest projects Convair had ever undertaken. Nonetheless, with changing technology even big contracts were vulnerable, and eventually the Department of Defense decided to replace the F-106 fighter with antiballistic missiles and stop building the fighter in 1961. With the Democrats in full cry about missile and bomber gaps in the late fifties, however, it was no easy time to cancel a major contract held by one of the nation's premier defense cities. Congressman Wilson knew that his town would get new contracts to replace the F-106, but he feared a three-year gap before the old contracts played out and the new began. So Wilson, too, joined the chorus of protest over the vulnerability of the United States in order to prolong and perhaps modify the F-106 while waiting for the new business to come on line.[30]

Modification came first. Wilson argued to the government that the F-106 could be modified to be used as a trainer for the B-70 bomber or to serve as a tactical fighter. The first ploy failed because the Kennedy Administration subsequently scrubbed that plane. In effect, Wilson had tried to piggyback one obsolescent technology onto another one. He had more luck with the tactical fighter, eventually persuading the government to buy thirty-five more F-106s for conversion. Beyond that, the congressman continually warned of the unemployment that cancellation would create, of the threat of the Soviet-manned bomber which made the F-106 still relevant, and of the even greater menace of Castro's Cuba within easy flying distance of the nation's southern shore. The congressman went so far as to try to help the fighter by attacking the newer technology, the Bomarc missile, manufactured by Boeing. The government eventually scrubbed the Bomarc, but that action did not save the F-106. Wilson argued forcefully enough to get more than $100 million put into the Eisenhower budget of 1961 to build more fighters, but the incoming Kennedy Administration, after a long and agonizing review, declined to spend the money. Although his constituents, especially the International Association of Machinists, fumed over the decision, Wilson felt that San Diego had done very well under Eisenhower. When Eisenhower came to office 35,000 San Diegans labored in defense industries; and by 1961, 110,000 did. The congressman foresaw similar success with the Democrats. He seemed to know whereof he spoke. In early 1962, just as the F-106 ran out, the government invited Boeing and Convair to make studies of a new fighter, the even more star-crossed TFX. And even if the F-106 disappeared, defense spending in the Port of the Palms had an overlapping quality to it. As the contractors phased out one system, they phased in another and were working on several others to phase in when the time was ripe.[31]

The Atlas missile overlapped the obsolete technologies very effectively. The immediate origins of that dreadnought weapon go back to early post–World War II days and ultimately to the success of San Diego in luring the then Consolidated Aircraft Corporation to the shores of its bay. In effect, Convair won the contract for America's first intercontinental missile, and San Diego won the firm that captured the contract.[32]

Interestingly enough, although San Diegans claimed the absolute necessity of building and keeping the Atlas, some well-informed scientists did not think it should have been built. According to Herbert York, Eisenhower's science advisor and one-time director of the Livermore Weapons Laboratory, the United States built about twice as many missile systems as it required to defend itself. Ultimately the country developed six different systems, whereas York thought it required only three. Among others, it did not need the Atlas, a liquid-fueled missile designed to fill a developmental gap until the more manageable solid-fueled weapons came on line. The rocket had other enemies. According to special assistant for science and technology George Kistiakowsky, the Ballistic Missile Division of the Air Force was one of them. However, both aide Bryce Harlow and Vice-President Richard Nixon favored them.[33]

Just after World War II, the government awarded Convair a contract to develop an American version of the German V-2 rocket, and the firm labored on this project until funding ran out in 1948. However, Convair kept together its team of scientists and was rewarded for its loyalty when the Korean War revived the contract for the missile as did the invention of the hydrogen bomb, which provided a much lighter but more powerful weapon. In 1953, Convair recommended that the government initiate a crash program to build missiles, and got the contract to do so. Several other defense giants shared the contract with Convair, but that firm held 22 percent of the prime contracts and let out 30 percent to subcontractors. Although local boosters talked of this weapon as a counter to the Soviets, city boosting played a large role too. The City of San Diego created the Kearny Mesa Industrial Park to house just this kind of project. Convair opened their Atlas plant there in mid-1958 on land sold to them by the City of San Diego. Beginning with a startup force of three hundred, the Atlas project soon employed over fourteen thousand, including six thousand on Kearny Mesa. From the outset, chamber officials believed that the Atlas would move beyond its purely military application to a more civilian one of boosting vehicles into space. Nor did city builders neglect the wider urban payoff of the missile. It would be a large construction job, attract skilled labor, lure smaller industries to the city, and "guarantee us leadership in growth for the new few years," argued the chamber president.[34]

Atlas did just that, as San Diego enjoyed record industrial growth in both 1956 and 1957. Even before the Kearny plant opened in July, 1958, San Diegans looked ahead for further windfalls from the weapon. A number of San Diegans suggested the necessity of a new West Coast site to test the dreadnought, a suggestion that the Navy snapped up. By mid-1958 the new Navy testing site near Lompoc was nearing completion, thus eliminating the necessity of testing the weapons on the East Coast and giving California another asset. None of the competing cities acquired the facility, but they all benefited by its proximity. Moreover, Convair alone received a $48 million contract to help ready the station. Eventually the Atlas became one of the country's ICBMs and also propelled the manned Mercury capsule into space, thus fulfilling the booster promise of beating swords into plowshares and gaining considerable publicity for their city in the bargain.[35]

Perhaps too much fame. By the end of the decade several converging pressures greatly increased the competition for military contracts. Two of these pressures were the defense contracting success of California and the losses of competing regions, especially New York state (that is, suburban Long Island). In addition, changing technology made relatively new weapons obsolete, and budget pressures by the President jeopardized them further. This loss triggered a free-for-all between the boosters of the Atlas and those of the Titan, built by Martin of Baltimore but manufactured in Denver with engines constructed in the Los Angeles area. Since the government did not need both missiles, and both would soon be replaced by the solid-fueled Minuteman, backers of the Atlas and the Titan felt insecure and each attacked the other. Wilson went on the assault against the Titan as early as 1959 and Convair moved to increase the range of their weapon from 5,000 to 9,000 miles, while increasing its warhead capacity. Wilson's effort did not beat out the Titan, and the 1959 ratio of thirteen Atlases to fourteen Titans smacked of a political compromise. Each side nullified the other, but both gained, since original projections for the missiles ranged from only six to eight squadrons. The Atlas also warded off competition from the Vega rocket for the chore of boosting space vehicles when the government canceled the Vega. In fact, military rockets boosted most of the original vehicles into space. Eventually, Secretary of Defense Robert McNamara would rule against the Atlas in the mid-1960s; but even before that, the principle of compensation seemed to be operating, as Convair was one of four defense conglomerates asked to bid on the Saturn II project and already in 1961 had a foothold in the Saturn I program.[36]

Simultaneously with the Atlas-Titan battle, a disgruntled New York delegation led by senators Jacob Javits and Kenneth Keating, miffed at the loss of that state's preeminence in war business, mobilized to reclaim its lost contracts from the Golden State. The New Yorkers charged that the close cooperation between California government and industrial leaders had resulted in that state's lead. California countered that its excellence in the martial arts explained its prominence. Both explanations were correct, but a third is important too. Douglas, Consolidated, and Lockheed, the core of the California weapons industry, were either lured to the Golden State in the 1920s and 1930s or persuaded to stay there by city boosters. Technical skill may explain how they prospered in the munitions business, but city boosting explains why urban California profited so inordinately from it. The California share of the industry had risen from 13.6 percent during the Korean War to 21.4 percent while that of the Empire State had fallen from 15.3 percent to 11.6 percent. This new battle was heating up just as 1961 ended, and its issue would await a later time.[37]

The period did witness the conclusion of the nuclear aircraft (ANP) episode. This time San Diego lost, but not before it had profited from the affair. The ANP was an attempt to mate two new technologies, nuclear and jet, which for a time seemed a promising venture. In fact, for a while, San Diegans were interested in powering the Atlas with nuclear propulsion, and Convair actually secured a contract to work on a space platform powered by controlled (we should hope) nuclear explosions. However, most of the city's political and economic clout went into the ANP. From the beginning, isoluble technical problems plagued what Herbert York called the "elusive nuclear airplane," not the least of which was how to shield the pilot and what to do if the plane crashed, especially in a residential neighborhood. Since San Diegans were already up in arms about the passage of North Island jets over Point Loma, one can only imagine their reaction to the thought of a crash of a nuclear-laden plane amid their palm trees and bungalows. Fortunately for them, the contractors never solved the technical problems. Yet, despite the obviously poor chances of the ANP, political and economic influences kept it alive. On one occasion Robert Wilson himself rebuffed the government's attempt to freeze funds for the ANP; and among politicians like Wilson, the AEC, the DOD, and the Joint Committee on Atomic Energy, this fated technology was kept alive from 1948 to 1961, when the Kennedy Administration accepted the Eisenhower recommendation to scale down the project to minimal research funding.[38]

However, the contractors and their competing cities, Convair and San Diego among them, must have taken some consolation from the one billion plus expenditures that the government literally sank into the ANP. Even in defeat, Convair's success illustrates its overall impact upon the Port of the Palms. In 1959, at the end of the period, Convair paid out $270,918,016 in wages to 47,150 area employees. As usual, one of the foot soldiers in the metropolitan-military host summed up this impact much more eloquently than any statistics could have. "I have watched San Diego grow from a sleepy semi-military, semi-retired peoples' town to a modern industrial city," wrote W. W. Whittier. During those years, "no single business or activity has contributed so dramatically as the Navy to our city's growth or its world-wide recognition as a center of industrial might." It was a role that demanded, Whittier insisted, a "recognition of the value of the company to the city, the United States and the free world."[39]

The elaboration of a more personal kind of welfare proceeded apace. As might be expected, Bob Wilson prided himself on being a conservative in politics, a man who owed nothing to unions. Nonetheless, they owed something to him, and so did other working people in San Diego's defense industries. Not only did he and other city boosters consistently fight to increase the number of jobs in the city, they struggled to prevent layoffs, to secure better services for employees, to raise military pay, to enhance service fringe benefits, and generally to secure decent working conditions for employees of the metropolitan-military complex.

Reductions in force (RIFs), especially at the two thousand–plus Repair Facility, a key building block in the naval oligopoly of San Diego, drew the instant attention of the city boosters. These layoffs illustrate well the conflict between welfare and warfare. When the

Navy had to cut back, it cited efficiency, budgetary, and especially military reasons for its reductions. The urban civilians countered this rationale in welfare language—they had kids in school, kids on the way, house payments, elderly parents, and could not afford to be laid off. However, the Navy, perhaps quixotically, insisted on operating on an efficient military basis and that insistence generated conflict. With what must be considered egregious timing, the Navy announced a big cut at the repair facility during the 1956 election campaign, a decision that local politics promptly forced them to rescind. They tried again in 1957 and had to accept another diminution of the cuts, but doggedly persisted into 1962 with another layoff, this time in the form of a reorganization. As usual, ideology did not complicate the city's attempt to transform further warfare into welfare. Despite his own distaste for unions, Wilson worked with the North Island Association, the International Association of Machinists, and the American Federation of Government Employees, just as he did with the conservative city booster press to avert the RIFs. The sometimes tearful thanks he received from these people illustrate both his success and his predicament. Whatever he called himself, the conservative, anti-union booster often functioned as a labor congressman.[40]

That necessity flew in the face of what the city considered the better strategy for gaining contracts.

> Today a considerable effort is being made in Washington by many states hard hit by unemployment to have defense contracts awarded on a formula of geographic distribution with emphasis on distressed areas. San Diego is not in a position to outcompete these other areas for these so-called hard luck contracts. As a result, the whole California delegation in the Congress has continually stressed the need that contracts be let on the well-established competitive basis practiced heretofore.

Thus, in spite of his many welfare activities, Wilson and his booster allies had to uphold publicly the larger good of competitive bidding and military qualitative excellence. Fortunately for the Harbor of the Sun, one could achieve other welfare gains in some realms while seeming to serve the national interest. Military pay, retirement benefits, job classifications, and fringe benefits opened an area for welfare efforts that could be justified on grounds of military efficiency, service morale, and fair play to the nation's defenders. As usual, the boosters could count on the cooperation of various San Diego pressure groups. The eight-thousand-member North Island Association, the Admiral Kidd Club, the American Legion, the *San Diego Bulletin,* the Navy Civilian Administrators Association, the Fleet Reserve Association, the IAM, and the Employees Association for the Naval Repair Facility could be counted upon both for support and pressure on bread-and-butter military matters. So could even civilian-seeming groups like the San Diego Chapter of the American Institute of Industrial Engineers. Of the sixteen officers, directors, committee chairmen, and members of the board of governors of that organization, fifteen worked for Rohr, Ryan, Convair, Narmco, Solar, and the Naval Air Station. Nor did this list of pressure groups come close to exhausting the reserve of political muscle in the city. Their agenda would have gladdened the heart of any New York City liberal; pay raises, retirement benefits, job classifications, equalization of benefits for active and retired personnel, travel allowances for military families, post commissary activities, and even the decrepit state of the North Island cafeteria claimed the attention of the martial metropolis. So did housing, since a shortage could lead to a turnover of the work force that might jeopardize contracts. Traditional welfare was perhaps not the boosters' favorite issue, but they took it very seriously where it had an impact on their metropolitan-military constituency.[41]

City builders were much more enthusiastic about the realm of education. In the late fifties, they put together one of the classic metropolitan-military campaigns on behalf of higher education. Southern California urban boosters had long believed that the California Institute of Technology in Pasadena was one of the key elements in the success of Los Angeles' defense industries. Cal Tech had lured new firms to the area, provided scientific advice, created new defense businesses, and generally made itself useful to the martial metropolis. It now became the model for a comparable institution in the Border City. The national shortage of trained scientists provided the ostensible reason for the creation of a new branch of the University of California, but the real reason lay much closer at hand. Convair and the other military businesses suffered from a shortage of trained scientists, one aggravated by their Atlas boom. They felt that their own businesses would be better served by the products of a new, world-class university, and their current scientists would have a place to upgrade their skills and develop their interests. Of course, the city builders also knew that such a center of learning would benefit the entire martial metropolis. As Robert Biron, sometime vice-president of Convair and later vice-president of the new University of California at San Diego, predicted, that place would ultimately have the same "dollar impact" on San Diego as Convair itself. And it was just the right kind of new dollar impact. Local leaders believed that research and development and education were largely recession-proof businesses and that they would provide the city entry into the age of automation, would attract the right kind of population — an elite one, would spin off innumerable new firms, and would be a clean industry (like the Navy) that would not throttle the city's flora.[42]

Exactly when the idea of the University of California at San Diego originated is not certain, but it surfaced in early 1955. It appears to have had quadrupartite origins with the city of San Diego, the San Diego Chamber of Commerce, Board Chairman John Jay Hopkins of General Dynamics, and assemblyman Sheridan Hegland. All campaigned, along with much of the city's elite, to get the California Board of Regents to accept the idea in mid-1956. However, the university then had neither the cash to initiate another branch nor the land to put it upon. Yet they got both, and, incidentally, got the university started, in a typical San Diego fashion. First, Hopkins offered to create a research laboratory, a new branch of General Dynamics, called General Atomic, in the San Diego area. However, he stressed the absolute necessity of having a major university close by to provide an appropriate resource for his nuclear scientists. He also needed land, and here the ever-shrewd and generous city government of San Diego chipped in about 300 acres. That gift satisfied a part of Hopkins's requirements, and when the regents agreed to create the university, the city donated another 450 to 500 acres next to the La Jolla campus of Scripps Institution of Oceanography for the new school. This donation got the university over one hurdle and Hopkins helped with the next. His business empire gave the university a million dollars to begin operations; by 1965, 2,258 students were in residence. One does not have to be a land economist to understand the value of these gifts, especially those of the city. Approximately 800 acres of prime real estate in the city's most prestigious suburb of La Jolla represented a large sum at the time and an even greater value for the future. This public contribution was decisive, as was its gift of land to General Atomic.[43]

No one should entertain any illusions that this campus was designed to serve the general educational needs of the community. San Diego State University already carried out that mission well. Nor UCSD did intend to be burdened with a lot of undergraduates trying to "find themselves"; rather it was to be an "atomic age graduate school," as the *Evening Tribune* termed it, or in the words of the other Copley paper, one designed for "ultrasonic, intercontinental, fissionable, fusionable 1956." Both President Robert Gordon Sproul of the University of California system and John Jay Hopkins recognized that the new university would create a very tight interface between itself and industry and both men stressed its national defense relevance. Roger Revelle, director of Scripps Institution, which served as the nucleus of the new school, argued that Americans must either "learn mathematics or learn Russian," thus giving the school a more general national defense twist. Of course students could learn mathematics at any number of California schools; the reason they would learn it at San Diego instead of Chico or Oroville, or Blythe or Lone Pine had more to do with corporate and urban ambition. "San Diego can give thanks to the satisfaction of moving forward with the assurance of a stability unequaled by most American cities," argued Mayor Charles Dail. "This is a model of progress, exceeded only by our continued efforts to keep San Diego at the top." Even an outsider like President Sproul understood that the "expansion of the Scripps campus would be a powerful stimulant to the already vigorous growth of this dynamic community." President Love of San Diego State put the matter in Turnerian terms when he noted that since the nation had reached its territorial limits, the new frontiers of the future were "upward, not outward." Perhaps that was so, but in a way the frontier was not so new after all. The frontier may have stretched upward instead of outward, but as Richard Wade pointed out many years ago in writing about the Ohio and Mississippi river valley cities, it was an urban one.[44]

The new John Jay Hopkins Laboratory of General Atomic also stimulated San Diego's development. The idea for this lab originated with John Jay Hopkins rather than the city, but that latter entity quickly grasped it when it became available. Hopkins was both a businessman and an idealist. Although his corporation manufactured many of the most deadly weapons of the Cold War, he did not believe in their ultimate effectiveness. Hopkins thought that communism fed off the uneven development in the world between have- and have-not nations and only the solution of the problems of the underdeveloped world could secure peace. As he put it, only an ethical balance of power, not a balance based on weaponry, would hold. Energy seemed the key to Third World development, and though fusion and solar power might ultimately help, he believed, only atomic power would be available in the near future. Hopkins became an evangelist for this form of energy, and his atomic laboratory represented a way to unlock the secrets of nuclear science for a developing world. He hoped for a world development agency to finance the purchase of nuclear reactors for the have-not nations, which would make them prosperous and therefore neither aggressive nor susceptible to communism. Of course such an institution would also subsidize the purchase of the goods that his company produced; nonetheless, he had a rather enlightened view of the Cold War. San Diego, however, viewed the laboratory as still another means to create further uneven development between itself and such American places as Montana and Utah and their cities and towns. As George W. Sears of the chamber put it, the "establishment of the laboratory can well mean that San Diego's future industry will be developed along the most up to date and most scientific lines, assuring the community a position of world leadership in the field of scientific and technological development." Needless to say, the city went after General Atomic with the usual magnificent gift of precious urban land, about three hundred acres of it, nearly half a square mile. In explaining the choice of San Diego, Hopkins stressed that a "combination of physical features needed for the laboratory, attractive surroundings, climate and the farsightedness of the San Diego community were the principal factors leading to the acceptance by the corporation of the San Diego area." Of course, with the exception of the farsightedness, all of these assets could have been obtained in many spots along the California coast. The laboratory came to San Diego because both the leadership and the masses of the city devoutly wished to have it and because it was a part of a package deal to acquire the university branch. The voters showed their own "farsightedness" when they ratified the magnificent land donation by a margin of six to one, as they had ratified the gift to the university.[45]

There seemed to be a cycle of defense investment in all of the many metropolitan-military endeavors. Perhaps the evolution was not predictable or consistent enough to be termed a model; nevertheless, a clear pattern seemed to exist. Initially, San Diego fought for some martial additions to their stock of contracts, bases, ships, berthing spots, laboratories, universities, amphibious bases, ship repair facilities, missile plants, and landing fields. Having gained them, the city builders sought to enlarge them, edging the naval repair facility ever upward toward the status of a full-fledged navy yard, expanding the capacity of the Atlas, and so on. If products were at stake, they would seek to sell more of them, often in contravention of government policy, as in the case of the F-106, while at the same time resisting any diminution of their prize. San Diego lost some contracts during the period, but it did not lose a single base or installation. Even when the city lost a contract, however, it usually reaped compensation or a consolation prize. Congressman Bob Wilson explained the process to Republican County Chairman Robert Finch when the latter wrote to Wilson to seek his help in keeping alive the Snark missile upon which twenty thousand Los Angeles County jobs supposedly depended. Wilson promised to do "everything I can to help," but pointed out the probability of the Snark's demise. "We have a similar crisis approaching in regard to Convair contracts but so far we in Southern California have been extremely fortunate in obtaining new contracts to replace jobs that become obsolete," consoled the San Diegan.[46]

Wilson spoke correctly on both counts. The Snark did disappear, and Southern California gained many new contracts both to replace it and to solve Convair's "crisis." From 1957 to 1961 the aircraft industry of California lost exactly 95,000 jobs but gained back 94,000 more defense jobs in aerospace, electronics, and missile industries, a net loss of only 1,000 positions. At that moment the Los Angeles Chamber of Commerce was trumpeting the decline of California defense industries as if a *real* crisis had overtaken the state.[47]

Obviously, a crisis had not occurred because the principle of compensation had taken effect. Further evidence of this process can be gleaned from the literal torrent of Defense Department contract verifications that flooded Congressman Wilson's desk in the early Kennedy years. Hardly a letter spoke of a dollar amount less than one million, and one exceeded $467 million, On October 17, 1962, the DOD announced it had "obligated" $29 million to Convair to develop test manuals for the Atlas; in July it announced an obligation of $467 million for the manufacture, delivery, and checkout of the Atlas; on May 29, 1962, it announced the obligation of $48 million for the development of the new Navy test site at Vandenburg Air Force Base; and on December 11, 1961, it announced the obligation of $78 million to General Dynamics under the Centaur program. These impressive totals represent compensation with a vengeance.[48]

Seen over a span of years since 1945, San Diego's martial empire strikes the observer as a very coherent one, and it was acquiring a coherent rationale to go with it. In short, the city had its own strategic theory to back its economic interests. Although he had plenty of support in the city, Congressman Wilson expressed this theory best. In fact, he had been one of the leading theoreticians for the Republican defense strategy put forth in the 1956 election. The representative was one of the most forceful spokesmen for the Eisenhower defense policies of getting more bang for the buck. However serviceable that idea may have been to a Republican administration, it was more useful still to an urban area whose industrial and commercial base was integrated with certain categories of military spending. Wilson spoke often of defense against the Russians, but the weapons that he advocated were almost always only those which his district manufactured or wielded. Overwhelmingly, he emphasized the importance of seapower and airpower and championed a concept of weapons balance between defense and offense, between fighters and bombers, between manned airplanes and unmanned missiles, between new and older weapons, and so forth. Here again, however, the coincidence between the interests of his district and its corporations and the weapons advocated was far stronger than the strategic logic that supposedly underlay his advocacy. For example, the Wilson logic of balance argued against phasing out the manned bomber (Convair manufactured the B-58 in Fort Worth) and in favor of a partnership of missiles (Convair built the Atlas in San Diego) and manned bombers. At the same time he favored a balance between Air Force and Navy nuclear weapons, which until 1961 meant an equilibrium between Polaris and Atlas missiles. He also argued for a solid fighter defense to defend against "total annihilation." Yet the congressman did not favor a new and upscale fighter to protect against the supposedly ever more sophisticated Soviet menace, but rather the tried and true F-106 made in San Diego. In 1961, the Soviets did not have a massive bomber and missiles threat, but they were notoriously fond of and ludicrously oversupplied with tanks and infantry. Yet the representative found no need to balance these weapons, the principal ones upon which the Soviets relied. By the same token, it made little strategic sense to have a strong Navy, even leaving aside the perennial behemoth carrier issue, to project American power if the United States had inadequate land forces to project.[49]

The most clever aspect of "balance" was that between new and obsolescent weapons. "Because of lead times, and other technical considerations it is constantly essential that we maintain a family of offensive weapons in various states of their life cycle," explained Wilson. "By the same token, it is equally essential that we have a similar family of defense weapons in the same stages." That kind of technological balance within the U.S. arsenal was at least as well calculated to promote an arms race as to increase security. However, this "balance" was very well designed to produce an endless supply of technological windfalls for the metropolitan areas that manufactured these "families" of weapons. As Wilson had explained to Robert Finch, Southern California had always had good success in replacing obsolete contracts with new ones, a process for which the representative's strategic theory was perfectly fitted.

NOTES

1. E. Robert Anderson to Bob C. Wilson, May 18, 1959, Robert Wilson Collection, Box 3, Archives Department, San Diego State University.

2. Robert Mitchell to Wilson, Mar. 16, 1961; Harve R. Dunlap to Wilson, Mar. 18, 1961, Wilson Coll., Box 33.

3. Mrs. Duane W. Anderson to Wilson, Mar. 21, 1961; Mrs. Paul W. Bergstedt to Wilson, Mar. 18, 1961, Wilson Coll., Box 33.

4. Mrs. Rose Bauer to Wilson, Mar. 17, 1961; Carl D. Bauer to Wilson, Mar. 17, 1961; William Nugent to Wilson, Mar. 17, 1961; Mrs. Joanne Thompson to Wilson, Mar. 22, 1961; Mrs. Helen Krumweide to Wilson, Mar. 22, 1961; Wilson Coll., Box 33.

5. Wilson to Ray Pekrul, Recording Secretary, International Association of Machinists, San Diego, California, Jan. 23, 1961, Wilson Coll., Box 56. "Convair Pays $936 Million to Suppliers," *San Diego Evening Tribune*, March 15, 1961, sec. b, p. 5.

6. J. H. Doolittle to Wilson, Aug. 13, 1953; "To/the/ 50th Anniversary Chairmen: Some of the 50th Anniversary Events . . ." Oct. 1, 1953, Wilson Coll., Box 12.

7. George May, San Diego Junior Chamber of Commerce, to Wilson, Aug. 13, 1953; Ray Booth, SD Jr. Chamber of Commerce, to Wilson, Dec. 4, 1953; Wilson to Ray Booth, Dec. 11, 1953; Wilson to Paul W. White, Executive Editor, Station KFMB, San Diego, Dec. 17, 1953, Wilson Coll., Box 12.

8. Commander R. H. Mereness, Assistant for Information, Twelfth Naval District, to Rear Admiral W. M. Eller, Director of Naval History, Navy Department, Washingon, D.C., Sept. 14, 1959, Wilson Coll., Box 43.

9. Marty Kingsbury to Wilson, Nov. 30, 1957; James W. Smith to Wilson, December 19, 1958; John H. Raifsnider to Wilson, Sept. 24, 1960, Wilson Coll., Box 33; Forrest Lockard, "Air Officer Views Gyrotor System," *San Diego Tribune*, Dec. 22, 1960; American Tunaboat Association to Wilson, May 11, 1961; Wilson to Captain Diego Xavier, May 22, 1962; American Legion "Memorandum to All Members of the United States Senate and House of Representatives," Mar. 12, 1959; William Bololen to Wilson, June 20, 1961; H. Jack Hardy to the Bureau of Supplies and Accounts, Material Redistribution Division, Washington, D.C., Feb. 3, 1955; Wilson to Admiral C. S. Cooper, Bureau of Aeronautics, Washington, D.C., May 17, 1957; Reverend W. L. Truman to Bob Wilson, Nov. 5, 1957; Wilson to Jim Snapp, Jr., March 12, 1959; Wilson to Charles Finucane, Assistant Secretary of Defense to Wilson, Mar. 2, 1959; Mrs. Martha Kirchmann to Wilson, Aug. 12, 1957; Dr. Ralph Schrock to Wilson, Feb. 2, 1960, Wilson Coll., Box 33.

10. Mrs. A. H. Keith to Wilson, June 17, 1959; Allan C. McAllister to Wilson, Sept. 14, 1960; William B. Macomber, Assistant Secretary of Defense to Wilson, Nov. 10, 1960; Dr. James W. Turpin to Wilson, July 31, 1961, Milton W. Nodacker to Wilson, June 25, 1962, Wilson Coll., Box 33.

11. Edward J. P. Davis, *The United States Navy & the U.S. Marine Corps at San Diego*, (San Diego: Pioneer Printing, 1955), pp. 32, 37–38, 47, 57, 60–61.

12. Wilson to Robert J. McPherson, Past President, San Diego Industrial Development Council, Inc., Apr. 16, 1958, Wilson Coll., Box 33.

13. G. C. Erickson, President, San Diego Council of the Navy League of the United States to Wilson, Mar. 13, 1959, Wilson Coll., Box 33; Lester Bell, "Nuclear Sub Base Proposed for S. D.," *San Diego Union*, Mar. 8, 1959, sec. a, p. 28; "A-Sub Pier Called 'Must' for City," *San Diego Tribune*, May 20, 1959, sec. a, p. 3.

14. Unsigned editorial, "Submarine Pier Vital: Keep Pace with Atomic Navy," *San Diego Union*, July 15, 1959, sec. b, p. 2; unsigned editorial, "We Need the Pier," *San Diego Independent*, Sept. 1, 1959, p. 4.

15. Wilson, "Statement of Congressman Bob Wilson: The Need for Nuclear Submarine Pier at San Diego, California," statement to the House Armed Services Committee, May 31, 1960, Wilson Papers, Box 33.

16. "Submarine Pier Vital: Keep Pace with Atomic Navy," *San Diego Union*, July 15, 1959, sec. b., p. 2; Oliver King, "NI 'A-Sub' Berth Out," *San Diego Independent*, Apr. 10, 1960, sec. a, p. 1; "Flotilla Commodore Rejects 'Choice' Idea," *San Diego Independent*, Mar. 3, 1960, sec. a, p. 1; "Kuchel's Support Asked On Sub Pier," *San Diego Union*, May 20, 1960, sec. a, p. 24; "Navy Bares Plan for Sub Piers Here," *San Diego Tribune*, Feb. 11, 1959.

17. Wilson to Rear Admiral E. W. Grenfell, Assistant Chief of Naval Operations, July 5, 1960, Wilson Coll., Box 33; "We Need the Piers," *San Diego Independent*, Sept. 1, 1959, p. 4.

18. Robert J. McPherson to Wilson, Mar. 17, 1960, Wilson Coll., Box 33; "Submarine Pier Vital: Keep Pace with Atomic Navy," *San Diego Union*, sec. b, p. 2. Edward G. Martin, "S. D. A-Sub Pier Project Postponed," *San Diego Union*, Apr. 4, 1963.

19. Anthony Martinolich to Wilson, June 23, 1953; C. Arnholt Smith, President, National Steel and Shipbuilding to Wilson, July 9, 1953; Charles ("Charlie") S. Thomas, Secretary of the Navy, to Wilson, July 8, 1955; Wilson Coll., Box 24. "Shipbuilding Firm

has Record Backlog, Plan to Hire 1,500," *San Diego Business* 26, no. 4 (1958): 3; Roger D. Fuller, Hydrodynamics Group Engineer, Convair, to Wilson, May 19, 1959, Wilson Coll., Box 56.

20. Edwin M. Hood, President, Shipbuilders Council of America, "The Case for the Private Shipyards," remarks before the Western Shipbuilding Association, Sept. [n.d.], 1961, pp. 2–4, Wilson Coll., Box 26.

21. Port of San Diego, Resolution, No. 8183 New Series n.d., attached to letter of John Bate, Director of the Port of San Diego, to Wilson, June 7, 1960; William F. Hood, Executive Secretary Local No. 9, Industrial Union of Marine and Shipbuilding Workers of America, Apr. 8, 1960, Wilson Coll., Box 59.

22. Rear Admiral Ray Tarbuck, USN, retired, "Analysis of the Transfer of Naval Vessels from San Diego," July, 1952, pp. 1–9, Wilson Coll., Box 57.

23. Wilson to John Bate, Director of the Port of San Diego, May 9, 1953; C. T. Leigh, President of the San Diego Chamber of Commerce, to Wilson, Nov. 2, 1953, Wilson Coll., Box 57.

24. "Many Benefits to San Diego Seen in Navy Harbor Dredging Project," *San Diego Business* 28, no. 18 (1960): 8; "Chamber Metropolitan Planning Committee Reactivated," *San Diego Business* 21, no. 3 (1953): 4; Richard F. Pourade, *The History of San Diego 7, City of the Dream* (La Jolla: Copley Press, 1977), pp. 200–201; Walter P. Davis to Bob Wilson, May 24, 1955; Wilson to Davis, June 10, 1955; Vice Admiral R. F. Good to Rear Admiral Chester C. Hartman, Commandant, Eleventh Naval District, Feb. 6, 1956, Wilson Coll., Box 57.

25. "Tremendous Investment in San Diego by Navy Emphasized in Tarbuck Report," *San Diego Business* 26, no. 7 (1958): 1–2. The San Diego Chamber of Commerce commissioned this latest Tarbuck Report, in which the admiral explained the city's good fortune with the Navy by its climate and operating conditions and "an overall receptiveness to the Navy and Marine Corps." He also reiterated the need for continued development of civil-military planning to ensure the Navy's future in the city. "Navy Increasing Investment in San Diego," *San Diego Business*, 26, no. 10 (1958): 1–2; Rear Admiral M. E. Arnold, Commandant of the Eleventh Naval District to Wilson, Mar. 21, 1962; U.S. Department of Commerce, Bureau of the Census, *Statistical Abstract of the United States: 1964* (Washington, D.C.: U.S. Government Printing Office, 1964), pp. 14–15; United States Department of Commerce, Bureau of the Census, *Eighteenth Decennial Census of the United States, Census of Population* I, *Characteristics of the Population* (Washington, D.C.: U.S. Government Printing Office, 1961), pp. 195–99.

26. Admiral Arleigh Burke to Wilson, Aug. 20, 1959, and attached draft of a Wilson speech to the House of Representatives entitled "Marine Combat Strength" n.d., Wilson Coll., Box 17.

27. J. W. Bond, Jr., to Wilson Feb. 2, 1958; W. H. Patterson to Wilson, Dec. 27, 1957, and attached untitled and undated speech, Wilson Coll., Box 56.

28. Wilson to Herb Hunzel Nov. 13, 1958, Wilson Coll., Box 59; Johnie [*sic?*] M. May to Wilson Nov. 27, 1961, Wilson Coll., Box 56.

29. Colonel Robert H. McCutcheon, USAF, Acting Director for Procurement Policy, Office of the Assistant Secretary of Defense to Wilson, Dec. 12, 1961; Wilson Coll., Box 56; "Collins Charges 'Wilson Fiddles While Constituents Burn,'" *Silvergate Union News: International Association of Machinists* 8; no. 4 (1962): 1.

30. "Industrial Buildup Seen for San Diego Area," *San Diego Business* 26, no. 4 (1958): 1; "Big Anti-Missile Job Restored to Convair," *San Diego Evening Tribune*, Mar. 28, 1958, sec. 1, p. 1; "In Dynamic San Diego," *San Diego Business* 27, no. 6 (1959):

5; Secretary of the Air Force, Memorandum to the California Congressional Delegation, untitled, undated, but probably 1959; Convair Memorandum, "Production Capacity Study: Wizard II," Oct. 1, 1957, Wilson Coll., Box 56.

31. Wilson to John V. Naish, President, Convair, Apr. 4, 1960, Box 56; Convair, Memorandum, "USAF F-106 All-Weather Interceptor: Status," May 20, 1960, Box 56; W. H. Patterson to Wilson, May 25, 1960; T. G. Pownall to Wilson, May 31, 1960; Wilson to Gerald R. Ford., Jr., June 21, 1960, Box 56; O. (Oliver) M. Gale to Wilson, Memorandum for Congressman Bob Wilson, June 16, 1960; Colonel Paul S. Deems, USAF, Memorandum for Mr. Gale, June 16, 1960, Wilson Coll., Box 56; Herbert York, *Race to Oblivion: A Participant's View of the Arms Race* (New York: Simon and Schuster, 1970), pp. 49–59; Wilson, to Richard Nixon, Memorandum, "Action on Convair F-106 Appropriation," June 29, 1960; Jim Wright to Wilson, Feb. 23, 1961; Wilson to Wright, March 1, 1961; Senator Dennis Chavez to Robert S. McNamara, Mar. 21, 1961, Wilson Coll., Box 56. Wilson to Thomas S. Gates, Jr., Secretary of Defense, Aug. 22, 1960; "AF Studies New Role For F-106," *Aviation Duty* (Feb. 14, 1961), p. 285; Assistant Secretary of Defense to Chavez, Mar. 9, 1961; Wilson to Mrs. C. E. Pennick, San Diego, Sept. 15, 1961; Major General Thomas C. Musgrave, Jr. to Wilson, Jan. 31, 1962; Wilson to Ray Pekrul, Jan. 23, 1961, Wilson Coll. Box 56.

32. Robert W. Lotchin, "The City and the Sword in Metropolitan California, 1919–1941," *Urbanism Past and Present* 7, no. 2 (1982): 1–16.

33. "In Dynamic San Diego," *San Diego Business* 27, no. 2 (1959): 5; Convair, "News Release," Jan. 4, 1960, pp. 1–2; "House Unit Backs B-52, B-58, Plans Cutback in B-70," *Wall Street Journal*, May 4, 1961, p. 26; York, *Race to Oblivion*, pp. 75–105; George B. Kistiakowsky, *A Scientist in the White House: the Private Diary of President Eisenhower's Special Assistant for Science and Technology* (Cambridge, Mass., and London: Harvard University Press, 1976), pp. 243–44, 271.

34. J. V. Naish, President, Convair Division of General Dynamics Corporation, "Statement before the Subcommittee for Special Investigations, Committee on Armed Services, House of Representatives, May 9, 1959," manuscript copy, Wilson Coll., Box 56, pp. 1–21; Kistiakowsky, *A Scientist at the White House;* "In Dynamic San Diego," *San Diego Business* 26, no. 7 (1958): 7.

35. Wilson to Rear Admiral J. S. Russell, Chief of the Bureau of Aeronautics, Department of the Navy, May 3, 1956; Rear Admiral C. S. Cooper, Acting Chief of the Bureau of Aeronautics, to Wilson, May 9, 1956; *San Diego Tribune*, May 22, 1958; Rear Admiral J. P. Monroe, Commander, Pacific Missile Range, Point Mugu, California, to Wilson, Mar. 31, 1959; Wilson Coll., Box 44.

36. Historians have documented the Eisenhower proclivity for a balanced budget, and Kistiakowsky's diary makes the point specifically for the B-70 and B-58 bombers, the nuclear carrier, and many other weapons. See, for example, Kistiakowsky, *A Scientist at the White House*, pp. 160–62; Naish, "Statement"; "Martin Girds for Titan Crisis," *Business Week*, Jan. 9, 1960, pp. 69–71.

37. Robert Harman, "New Yorkers in Drive for California Missiles Business," *Los Angeles Times*, Feb. 4, 1959; "Work on Titan Will Proceed, Wilson Advised," *San Diego Union*, Feb. 10, 1959; "N.Y. Moves to Halt 'Trend' of Arms Work to California," *San Diego Union*, May 8, 1959, sec. a, p. 5; Lester Bell, "Missile Budget Is Sufficient, Pacific Range Chief Says," *San Diego Union*, Feb. 10, 1959.

38. "Wilson Encouraged on Atom Seaplane," *San Diego Union*, Dec. 11, 1957; Frank Macomber, "Rep. Wilson Plans Parley on A-Plane," *San Diego Evening Tribune*, Dec. 9, 1957, sec. a, p. 5; Wilson to Eisenhower, Dec. 1, 1957; Eisenhower to Rep. Mel-

vin Price, Mar. 5, 1958; Eisenhower to Wilson, Mar. 10, 1958, Wilson Coll., Box 33; untitled Convair press releases, July 2, 1958, Apr. 10, 1958, Aug., 31, 1959, Wilson Coll., Box 43; Kistiakowsky, *A Scientist at the White House*, pp. 123, 146, 182, 204; York, *Race to Oblivion*, pp. 160–74. Both York and Kistiakowsky document the enormous political pressure surrounding this project, and, for that matter most others.

39. W. W. Whittier to Wilson, Feb. 23, 1962; Convair News Release, Jan. 4, 1960, Wilson Coll., Box 56.

40. E. O. Arnold, Employees Association, United States Navy Ship Repair Facility, to Wilson, Sept. 7, 1956; Rear Admiral A. G. Mumma, Chief of the Bureau of Ships, to Wilson, Sept. 7, 1956; E. O. Arnold to Wilson, Sept. 9, 1956; Joseph A. Breault [sp.?] to Wilson, Sept. 12, 1956; Arthur M. Johns to Wilson, Sept. 15, 1956; A Future RIFee to Wilson, Sept. 18, 1956; Memo from E. O. Arnold to Wilson, Aug. 24, 1956; Frank Macomber, "Navy to Reduce Civilian Staff at Repair Facility," *San Diego Evening Tribune*, Sept. 15, 1956; Robin Goodenough, Mayor of Coronado, to Wilson, Sept. 10, 1956; Wilson to Goodenough, Oct. 3, 1956; F. H. Watts, President, Southwest Iron and Steel Corporation, to Wilson, Sept. 6, 1956; Wilson to C. A. Brooks, Sept. 28, 1956; Senator Thomas Kuchel to E. O. Arnold, Feb. 14, 1957, Wilson Coll., Box 33.

41. Wilson to Robert B. Freeman, Mar. 15, 1962, Wilson Coll., Box 56; U.S. Congress, House, extension of the remarks of Representative Bob Wilson speaking on service academy pay, Cong., 1st sess., July 27, 1953, *Congressional Record* 99, pt. 12, p. A4924; U.S. Congress, House, extension of the remarks of Representative Bob Wilson speaking on fringe benefits in the armed forces, 83rd Cong., 2d sess., May 24, 1954, *Congressional Record* 100, Appendix, p. A3789; *San Diego Bulletin*, June 11, 1954; Michael F. Catania, National President Fleet Reserve Association to Wilson, Mar. 7, 1955, Wilson Coll., Box 57; R. L. Becht, President, San Diego chapter of the American Institute of Industrial Engineers, May 6, 1958, Wilson Coll., Box 33; Wilson to W. Kirby Vaughan, President, North Island Association, May 27, 1975; W. Kirby Vaughan to Wilson, May 18, 1957; Wilson to Rear Admiral George A. Holderness, Chief of Industrial Relations, U.S. Navy, May 12, 1955, Wilson Coll., Box 33; Wilson to Ernest C. Pherson, Two-Time Veterans Association, Feb. 13, 1958, Box 3; draft copy of a "Statement of Congressman Bob Wilson Before the House of Representatives," on May 12, 1960, pp. 1–2; Harry L. Wingate, Jr., Chief Clerk, Senate Committee on Armed Services, to Wilson, June 29, 1960, Wilson Coll., Box 33; U.S. Congress, House, extension of the remarks of Representative Bob Wilson speaking on pay increases for personnel of the Armed Services, 83rd Cong., 2d sess., Mar. 15, 1954, *Congressional Record* 100, Appendix, p. A1954; "Sub Pay Denied Bathyscaph Diver," *San Diego Union*, May 28, 1960. "Initial Chamber Housing Survey Completed," *San Diego Business* 20, no. 3 (1952): 1, 3; "Critical Shortage Over According to New Report," *San Diego Business* 21, no. 7 (1953): 1; "Housing Report Indicate Upturn in Single Family Dwellings Here," *San Diego Business* 22, no. 6 (1954): 5; "Rental Housing Shortage Seen as Labor Force Here Increases," *San Diego Business* 24, no. 6 (1956); 12; "Wilson Gets Conferee Assignment," *San Diego Union*, Aug. 1, 1958.

42. Richard Pourade, *City of the Dream*, p. 223; editorial, "San Diego Enters the Era of Science," *San Diego Union*, Aug. 25, 1956, sec. b., p. 2.

43. Henry Love, "Expanded Scripps Graduate School of Science Approved by Regents;" "Initial Need Is 12 Million, Revelle Says," "New Industrial Horizon Foreseen," "State College Unaffected by Scripps Plan," "San Diego Enters Era of Science," *San Diego Union*, Aug. 25, 1956, sec. a, pp. 1–2, sec. b., p. 2,

44. "Community Unites to Put Over Idea; 12 Million Expansion Okayed; Civic

Leaders Join in Lauding Action," "Revelle Voices Thanks for Aid," "Regent Vote Wins Praise of Hegland; Expansion of Campus Bright News for Area;" editorial, "Community, State and Nation Can Rejoice in U.C. Decision," *San Diego Evening Tribune*, Aug. 25, 1956, sec. a., pp. 1–2, 8; "Chamber Applauds U. of C. Action: Science, Technology School at La Jolla Wins Approval," *San Diego Business* 24, no. 9 (1956): 1–2. The City of Coronado also made a bid for the new university, which apparently never received serious consideration. Walter A. Vestal, Mayor of Coronado, to the Board of Regents, University of California, Jan. 25, 1956; T. H. Hugford, assistant director, budget and fiscal, University of California, to Sheridan Hegland, Mar. 1, 1956; Patrick J. Sullivan, director of public relations, General Dynamics Corporation, to R. K. Kelly, University of California, July 18, 1956; General Dynamics press release, July 18, 1956, pp. 1–3; memo from Robert G. Sproul to the Regents Committee on Education Policy (recommending the expansion to San Diego), Sept. 10, 1956, Presidents' Files, University of Califonia Archives, Bancroft Library (UCB). "City Moves for A-Lab on Torrey Pines Mesa," *San Diego Evening Tribune*, Feb. 10, 1956, p. 1; James W. Archer to Robert Gordon Sproul, president, University of California, Feb. 23, 1956, Presidents' Files, UCB; "University Campus Plans Get Backing," *San Diego Business* 26, no. 9 (1958): 1–2; editorial, "Community, State and Nation Rejoice in U.C. Decision," *San Diego Evening Tribune*, Aug. 25, 1956, sec. a, p. 8; Pourade, *City of the Dream*, pp. 222–23; Charles C. Dail to Sproul, Sept. 28, 1956, Presidents' Files, UCB; Dr. Malcolm Love, "A Nation's Progress: Science Conquers U.S. Frontiers," *San Diego Union*, Feb. 19, 1956, sec. c, pp. 1, 3.

45. John Jay Hopkins, "Toward a New Heaven and a New Earth," a proposal for the creation of a World Energy Community presented at the World Symposium on Applied Solar Energy, Phoenix, Arizona, Nov. 3, 1955, pp. 1–16; John Jay Hopkins, "The Truth Shall Make You Free," Founders' Day address at Occidental College, April 21, 1955, pp. 1–14. James W. Archer to Robert G. Sproul, Feb., 23, 1956, Presidents' Files, UCB; "City Moves for A-Lab on Torrey Pines Mesa," *San Diego Evening Tribune*, Feb. 10, 1956, p. 1; "In Dynamic San Diego: General Atomic Dedication, Guided Missile Plant Plans are July Highlights," *San Diego Business* 24, no. 8 (1956): 8; "In Dynamic San Diego: Record Atomic Reactor Flash Marks Lab Dedication," *San Diego Business* 27, no. 7 (1959): 3; "Nuclear Lab for San Diego Is Approved," *San Diego Business* 24, no. 3 (1956): 1.

46. Robert H. Finch to Wilson, Mar. 31, 1958; Wilson to Finch, Apr. 5, 1958, Wilson Coll., Box 44.

47. Los Angeles Chamber of Commerce, "Report to the California Congressional Delegation," Mar. 14, 1961, pp. 1–7, Wilson Coll., Box 12; Wilson to Ray Pekrul, Jan. 23, 1961, Wilson Coll., Box 56.

48. Robert H. McCutcheon, Acting Director for Procurement Policy, DOD, to Wilson, Dec. 12, 1961; Thomas G. Corbin to Wilson, Oct. 17, 1962; Perry M. Hoisington II to Wilson, July 13, 1962; Hoisington to Wilson, May 29, 1962; Hoisington to Wilson, Dec. 11, 1961, Wilson Coll., Box 56.

49. Robert Wilson, "Marine Combat Strength," manuscript version of a speech Wilson delivered to Congress, attached to a letter from Arleigh Burke, Chief of Naval Operations, to Wilson, Aug. 20, 1959; Robert Wilson, untitled manuscript version of a speech to the House of Representatives, Aug. 15, 1961, pp. 1–6, Wilson Coll., Box 17; U.S. Congress, House, extension of the remarks of Wilson speaking on defensive problems, the Cong., 2d sess., Aug. 17, 1961, *Congressional Record* 107, pt. 25, Appendix, pp. A6476–77.

ROBERT B. FAIRBANKS

The Good Government Machine:
The Citizens Charter Association and
Dallas Politics, 1930–1960

THE HISTORIOGRAPHY of recent urban America—particularly sunbelt America—poses a certain paradox. Studies of the post–World War II urban South and West have noted the dominance of the business community in both civic and political leadership. According to some accounts, these leaders set and maintained urban agendas that reflected their own special concerns, especially economic growth and the revitalization of the central business district. Meanwhile, they ignored the social needs of the city and neglected its physical problems.[1] Nevertheless, these leaders were able to sustain widespread support from large sements of the population or at least avoid serious challenges to their dominant position. Such conclusions leave several questions unanswered. Why, for example, were business-backed governments able to dominate urban politics in so many sunbelt cities after World War II? And why, if business leadership was selfish, did voters in city after city elect full slates of candidates, as they did in Dallas, Texas, chosen by the business-dominated groups?

Traditional explanations for the emergence and tenure of business-run government emphasize the relative homogeneity of sunbelt cities, the dissatisfation with the old-guard political leadership as it failed to cope adequately with the demands brought on by rapid growth, and the infusion of newcomers not tied to the political traditions of the city. Other explanations point to the elite's dominance of the media and the advantage given to business-backed candidates through at-large and nonpartisan local elections common to sunbelt cities after the war.[2]

While these explanations are helpful, closer attention to the actual rhetoric and actions of the business leadership might provide a different perspective to understand their successful domination of urban leadership roles during the 1940s and 1950s. Dallas, identified by Bradley Rice and Richard Bernard as the archetype of business-dominated sunbelt cities, provides an ideal setting in which to examine the popularity of business-backed government.[3]

Compared to New York, Chicago, or St. Louis, Dallas in 1930 was demographically a homogeneous city. Of the 260,475 people living in 45.6 square miles of the city, 82.6 percent were native-born whites. Blacks made up nearly fifteen percent of the city's population while the foreign born, primarily Mexican, composed a mere 2.5 percent.[4]

Despite its homogeneous composition, Dallas was not unified in 1930. The rapidly growing city, which escaped the worst of the Great Depression, still exhibited extremes of wealth and poverty not uncommon in most cities. Severe controversy between neighborhoods over the placement of public works, and tensions between open and closed town factions also appeared in Dallas during this time. Even the downtown business community was divided between west and east central business district interests.

Dallas had experienced a decade of growth during the 1920s more commonly associated with post–World War II sunbelt years. Not only did its population increase by more than 100,000, but the city nearly doubled its physical size when it annexed 21.6 square miles.[5] Such growth and the corresponding demand for services help explain reform efforts in 1927 aimed at changing the structure of urban government.

The city operated under the commission form of government adopted in 1907 as a consequence of an earlier business-sponsored reform movement. By the twenties, however, many of the same leaders faulted the government's lack of centralized coordination, and complained about the rapid turnover in commissioners due to the heavy work demands. Although some later accounts would claim Dallas suffered from machine politics in the 1920s, Harold Stone, writing for the Social Science Research Council, would best articulate the city's real problem: "The commission's major political trouble," Stone observed, "was not spectacular graft or patronage but the disintegration produced by the private political ambitions of five administrative heads who, after being independently elected, managed their departments separately rather than collectively."[6] The commission form of government had failed to give Dallas the type of centralized and responsive government that many felt the city needed. According to the *Dallas Morning News*, "A city is a business institution and should be operated under business methods." To the *News*, the city manager– council form of government provided the best type of business-like government, since "the city manager is the executive of a corporation under the board of directors. And Dallas is the corporation."[7] Others joined in with the *News* and formed the Citizens Charter Association to take politics out of Dallas government. In 1930 Dallas voters approved charter amendments that established a nine-member city council (all elected at large but six repesenting different districts), a city manager, and civil service for many government jobs. The nine council members would select a mayor from their number. Proponents of the new government form argued it provided not only a more effective structure to run Dallas but that the council posts would attract top-notch businessmen too busy to serve as full-time commissioners, but able to participate in the less time-consuming council.[8]

Shortly after Dallas citizens approved the new government, the Citizens Charter Association (CCA) decided to maintain its organization to make sure the "right type of men" were elected. The CCA would organize several months before the April election, select council candidates, rally public support, and then disband until the next municipal election. Although the good government group sought participation and support from all segments of the Dallas population, businessmen and professional men, and their wives, dominated leadership roles. And this elite group, rather than the CCA's other supporters, selected the slate of candidates to run under the charter ticket. The candidates, whose campaign was financed entirely by the CCA, were not allowed to make speeches. Nor did the CCA write a campaign platform. Rather, it simply promised its candidates would bring Dallas "an efficient, non-political administration."[9]

The strategy worked, as all nine CCA council candidates won by a landslide in the April, 1931, election. Shortly after the election the council met and elected as mayor T. L. Bradford, chairman of the Southwest Life Insurance Company, and appointed John N. Edy city manager. Edy, former head of the International City Managers Association, had managed Berkeley, California, and Flint, Michigan, before coming to Dallas. He took the Dallas job on two conditions: that he would be allowed to promote strict law enforcement and that he would have sufficient budgetary control to force Dallas to live within its income.[10]

Despite the realization of the city manager form of government and a clearly cost-effective first administration, partisan politics did not disappear from the city. Edy's cost-cutting measures, including the firing of nearly three hundred city employees (10 percent of all city workers) and tighter department supervision, caused controversy both inside and outside city hall. So did his cold and aloof manner and his close enforcement of liquor and gambling laws. As a result, Edy became the major issue in the city election of 1933. Thirty-seven candidates vied for council seats including full slates by the CCA, the newly founded Home Government Association (HGA), and the Progressive Voters League. Apparently business-like government did not appeal to everyone in Dallas during the depression.[11]

Although much of the opposition to the CCA slate, up for re-election, came from discharged employees and businessmen interested in a more open town, the campaign also showed other divisions in the city. The HGA, which pitched its campaign to the working classes of the Oak Cliff, South Dallas, and East Dallas neighborhoods, attacked Edy because "he [had] . . . neglected the interests of the forgotten man while safeguarding the vested interests." Others questioned the role of outsiders in governing Dallas. HGA supporter Judge George Burgess feared Edy represented a new type of carpetbagger. Burgess believed "it [was] the intention of the National [sic] City Managers Association to dominate the affairs of every principal city of this country." Edy, he noted, had "spent a great deal of his time since he has been in Dallas attending to the affairs of the City Managers Association." Nor did the Progressive Voters League like outsiders. It too called for a council willing to replace Edy with "someone who is imbued with the Dallas Spirit, breathes the Dallas atmosphere, someone who is in sympathy with our aspirations and has reverence for our traditions."[12]

Even the Dallas Morning News lost its ardor for the CCA, remaining neutral in the 1933 campaign because of disagreements with the city manager. Edy's unwillingness to allocate bond money to facilitate the Dallas Levee Improvement District's efforts to convert the swampy bottoms of the Trinity River into industrial land particularly angered the News. Such a commitment would not only provide more

room for industrial expansion, but would help revitalize the deteriorating west side of the central business district, home of the *News*. Despite the neutrality of the *News*, and despite the vitriolic attack on
Edy, the CCA again won all nine council seats in 1933. Growing dis-
satisfaction during the next two years, however, would defeat the CCA
in 1935.

Probably no single issue worked against the continued success of
the CCA more than the Texas Centennial Exposition. The city's civic
leaders had in 1935 secured the massive celebration of Texas Indepen-
dence only after pledging $3.5 million to help the state defray costs.
The city's contributions to the Centennial pushed the city's revenue
needs beyond the real estate tax limits allowed by state law. To com-
pensate for this shortfall, Edy proposed and council passed a controversial sewer tax which charged citizens for connecting to the sanitary
sewer system based on the amount of water used. That tax alienated
much of the city's working classes and became a major issue in 1935,
as was Edy's refusal to ease up on his efforts to keep Dallas a "blue-
nose town." Such committment alienated influential business leaders
wanting to make Dallas as attractive as possible to exposition visitors.
The decrease in support from the business community was particularly disastrous for the CCA, which lost all nine council positions in
1935 to an opposition slate sponsored by the Catfish Club.

The Catfish Club, a secretive political organization, appeared soon
after the 1933 elections. Organized by former city employees, this
ritualistic club built a strong following among the city's working class.
Using campaign donations from a variety of sources, including utility
and gambling interests, and a political organization that included
precinct captains and block lieutenants, the Catfish Club ran its own
slate of lawyers and businessmen under the Civic Association ticket.
Its victory, however, did not radically change Dallas's government.

Although the new council did replace John Edy with Hal Moseley,
former commissioner of streets and public property, Catfish Club efforts
to secure patronage and dictate policy met with strong resistance from
council members as well as from Moseley, who embraced the norms
of his profession. The council repealed the sewer tax, and the city
manager allowed a more lax enforcement of vice and gambling laws
during the Centennial year, but no machines appeared in Dallas as
the council feuded internally over a number of growth-related issues.

Two councilmen became so upset with their colleagues that they left the Civic slate that had elected them and joined the CCA in 1937.[13]

Despite internal dissension in the Catfish Club, and the endorsement of all the city's daily newspapers in 1937, the CCA managed to elect only two councilmen in addition to the two who had defected from the Catfish Club–sponsored Civic Association. As in 1935, the enforcement of drinking, prostitution, and gambling regulations emerged as the major issue. The CCA's call for strict control of vice gained it the enthusiastic support of the Dallas Pastors' Association but alienated some of its big business supporters from earlier times. As a result, opponents outspent the CCA in the 1937 election.[14]

Loss of business support may have not been the critical factor in the CCA's 1937 defeat, however. The newly formed black Progressive Voters League (not to be confused with the 1933 slate) registered four times as many blacks for the 1937 municipal election as had been registered in 1934. The League endorsed the Forward Dallas Association (formerly the Civic Association) after that group promised to hire black policemen and improve black schools. Forward Dallas Association also received strong support from white working-class voters in the South Dallas, East Dallas, and Oak Cliff neighborhoods.[15]

Two events occured following the 1937 election which would not only change the fortunes of the CCA but profoundly affect the development of Dallas. First was the establishment of the Dallas Citizens Council (DCC) by the city's leading bankers. An outgrowth of the movement to secure the Texas Centennial, the Dallas Citizens Council had been initiated by Robert L. Thornton, chairman of the Mercantile National Bank. Frustrated by the delays in raising money for the Texas Centennial Exposition, Thornton decided Dallas needed an association of the city's most powerful business leaders to act for the city's good. Membership of the one-hundred-man committee chartered "to study, confer and act to help Dallas" was limited to company presidents and board chairmen.[16]

Interested in promoting ordered growth, the Dallas Citizens Council's early programs included support for airport improvement, a new comprehensive city plan, canalization of the Trinity River, improvement of the State Fair grounds, and a downtown auditorium. Members also sought to promote the revival of the "Old Dallas Spirit" which emphasized unity and cooperation "in matters affecting the progress and development of this city." Sectional interests would give way to commitments for the city as a whole.

Less than a year following the organization of the Dallas Citizens Council, the Citizens Charter Association reorganized under the leadership of Roscoe L. Thomas. The insurance man and former schoolteacher accepted the presidency of the CCA in 1938 after other civic leaders rejected the post. What he inherited was not the vital organization of 1931, but a good government association, according to the *Dallas Times Herald*, "shattered by defeats in the 1935 and 1937 elections." Yet Thomas's strong leadership and his close cooperation with the city's business community allowed him to secure the teetering CCA.[17]

Soon after assuming the presidency of that group, Thomas approached Robert Thornton seeking contributions for a yet unnamed council slate. He secured money only after placing Thornton on the CCA's nominating committee—a committee that eventually included six bank presidents or vice-presidents, a financier, an insurance company president, an attorney, a former mayor, and a securities broker.[18] Althouth so many members of the Dallas Citizens Council participated in the CCA that the latter would be characterized as the political arm of the business civic group, no formal relationship ever existed. It is clear, however, that certain Citizens Council leaders played critical roles in candidate selection for the CCA council ticket.

Not surprisingly, the CCA's interests reflected the same interests as the Dallas Citzens Council, including city planning, airport improvement, and other growth promoting programs. This, however, stems more from a shared vision of priorities than from business supporters pressuring councilmen to vote for specific issues. Indeed, the CCA executive committee kept the source of all contributions from individual council candidates and forbade its business-dominated executive committee from ever requesting "services or favors" from the administration it backed.[19]

Beyond its efforts to secure monied Dallas backing, the CCA realized it needed to appeal to other Dallasites, and so it worked closely with the city's women's clubs, appointing prominent women to leadership positions and also named important clergy to its executive committee in an attempt to cultivate the religious vote in Dallas. And in 1939, the CCA secured the endorsement of the Progressive Voters League, the powerful black group that had helped defeat the CCA in 1937. Promises of better services to black neighborhoods played a crucial role in gaining black support.[20]

With its new coalition the CCA won all nine seats in the 1939 election. In its campaign against two slates of candidates and several independents, the CCA emphasized the need to elect a council willing to "forget selfish sectionalism" and one which would "represent all of Dallas." The CCA asked voters to elect all nine of its candidates to avoid the bickering and division characteristic of the current administration. According to CCA head Roscoe Thomas, Dallas voters were "tired of politics instead of business methods at city hall." As a result, Thomas predicted that voters would select CCA-sponsored council candidates because "Dallas people know teamwork and a business administration will increase the city's prosperity." Politics, according to the CCA, had caused a scandal in the Park Department the previous year, resulting in the indictment of two Park Board Members by a Dallas County Grand Jury. Partisan politics also threatened Dallas's well-being by "raising class and race hatred." Discussing a formula that the local newspapers adopted, the CCA in effect argued that harmony rather than division, efficiency rather than democracy were the keys to effective city government. Such conditions promoted the urban growth that would allow "the people of Dallas, laboring classes and office workers alike, to accordingly prosper."[21]

Opponents of the CCA viewed the call for consensus and cooperation differently. According to the leaders of the other two slates, the CCA was not interested in serving Dallas as a whole. Rather, wealthy businessmen, powerful bankers, and influential newspaper publishers, many of them residents of suburban Highland Park, sought to use city government for their own selfish ends. Jack Burroughs of the Non-Partisan Association singled out Fred F. Florence, chairman of the Republic National Bank, as the mastermind behind the CCA. According to Burroughs, the race pitted the people's ticket against the bankers' ticket.[22] The opposition campaign strategy failed, however, for on April 4, 1939, more than twenty thousand voters turned out to elect each CCA council candidate to office by more than a 2 to 1 margin. A heavy turnout by blacks gave CCA candidates more than five thousand votes each. Shortly after the election, the council selected lawyer J. Woodall Rodgers, a planning enthusiast, as mayor, and replaced

City Manager Hal Moseley with James Aston, former assistant to John Edy. The twenty-seven-year-old Aston came to Dallas from Bryan, Texas, where he had just been appointed to a similar post.[23]

The CCA regained public office at a propitious time. Wartime mobilization across the nation promised vast opportunities for new growth and development. Working closely with the Chamber of Commerce and the Dallas Citizens Council, the city government helped land not only a $1 million naval reserve aviation base for the city but secured a massive airplane factory as well. Groundbreaking for the North American Aviation plant took place on September 28, 1940. By the end of the following year the plant employed more than seven thousand workers, a figure which would increase to forty-three thousand by 1943.[24]

Not only did the Charter-dominated city government get things done, but it succeeded without the public squabbling that had characterized the earlier council. Closed-door sessions were held before the actual council meeting to allow council members time to iron out their differences in private.[25] Just as the Dallas Citizens Council had brought about greater unity among the city's leading businessmen and bankers, the 1939 CCA-dominated council promoted the same image of unity. At a time when politics and parochialism were viewed as evils in urban government, the CCA's ability to work in harmony for the city as a whole did indeed seem fortunate to many Dallasites.

The Council's actions between 1939 and 1941 did not please everyone, however, and clearly reflected shortcomings in a business-controlled government interested primarily in order and growth. When black residents of North Dallas, forced to relocate by a federal slum clearance project, moved into a South Dallas white neighborhood bordering a black section, violence erupted. Between September, 1940 and April, 1941, blacks suffered thirteen bombings and other acts of violence. Mayor Woodall Rodgers responded to the violence by chastising blacks for upsetting the city's order by invading white neighborhoods and appointed an all-white "interracial committee" to help work out the difficulties to the best interests "of all the citizens of Dallas." That committee responded to the conflict by recommending that the city council buy out blacks already living in white areas and designate "white only" areas in both the city's south and north sides. Council unanimously passed such a resolution and rescinded it only after being reminded that the Supreme Court had already declared racial zoning unconstitutional.[26]

This action cost Rodgers and six other CCA members the support of the Progressive Voters League in the 1941 municipal elections, although it did not cost them the election. Had all of the eight thousand blacks who paid their poll tax voted, they could have easily defeated the CCA candidates. However, fewer than eleven thousand voters throughout the city turned out, electing nine CCA candidates to the council, including the eight incumbents.[27]

The election campaign, according to the *Dallas Morning News*, was one of "the dullest in years." It pitted the CCA against the Dallas Citizens Association slate, which included former Catfish Club supporters and others dissatisfied with "banker control of city hall." The CCA ticket ran on its record and re-emphasized its commitment to harmony and government for all the people of Dallas. Although the CCA lost support from Dallas blacks, it gained an endorsement from organized labor when the AFL's *Dallas Craftsman* backed the entire CCA council slate. According to the *Craftsman*, the CCA had "come to a better understanding with organized labor," and had recognized it "in many ways."[28]

The continued support of the city's leading businessmen and newspapers, promoted in part by the accomplishments of a CCA-dominated city government exhibiting unity and efficiency, helped propel the CCA to unprecedented heights of success. During the next two elections, the CCA ran candidates for the council unopposed for the first time in the city's history. The *News* credited "the war and an apparent public confidence in the present administration" for the "quiet" nature of city politics.[29]

CCA's efforts during these years were clearly helped by the well-publicized Dallas Master Plan developed for the city by Harland Bartholomew. The plan, the brainchild of the Dallas Citizens Council, called for a wide variety of improvements for the entire city. Not only did the plan propose more parks, roads, and sewers for the city's various sections, but it outlined a neighborhood community strategy to promote greater civic consciousness among the city's residents. Although the master plan contained a number of suggestions for improving downtown Dallas, not one volume of that document focused exclusively on the downtown. The Dallas Master Plan, according to one observer, was an "all-for-one program — equitable to all sections of Greater Dallas."[30]

The plan also recommended that all of Greater Dallas be united under one government since "all areas are physically, civically and socially interrelated." Just as neighborhood parochialism in Dallas worked against the interests of the whole, so would suburban parochialism work against prosperity for Greater Dallas. Despite the rhetoric, an impressive Greater Dallas campaign in 1945, and the support of many of its leading citizens, Dallas was unable to lure wealthy Highland Park or University Park into the city.

The popularity of both metropolitan planning and a city manager–council form of government in Dallas reflects a vision that emphasizes the city's complexity — and the need for professionals to administer and guide growth for the city as a whole. Within this vision, neighborhood politics equaled parochialism, and only businessmen and professionals with a citywide vision could serve in the city council and help make the policy that would then be administered by city-management professionals. Only the kind of citizen participation that produced a civic consciousness for the greater whole was healthy; other citizen involvement might be too shortsighted and destructive to civic harmony. Within this vision, moreover, conflict over specific issues was disruptive, and advocacy groups were seen as a threat to government interested in the city as a whole. Such a vision helps explain much of the rhetoric and action of the CCA, particularly after World War II.

During this time, the CCA continued to dominate Dallas city government, but not always without opposition. Rapid population growth nearly doubling the city's size during the war years created a variety of challenges to the re-elected city council of 1945. Tensions over master plan priorities and controversy related to new zoning legislation divided the city's business leadership as well as its city council. Other disputes focusing on water needs, spending, and vice control fragmented the council. That fragmentation was reflected in the council's first vote to decide whether or not to retain acting city manager V. R. Smithan, a vote Smithan narrowly won in a 5 to 4 decision.[31]

The Citizens Charter Association responded to this division in 1947 by instigating a complete change in its organization's leadership and by drafting a new council slate. As in the past, the CCA selected busi-

ness leaders and professionals it deemed able to work for the city as
a whole. According to a CCA flyer, "all the candidates [were] mar-
ried, all church members, all taxpayers . . . and all [were] pledged to
fair impartial businesslike administration of city affairs."[32]

Sensing that the CCA might be in trouble, four opposition parties
formed and entered slates in the 1947 election. Although the specifics
of each party differed, all charged that the city's business and banking
elite controlled the CCA, and thus that group was not responsive to
the needs of the people. Realizing such charges had not been particularly effective in the past, opposition groups also challenged the CCA's
efficiency, impartiality, and honesty. The Greater Dallas Association
claimed, for instance, that the CCA did little for South Dallas, and
attacked the CCA's selection of twenty-three-year-old Joe Golman to
represent that area. The newly formed All Dallas, GI and Veterans
Party flayed the CCA for its "neglect of the paving and sewer needs
of the smaller communities." Others accused the CCA of "squander-
ing and waste," "wild-eyed bond selling" and the "wasteful practice
of engaging high salaried experts from out of town" to tell them how
they should build their city. Unfair garbage taxes and a taxi monopoly
also were issues scored by CCA opponents.

Despite the onslaught of criticism, and the earlier divided council, the CCA dominated the election. Two CCA candidates won out-
right and six others won in run-off elections. Only the young Joe Golman lost to G. G. Stabbs, Sr., a candidate endorsed by South Dallas's
incumbent councilman, L. L. Hiegal.[33]

The CCA won eight of the nine council seats in part because it
successfully promoted its image as an efficient, businesslike organization working for Dallas as a whole. The strong endorsement of the
city's newspapers helped to maintain this image as well. The *Dallas
Times Herald* reminded its readers of the non-political nature of the
CCA, observing how its candidates were drafted and had "never even
dreamed about going into politics" before the CCA contacted them,
and so their only ambition was "to promote the welfare of Dallas to
the best of their ability." The *Dallas Morning News* mirrored similar
sentiments when it editorialized, "If personal qualifications were solely
determining, it might be difficult to choose in a number of individual
cases. . . . But the issue is much larger when viewed from the best interest of Dallas. That issue is whether we shall have a united, harmo-

nious governing body at city hall, or one composed of two warring factions."[34]

The CCA's victory came despite its inability to gain widespread support from either labor or blacks in 1947. The Progressive Voters League, for instance, supported seven opposition candidates for council. And organized labor — particularly the CIO — worked against the CCA because of its refusal to allow municipal workers to unionize. Despite these defections, general voting followed earlier patterns with heavy CCA support coming from the upper- and middle-class neighborhoods of North Oak Cliff and North and Northeast Dallas.[35]

The 1947 election marked the last time the CCA would lose a council seat for more than a decade. The remarkable record of election victories stemmed from several factors, first among them the CCA's willingness to act in a way that supported its claim to be for Dallas as a whole. Not only did its close cooperation with the Dallas Chamber of Commerce and the Dallas Citizens Council help propel Dallas into an unparalleled economic boom in the 1950s which benefited a variety of Dallas residents, but the CCA made special efforts to recognize the particular needs of certain Dallas groups. When Bill Harris, president of the local AFL, ran for city council on an opposition slate in 1949 the CCA attacked his backers, arguing that they were not interested in Dallas but were "a political bunch seeking to grab power for the big national labor bosses." In 1953, however, the CCA nominated the same Bill Harris for city council, arguing that the AFL deserved representation. As a result, the *Dallas Craftsman*, mouthpiece of the AFL, provided strong support for the CCA, citing not only the selection of Harris but the benefits from the city's massive programs of public works generated by the incumbent CCA council.[36] In 1957 the CCA nominated Mrs. Carr P. Collins as its first woman council candidate. The *News* supported the move, observing that "with the substantial voting strength in Dallas of the distaff side, the wisdom of representing Dallas women directly on the council must be clearly apparent."[37]

Although no blacks received the CCA nod in the 1950s, they were appointed to the CCA executive committee and generally treated with respect. Not only did the CCA open up more public job opportunities for blacks, including law enforcement, but during the early 1950s the city undertook one of the largest public housing programs in the country in an attempt to resolve blacks' desperate housing needs, and the community tensions which went with them. An unprecedented number of public services, including roads and sewers, were further provided for the city's black neighborhoods. Finally, the CCA worked to carry out court mandates for integration through compromise rather than confrontation with the black community and, consequently, the Progressive Voters League usually supported the CCA during this time.[38]

In the 1950s, the CCA also made a special effort to provide public projects for the white working-class sections of Oak Cliff, south and west of the downtown area. That area had long been jealous of the rapid growth and prosperity of North Dallas. As a result, even the usually critical *Oak Cliff Tribune* acknowledged in 1957 how the present administration had been "most generous to Oak Cliff." Such action helped the CCA maintain its image throughout this period as the party for Dallas as a whole, an image that caused the *News* to ask in 1949, "shall we continue nonpartisan municipal government of, for and by all the people of Dallas? Or shall we revert to old-style politically controlled government primarily for the interests of a small block of political leaders?" As long as Dallas identified good municipal government as "business-like, efficient, economical and nonpartisan" government, the CCA was hard to defeat. In the 1951 election, for example, despite the entry of two opposition slates, CCA candidates won ninety-two of the city's ninety-three precincts.[39]

The ability of the CCA to maintain a united front also helped it dominate local government. Unity did not come easily, however. When council candidate J. B. ("Tiste") Adoue, Jr., proved the top vote-getter in 1949 and was not then elected mayor by council, the usual procedure, trouble broke out. Adoue, a banker who had earlier presided over the Chamber of Commerce, was, according to one observer, "an intensely individualistic business leader" who tended to treat his peers as inferiors. Whether it was his treatment of council members, his unpredictability, or his unwillingness to be a team player, Adoue failed to get the post. Supporters immediately started a campaign to make the mayor's office an elected position, an issue that split the CCA leadership and polarized the two leading newspapers. The campaign for an elected mayor succeeded, but such a breach did not result in any permanent damage to the CCA. In the subsequent 1951 election it posted an impressive election victory as Dallas voters elected Adoue mayor.[40]

Under Adoue's leadership, local government experienced great turmoil, according to one source, "sparked largely by Adoue's tempestuous nature." Adoue warred both with council members and with city manager Elgin E. Crull, at one point calling the latter a liar. Such conflict threatened to alienate many of CCA's supporters, including business leaders, and also tarnished the CCA's image as a harmonious and efficient organization interested in serving the entire city. Although Adoue's administration actually had an impressive record of achievement, it bungled the city's water crisis and approved significant increases in the city's utility rates. Because of these actions, and the public squabbling for the first time in years, the CCA in 1953 faced an election with apprehension.[41]

The CCA responded to its tarnished reputation by selecting all new candidates to run for council. Even more important, it convinced one of the city's most prominent citizens, seventy-two-year-old Robert L. Thornton, to run for mayor. Thornton, who had played a major role in every civic endeavor in the city since the 1930s, proved a brilliant choice for an organization trying to overcome factionalization and retain its image of being for Dallas as a whole. In his acceptance speech Thornton promised if elected to promote "a progressive, vigorous city, that will attract businesses, large and small, in our city." He also called for a "clean and well-rounded city."[42]

Thornton's candidacy helped punctuate the civic image which CCA leaders wished to project. When Marvin Williams, candidate for mayor from the Greater Dallas Party, challenged Thornton to a debate, the banker reminded Williams that he was not a politician and would not debate with anybody. "I think that a man who engages in a political debate," Thornton observed, "has to have some elements of a politician, and I have none." Thornton and the CCA council candidates also rallied behind the familiar slogans linking their party with business-like, efficient, and economical city government. With the very popular Thornton heading its ticket, the entire CCA slate swept to victory by more than a 2 to 1 margin. Only sixteen precincts in the city gave majorities to CCA opponents. Two years later, the Thornton-headed CCA slate ran unopposed.[43]

Despite these impressive victories the CCA faced growing opposition in the late 1950s as many Dallas voters apparently embraced a new definition of good city government, one emphasizing democracy rather than efficiency. Under this definition, the CCA's business-dominated party leadership became increasingly vulnerable to attack. In the 1957 municipal campaign, for instance, opponents claimed that the CCA governed Dallas with "dictatorial and boss-like control." Laurence Melton, president of the CCA, became a favorite target for such charges. The former journalist and cofounder of the Melton Printing Company in 1936 assumed the presidency of the CCA in 1949 and retained that position for the next eleven years. Through his long tenure Melton gained both power and prestige, but also left himself vulnerable to charges of bossism.[44]

The changing nature of Dallas politics also affected the fortunes of the CCA. In 1954, Dallasites elected ultraconservative realtor Bruce Alger to Congress, the first Republican ever voted to that post from Dallas County. That victory helped accelerate the rise of the Republican party in Dallas, and promoted a partisan politics that would eventually challenge the dominance of the CCA and its philosophy of working for Dallas as a whole. In 1957, for example, North Dallas Republicans challenged the CCA-controlled council and park board for allowing the city's Museum of Fine Arts to exhibit paintings by known communists. And during the 1957 election, one opponent accused CCA council candidates of coddling communists.[45]

In response to its opposition, the CCA maintained its usual approach to local campaigns, emphasizing how it had given the city "harmonious teamwork and good, efficient city government." CCA literature labeled Dallas a "progressive city" and reminded voters that a "progressive city attracts industry. Progress," according to the CCA, also "meant larger payrolls, more jobs, increased prosperity for all citizens, no matter who they are."[46]

Although the Citizens Charter Association won convincingly in 1957 in an election which saw over sixty-two thousand ballots cast, more than twenty-eight thousand voted against CCA candidates—the largest number of votes cast against the CCA since its creation. Shaken by the growing numbers opposing the good government organization, CCA head Laurence Melton called for the reorganization of the CCA after the election. Melton proposed a full-time CCA organized year round on a precinct basis to "take the CCA closer to the people." The CCA needed a grassroots organization, according to Melton, because it had been "getting out of touch with the people." Melton, who for all intents and purposes had *been* the CCA except at election time, called for an active executive committee of thirty-five to forty members representing all parts of the city and remaining active throughout the year. He also recommended formal card-carrying membership in the CCA, and the development of an organization to keep citizens informed and involved in good government goals year-long.[47]

Even greater changes occurred in the CCA after the 1959 municipal election. That election marked an important watershed in Dallas local politics not only because of the strength demonstrated by CCA opponents but also because it underscored the importance of a relatively new actor to local politics — neighborhood political organizations. Groups with specific neighborhood goals, such as the North Dallas–Walnut Hills Improvement League and the White Rock Committee for Conservative Legislation, would challenge the dominant "for-Dallas-as-a-whole" rhetoric and rally support around neighborhood quality-of-life issues rather than city-wide growth issues.[48] Furthermore, the 1959 election reflected a growing unhappiness in the city about the distribution of services, federal-urban relationships, and the problem of CCA boss rule. Indeed, the whole concept of the select few knowing what was best for the city as a whole came under increasing attack.

The race for mayor in 1959 clearly demonstrated the new dimensions of local politics. Although Earle Cabell, son and grandson of former Dallas mayors, had expected the CCA's nomination for mayor in 1959, a last-moment decision to draft the seventy-eight-year-old Thornton for a fourth term changed all that. Cabell decided to run against his old friend anyway, particularly at the urging of Republican leaders from North Dallas and the White Rock Lake area who believed that the CCA had become too liberal and dominated by Democrats.[49]

Cabell, who himself had been a member of both the CCA and the Dallas Citizens Council, focused his campaign rhetoric not on Thornton but on the CCA. The dairy store owner charged that CCA leaders had abdicated their responsibilities to Dallas as a whole and had created "a ward heeling type of political machine. The early patriotic and unselfish leaders of that group," according to Cabell, had "given way to a handful of would be kingmakers, under the longtime domination of a full time Political Boss."[50]

Cabell not only challenged the CCA's organization, but questioned its campaign rhetoric, emphasizing that only a unified, all-CCA administration producing a harmonious and efficient council could best serve Dallas. Cabell suggested that "a mixed council would be in the finest tradition of a representative democracy." Moreover, Cabell challenged the very notion that individuals should sacrifice their particular concerns for Dallas as a whole. For instance, Cabell opposed the fluoridation of Dallas water out of concern for the few. "Regardless of the alleged benefits of such mass-medication," Cabell observed, "it is wrong in principle. Where matters of vital public health are concerned," he continued, "the wishes of any group, even though a minority, should not be subordinated to the arbitrary will of any other group."[51] Government, then, according to Cabell's vision, owed its first commitment to the individual rather than to the city as a whole.

Cabell opposed federally subsidized urban renewal in Dallas for the same reasons. Because it took land away from property owners and sold it to other business interests for improvement, Cabell called urban renewal "the most socialistic measure to be ever passed onto the citizens of Dallas." The growing anti-federal government posture of the *Dallas Morning News,* which had earlier supported New Deal measures, as well as the popularity of Congressman Bruce Alger, who continued to win re-election during the 1950s despite the opposition of some of the city's prominent bankers and business leaders, suggests a growing parochialism by Dallas citizens unwilling to see their city's ties to the larger nation.[52] This new orientation of many Dallas citizens in the 1950s contrasted with the tradition of the Citizens Charter Association and the Dallas Citizens Council, which had viewed both urban renewal and public housing as effective tools for Dallas as a whole.

Despite the CCA's continued rhetoric about working for Dallas as a whole, opponents of that organization found it much easier by the late 1950s to portray the good government organization as a special interest group. The CCA's growing concern with revitalizing downtown made it particularly vulnerable to charges of geographic favoritism. With intense competition from suburban retail centers, and with real signs of decay appearing in the central business district's (CBD) west end, civic leaders launched several well-publicized programs to address the needs of the city's core. But a new comprehensive plan for the CBD fanned charges of geographic favoritism as Cabell and other independent candidates pointed to a disproportionate amount of tax money being spent on downtown street expansion. Even more alarming, according to Cabell, was that "certain CCA leaders supported urban renewal in Dallas, which was nothing but a vicious conspiracy of a group of business leaders . . . to make millions on the downtown area west of Field Street."[53]

Even the accusations of bossism and machine rule that were hurled with increasing regularity now seemed more plausible. Not only had one man, Laurence Melton, dominated the CCA for more than ten years, but claims that the CCA punished its enemies through economic reprisals and rewarded its supporters with economic perks were heard often during the campaign. Cabell's supporters noted, for instance, that only two days after the *Times Herald* endorsed the entire CCA slate, city workers made important street improvements near the newspaper's offices. Such charges of banker control and favoritism continued to alienate at least part of the city's more liberal element, while at the same time the ultraconservative vote went for Cabell, thereby cutting into traditional CCA strongholds in North Dallas.[54]

Despite growing defections, the AFL-CIO Labor Council's special committee on the Dallas city election recommended the re-election of Thornton and his CCA slate. Dallas black leaders maintained their support of Thornton and other CCA candidates even after C. B. Brinkley, Jr., a black, entered the race for council.[55]

Thornton and his CCA running mates needed all the support they could garner in this hotly contested election in which more than seventy thousand Dallasites voted. For the first time since 1947, four CCA candidates failed to receive a majority vote and were forced into runoffs, like the popular Thornton who, though he outdistanced Cabell by seventeen hundred votes, was deprived of the necessary majority by a third candidate. In a second election more than thirty-four thousand voted for Cabell, and Thornton won by a margin of only three thousand votes. Two other CCA candidates won tightly contested runoffs, while lawyer Joe Geary, a former CCA supporter, won his runoff bid against a CCA candidate by nearly eleven thousand votes.[56]

The closeness of the 1959 election and the type of campaign waged by its opponents left their marks on the CCA. Several days after the run-offs, Laurence Melton, stung by the charges of boss rule, announced that the CCA would launch a massive educational program to clarify its goals: the preservation of the city manager form of government and efficient government. If the CCA resembled a "machine" at all, Melton noted, it was "a machine interested only in perpetuating good government." Melton, a controversial figure and a growing liability to the CCA, also announced that he would not serve past his current term ending in January of 1961.[57]

Education, according to some CCA supporters, would not be enough. They called for still another complete reorganization of the CCA to develop a greater groundswell of support. Lawyer Robert L. Clark proposed a variety of changes to the CCA leadership in October, 1959, to combat what he viewed as a "loss of prestige" by the CCA. That group suffered most from the limitations it placed on political participation, according to Clark, who observed that although the CCA had always encouraged widespread public support for its candidates, its rank-and-file members had played little part in candidate nominations and association decisions. By the late 1950s, such action had become a liability, the lawyer said because "citizens are just plain tired of being told who is going to run for what."[58] Local politics should no longer be a spectator sport, but rather, should encourage participation and the power that goes with it.

Toward this end, Clark recommended that the CCA leadership reorganize to include meaningful participation by the city's various neighborhoods. Noting that the "newly asserted strength of self-starting neighborhood groups" had proved an important factor for the opposition's strength during the last election, Clark called for more opportunities for this "newstyle voter worker" in the CCA. Not only would such action provide new faces and new ideas for the CCA, but it might prove to be an effective way to educate the public about CCA goals. Going to the voter for advice and involvement was a must, Clark warned, because times had changed. For too long, the CCA had "closed [its] eyes and ears to changing political moods, behavior, and actions in the city's elections." Now was the time to acknowledge new conditions since the city's political geography, its political environment and its political community had all changed. Others echoed Clark's sentiments. The *Dallas Morning News*, for example, argued that the

Charter Association needed new blood and a new program to "dispel
the public notion that it is run by a handpicked few of the city's big
shots."[59]

The CCA responded to such recommendations by naming a
twenty-two member committee to study the reorganization of the CCA.
W. H. Cothrum chaired the committee, which conducted a series of
"grass roots neighborhood meetings throughout the city to hear what
the city's residents thought the CCA should do." From those meetings
it recommended CCA reorganization by council districts. Each district would have a twenty-one member committee, representing the
different geographic parts of the district. It would be allowed not only
to propose officers for the CCA, but to forward names for CCA council positions to a nominating committee composed of the CCA president and the six district vice-presidents. That group could make its
nominations only from among the names submitted by the district
groups. The new CCA plan also required council candidates to hold
neighborhood meetings so the people could help draft the CCA platform. These resolutions marked a major change of direction by the
CCA.[60] Earlier, a small group of bankers and other business leaders
dominated CCA leadership; now, the CCA turned to the citizens for
guidance and leadership, following the tone if not the specifics of Clark's
recommendations.

Despite its new emphasis on grassroots participation, the CCA
never regained the kind of support it had experienced in the 1940s.
Indeed, the CCA lost the mayoralty to Earle Cabell in 1961, in part
because of the growing fragmentation among CCA financial supporters. Problems appeared after the new nominating committee, responding to strong grassroots support, named Joe Geary its candidate for
mayor. Originally a CCA member, Geary had bolted from the group
in 1959 to run successfully for council as an independent. Meanwhile,
Elgin B. Robertson, mayor pro tem and an Oak Cliff realtor, was the
choice of many CCA supporters. Fearful that Robertson had neither
the charisma nor the name identification necessary to carry North
Dallas, now home to 42 percent of the city's population, the CCA
nominating committee selected Geary. This decision so angered some
CCA supporters that they abandoned the good government group,
shifting their financial backing to Cabell.[61]

Not only did major contributors abandon the CCA, but so did the

Dallas Morning News. In an unprecedented move, the *News* endorsed Earle Cabell. Although publisher Ted Dealy's close relationship with the Cabell family helped explain that endorsement, so did Cabell's conservatism. According to a *News* editorial, the paper particularly liked Cabell's "pledge to fight dictation from Washington."[62] At a time when a growing number of Dallas groups were becoming more conservative and opposed to cooperation with Washington, the CCA's business progressivism became a liability.

Cabell went on to win re-election in 1963 without opposition from the CCA. Independents also won three council seats. The defeats of 1961 and 1963 did not mark the end of the CCA, however. That organization regained new strength after the Kennedy assassination in 1963. But the election of 1961 clearly closed an era in Dallas politics — an era that had equated good government with business-like efficiency rather than democracy, an era that had focused on the city as a whole rather than the desires of individuals, an era that had seen Dallas bankers and business leaders use the federal government as at least an occasional ally rather than picture it as the city's greatest enemy.

Simply dismissing the CCA as a conservative, business-dominated political organization formed to promote downtown development, then, overlooks one of that group's legacies to Dallas. The CCA's growth-oriented business progressivism sought a type of "good government" which would benefit the entire city through low taxes and the efficient delivery of services by a business-like city administration. A growing, well-ordered city, not just a prosperous downtown area, seemed to be the goal of business leadership in the 1940s and early 1950s. Not only did the CCA appear committed to responding to the physical needs of the entire city, but it also provided at least token recognition of the city's various citizen groups such as blacks and organized labor, whose needs had been previously ignored by city government. Coupled with Dallas's phenomenal growth during this period, which provided new economic opportunities to a variety of groups, the CCA's popularity should not be surprising. The CCA's conservatism, as well as the Dallas Citizens Council's conservatism, proved flexible enough to allow Dallas leaders even to promote socially beneficial programs when they could be linked to the city's broader goals of ordered growth. The popularity of the CCA and its flexible conservatism lessened in the late 1950s as a new preoccupation with a more democratic municipal government challenged the CCA's hegemony. The irony, of course, is that ultraconservative groups benefited most from the changing definition of good government from efficiency to democracy, rather than the city's racial minorities or working classes. Those groups would eventually reap the dividends of such change, but not before Dallas earned the reputation of being the city of hate and the assassin of John F. Kennedy.

NOTES

1. Carl Abbott, *The New Urban America: Growth and Politics in Sunbelt Cities* (Chapel Hill: University of North Carolina Press, 1987), pp. 123–45, 247–52; Richard M. Bernard and Bradley R. Rice, *Sunbelt Cities: Politics and Growth since World War II* (Austin: University of Texas Press, 1983), pp. 21 22; John Mollenkopf, *The Contested City* (Princeton, N.J.: Princeton University Press, 1983), p. 246.

2. Abbott, *New Urban America*, pp. 247–52; Bernard and Rice, *Sunbelt Cities*, pp. 21–22; Stephen L. Elkin, "State and Market in City Politics: or, the 'Real' Dallas" in *The Politics of Urban Development*, ed. Clarence N. Stone and Heywood T. Sanders (Lawrence: University Press of Kansas, 1987), pp. 25–31.

3. Bernard and Rice, *Sunbelt Cities*, p. 21.

4. U.S. Department of Interior, Bureau of Census, *Fifteenth Census of the United States, 1930: Population*, 3:1082; William Neil Black, "Empire of Consensus: City Planning, Zoning and Annexation in Dallas, 1900–1960," Ph.D. diss., Columbia University, 1982, p. 286.

5. U.S. Department of Interior, Bureau of Census, *Fifteenth Census of the United States, 1930: Population*, 1:1056; Black, "Empire of Consensus," p. 286.

6. Harold Stone et al., *City Manager Government in Dallas* (Chicago: Public Administration Service, 1939), pp. 8–17; the quote is on p. 13.

7. Quoted in Carolyn Jenkins Barta, "The Dallas News and Council-Manager Government," M.A. thesis, University of Texas, 1970, p. 36; Quoted in Stone, *City Manager Government in Dallas*, p. 24.

8. Stone, *City Manager Government in Dallas*, p. 21; Elkin, "State and Market in City Politics," pp. 28–30; "Stephen J. Hay: An Oral History Interview by Alan Mason on June 24, 1980," Dallas Mayors Oral History Project, Dallas Public Library (DPL), pp. 25–26.

9. Carl B. Callaway to Glenn G. Wiltsey, June 4, 1934, Carl B. Callaway Papers, Manuscript Division, DPL.

10. Stone, *City Manager Government in Dallas*, p. 27; Roscoe C. Martin, "Dallas Makes the Manager Plan Work," *Annals* 198 (July, 1938): 64–70; "James Aston: An Oral History Interview Conducted by Alan Mason on Mar. 20, 1981," Dallas Mayors Oral History Project, DPL, p. 37.

11. Stone, *City Manager Government in Dallas*, pp. 28, 51, 61–62, 68; Barta, "The Dallas News," pp. 44–45.

12. Campaign pamphlet, Home Government Association, Callaway Papers, DPL;

Stone, *City Manager Government in Dallas*, p. 62; Judge George Burgess, untitled speech at the initial rally of the Home Government Association, Mar. 18, 1933, Callaway Papers, DPL; Pamphlet of the Progressive Voters League, Callaway Papers, DPL.

13. Stone, *City Manager Government in Dallas*, pp. 52–56, 65–71, 76; *Dallas Morning News*, Mar. 4, 1937.

14. Stone, *City Manager Government in Dallas*, pp. 77–78; *Dallas Morning News*, Apr. 21, 1937.

15. *Dallas Express*, Feb. 20, 1937, Mar. 20, 1937; Stone, *City Manager Government in Dallas*, p. 79; W. Marvin Dulaney, "The Politic of Disfranchisement: Black Politics in Dallas, 1930–1960," paper delivered at the Southwestern Social Science Meetings, Mar. 20, 1987; Stone, *City Manager Government in Dallas*, p. 68; *Dallas Morning News*, Apr. 21, 1937.

16. Quote from Carol Estes Thometz, *The Decision-Makers: The Power Structure of Dallas* (Dallas: Southern Methodist University Press, 1963), pp. 30–60; Warren Leslie, *Dallas Public and Private: Aspects of an American City* (New York: Grossman, 1964), pp. 68–71.

17. *Dallas Morning News*, Feb. 8, 1939; Sam Acheson, *Dallas Yesterday* (Dallas: Southern Methodist University Press, 1977), pp. 194–95; *Dallas Times Herald*, Apr. 2, 1939.

18. Acheson, *Dallas Yesterday*, p. 195; *Dallas Morning News*, Oct. 4, 1946.

19. *Dallas Morning News*, Feb. 8, 1939, Feb. 28, 1939; Oct. 4, 1946.

20. Ibid., June 30, 1938, Jan. 4, 1938; *Dallas Express*, Apr. 1, 1939; Acheson, *Dallas Yesterday*, p. 196.

21. *Dallas Morning News*, Feb. 12, 1939, Apr. 4, 1939; Henry Jebsen et al., "Centennial History of Dallas, Texas Park System, 1876–1976," Texas Tech University, 1976, 2:498–500 (typescript); *Dallas Times Herald*, Apr. 2, 1939; *Dallas Craftsman*, Mar. 17, 1939.

22. *Dallas Times Herald*, Apr. 2, 1939; *Dallas Morning News*, Mar. 25, 1939, Apr. 2, 1939.

23. *Dallas Morning News*, Apr. 5, 1939, Apr. 1, 1939; *Dallas Express*, Apr. 8, 1939; "James Aston: An Oral History Interview," pp. 6–16.

24. "Dallas Gets Naval Base," *Southwest Business*, Oct., 1940, p. 6; "North America Comes to Dallas," ibid., p. 9. By 1944, Dallas housed two hundred prime contract war industries which employed 100,000 workers. *Dallas*, Feb., 1944, p. 6.

25. *Dallas Morning News*, Mar. 2, 1941.

26. "Acts of Violence Against Negro Homeowners," American Civil Liberties Union Archives (ACLU), Princeton University Library (PUL); Memo to American Civil Liberties Union from Thurgood Marshall, July 28, 1941, ACLU Archives, PUL; *Dallas Express*, Jan. 18, 1941, Oct. 17, 1940.

27. *Dallas Express*, Mar. 29, 1941; *Dallas Morning News*, Apr. 5, 1941; Ann P. Hollingsworth, "Reform Government in Dallas, 1927–1940," M.A. thesis, North Texas State University, 1971, appendix D, p. 104.

28. *Dallas Morning News*, Mar. 14, 1941, Mar. 1, 1941; *Dallas Craftsman*, Mar. 28, 1941.

29. *Dallas Morning News*, Apr. 6, 1943.

30. Harland Bartholomew and Associates, "A Master Plan for Dallas, Texas," 13 pts., 1943–1945 (typescript); *Dallas Craftsman*, Mar. 16, 1945. For more on the plan see Robert B. Fairbanks, "Metropolitan Planning and Downtown Redevelopment: the Cincinnati and Dallas Experiences, 1940–1960," *Planning Perspectives* 2 (Sept., 1987): 245–47.

31. *Dallas Craftsman*, Mar. 23, 1945; *Dallas Morning News*, Apr. 4, 1945, May 2, 1945.

32. *Dallas Time Herald*, Sept. 22, 1946; *Dallas Morning News*, Apr. 1, 1947; Citizens Charter Association campaign flyer, CCA clippings file, DPL.

33. *Dallas Morning News*, Mar. 20, 1947, Mar. 26, 1947; Apr. 2, 1947, Mar. 17, 1947, Apr. 16, 1947.

34. *Dallas Times Herald*, Apr. 11, 1947; *Dallas Morning News*, Apr. 3, 1947.

35. *Dallas Express*, Mar. 29, 1947; *Dallas Morning News*, Mar. 26, 1947, Apr. 16, 1947.

36. *Dallas Morning News*, Apr. 4, 1949; *Dallas Craftsman*, Apr. 3, 1953.

37. *Dallas Morning News*, Apr. 4, 1957.

38. *Dallas Housing Authority. What It Is and How It Works*, n.d., p. 3; "West Dallas," *Journal of Housing*, 11 (Feb., 1954): 54–55; Editors of Fortune, *The Exploding Metropolis* (Garden City, N.J.: Doubleday Anchor Books, 1958), p. 72; *Dallas Express*, Mar. 24, 1951; Leslie, *Dallas Public and Private*, pp. 71–74; Jim Schutze, *The Accommodation: The Politics of Race in an American City* (Secaucus, N.J.: Citadel Press, 1986).

39. *Oak Cliff Tribune*, Mar. 29, 1957; *Dallas Morning News*, Apr. 4, 1949, Apr. 4, 1951.

40. "Stephen J. Hay: An Oral History Interview," pp. 53–68; "Wallace Savage: An Oral History Interview conducted by Alan Mason on September 18, 1980," Dallas Mayors Oral History Project, DPL, pp. 19–20; Acheson, *Dallas Yesterday*, pp. 197–201.

41. *Dallas Morning News*, Jan. 3, 1953, Dec. 3, 1952, Jan. 31, 1953; *Dallas Times Herald*, Dec. 14, 1952.

42. *Dallas Times Herald*, Feb. 11, 1953.

43. *Dallas Morning News*, Mar. 29, 1953, Apr. 8, 1953; Apr. 6, 1955.

44. Ibid., Mar. 19, 1957, Mar. 21, 1957; Mar. 20, 1978; *Oak Cliff Tribune*, Dec. 18, 1959.

45. *Dallas Morning News*, Nov. 3, 1954, Mar. 31, 1957; "One Among 22," *Newsweek*, Jan. 17, 1955, pp. 22–24.

46. *Dallas Morning News*, Apr. 1, 1957.

47. Ibid., Apr. 3, 1957, July 21, 1957. A special U. S. Senate election helped inflate the voter turnout.

48. Ibid., Jan. 22, 1959; Robert L. Clark, "Times Have Changed: A Discussion of Municipal Politics and Elections in the City of Dallas," Oct., 1959, Earle Cabell Papers, DeGolyer Library, Southern Methodist University (SMU).

49. *Dallas Times Herald*, Feb. 18, 1959.

50. "Stephen J. Hay: An Oral History Interview," pp. 70–73; Statement of Earle Cabell, Feb. 19, 1959, Cabell Papers, SMU.

51. Statement of Earle Cabell, Feb. 19, 1959, Cabell Papers, SMU.

52. Cabell news release, Mar. 10, 1959, Cabell Papers, SMU; "Cabell Makes Mental Note," undated *Dallas Morning News* article, clipping file, DPL; *Dallas Morning News*, Nov. 3, 1954; Leslie, *Dallas Public and Private*, pp. 113–14.

53. *Dallas Morning News*, Apr. 4, 1959; Fairbanks, "Metropolitan Planning and Downtown Redevelopment," pp. 249–50; Cabell news release, Mar. 10, 1959, Cabell Papers, SMU.

54. *Oak Cliff Tribune*, Dec. 18, 1959; Cabell news release, Mar. 15, 1959, Mar. 18, 1959, Cabell Papers, SMU; *Dallas Craftsman*, Apr. 3, 1959; Cabell, untitled speech, Apr. 6, 1959, Cabell Papers, SMU.

55. *Dallas Craftsman*, Apr. 3, 1959; *Dallas Express*, Apr. 4, 1959.

56. *Dallas Morning News,* Apr. 9, 1959, Apr. 22, 1959.
57. Ibid., Apr. 24, 1959.
58. Clark, "Times Have Changed," p. 5.
59. Ibid.; *Dallas Morning News,* Dec. 15, 1959.
60. *Dallas Times Herald,* Dec. 13, 1959, Jan. 8, 1961; *Dallas Morning News,* July 7, 1960, Dec. 9, 1960.
61. *Dallas Morning News,* Apr. 5, 1961, Jan. 30, 1961.
62. Ibid., Mar. 19, 1961.

ZANE L. MILLER

Pluralizing America: Walter Prescott Webb, Chicago School Sociology, and Cultural Regionalism

IT MAY SEEM odd and ironic to link Walter Prescott Webb, who we remember as a historian, with sociologists, especially the so-called school of sociologists from the University of Chicago, the institution at which Webb tried but failed to earn a Ph.D. in history. The connection may seem stranger still for those who remember Webb as a student of the frontier and who recall the Chicago school sociologists as students of the urban way of life in twentieth-century industrial society. And it may seem odder still, at least to some, to take seriously either Webb or the Chicago school sociologists. Their works, after all, appeared during the second quarter of the twentieth century and may be seen now as hopelessly and even amusingly out-of-date, relics of the past so irrelevant to our concerns that they might safely be treated as post-modern architects treat "historic" architecture, as essentially meaningless but "interesting" contextual elements with which to embellish our living-room bookshelves or conversations as we craft whatever "life-style" we may at the moment have decided to pursue to make us feel good about ourselves.

Yet an attempt to make such a linkage might yield both a new understanding of Webb and the Chicago school and illuminate that recent past in which we yet live, that period since 1950 when we began to talk about the "Sunbelt" and its cities as distinctive and significant phenomena, forward-looking localities populated by liberated individuals pursuing in a variety of ways their own self-fulfillment by choosing their own life-styles.[1] In this view Webb and the Chicago school deserve our attention because of the status of their work as symptomatic of a major theme in the history of the United States from the late nineteenth century into the last decade of the twentieth century:

the question of how to handle regional and/or racial and ethnic diversity in American civilization.

As it turns out, Webb's life spanned three eras characterized by different modes of dealing with that question. During the first, which ran from 1870 to about 1920, regional and racial diversity seemed a problem, something to be overcome in order to achieve national unity and cultural homogeneity. During the second, which lasted until the 1950s, the embedding of culture in place and the advent of cultural pluralism suggested the "normality" of regional and ethnic diversity but raised the issue of how, with justice, to foster regional and ethnic integrity, equality, and national coherence. Since 1950 a revolt against cultural determinism has liberated us from the necessity of conforming to or putting up with regional, ethnic, or other cultural "stereotypes." But it has also given each of us, as individuals bereft of "given" cultural imperatives with which to conform or against which to rebel, the problems of selecting and maintaining our identities and of deciding how together we might define, create, and sustain a satisfying and viable territorial community life in neighborhoods, cities, regions, and the nation.

This story about Webb and the shift from homogeneity, to cultural group pluralism, to individual pluralism in the definition of American society, begins in the summer of 1893 in Chicago, where Frederick Jackson Turner, a historian often associated with Webb (and occasionally by Webb himself),[2] appeared at the World's Columbian Exposition to present a paper at the Congress of Historians and Historical Students held in conjunction with the Exposition.[3] A young and freshly minted Ph.D., Turner sought in his paper to make history useful in developing a scientific social theory that would guide social planning and practice for the present and the future, and especially useful in dealing with the problem of regional and racial diversity in a nation that he and others assumed ought to be united and homogeneous. His paper, entitled "The Significance of the Frontier in American History," suggested how this might be done but stopped short of making an application of theory to practice. The thesis of the paper proposed that the frontier process, the moving line of settlement that had traveled across the continent from the Atlantic coast to the West of William Jennings Bryan and the Populists, explained two things. It showed that American civilization had replicated the development of any civilization in passing by continuous stages through the familiar hunting and gathering, pastoral, agricultural, and mercantile-industrial phases of development. In this sense America was not unique.

But Turner also contended that the frontier represented the place — albeit a moving one — in which a cultural alteration occurred, a place in which diverse European races redesigned their cultural baggage as they adapted to a landscape that had been defined by Indians, from whom the diverse European races borrowed as they made their adaptation. For the young Turner, then, the frontier functioned as a force that determined American nationality, a force that galvanized European races into a wholly new population characterized by frontier traits that transcended enduring racial distinctions, a united population of diverse origins which exhibited that

> coarseness and strength combined with acuteness and inquisitiveness; that practical, inventive turn of mind, quick to find expedients; that masterful grasp of material things, lacking in the artistic but powerful to effect great ends; that restless nervous energy; that dominant individualism, working for good and evil, and with all that buoyance and exuberance which comes with freedom.[4]

This deterministic account of the effect of the frontier on American culture and character provided a tool which Turner found useful in "solving," usually by explanation, particular social problems. It could be used, for example, as Turner used it in 1896, to explain away the anomaly and "un-Americanism" of the Populists and their candidate for president, Bryan of Nebraska. To many at the time these native-born, white Americans seemed "radical" and out of place in a presumably homogeneous America that preferred to discuss the tariff or banking questions rather than the monetarization of silver or socialistic proposals for federal government ownership of railroads, telegraphs, and telephones, or the graduated income tax. But Turner assured his readers that the Populists represented merely another expression of the rowdy exuberance and youthful idealism of the frontier, and that they, like the frontier itself, would pass as the West moved up the ladder of American social development toward a democratic industrial capitalism compatible with the older and more mature parts of the country.[5]

Yet there was another Frederick Jackson Turner, the one who between 1896 and 1926 wrote a series of articles published in 1932 as a book entitled *The Significance of Sections in American History,* whose title implicitly and contents explicitly contradicted the theme of American homogeneity projected in his frontier thesis of 1893.[6] This second Turner emphasized the similarities between American and European development, accorded a greater importance to the nexus of place and culture so that they became inextricable, and stressed the interchange of cultural traits among cultural groups, emphases which softened the late-nineteenth-century notion of race and which by the 1920s had come to be grouped together under the labels of place-based "ethnicity" and "assimilation."[7]

In these articles on the significance of sections in American history Turner contended that American civilization stemmed from the settlement and separate development of several distinct and successive frontiers, each of which stamped its European and American settlers with a particular and persisting regional culture.[8] Turner found no short- or long-term threat to national coherence in this Balkanized view of America, however, for he expected in the short run that balance could be maintained through Congress and through interregional associations, and in the long run through a vaguely defined process of "assimilation"[9] by which American culture became a pluralistic mixture of regional traits. This construction of American history provided a role both for ethnicity and frontiers in determining American regional pluralism and preserved the notion of a continuously developing American civilization passing through a series of stages in space and time as the frontiers marched across the country and the regions moved up the American ladder of social evolution toward a mature, coherent, and culturally assimilative regional pluralism and a democratic urban industrial capitalist society.[10]

By the 1920s, when Webb began his career as a student of American civilization, the idea of the American frontier and the idea of American *frontiers* had become conventions of American social theory and practice most familiar to historians through the historical essays of Turner. In the hands of Turner, those ideas had yielded two versions of American history, both of them constructed in terms of a ladder of continuous social development culminating in a democratic and capitalist urban industrial society. But the frontier version pointed to the emergence of a culturally homogeneous America while the *fron-*

tiers version pointed to the emergence of a culturally pluralistic America of regions which retained its balance and equilibrium — its coherence — through the operation of political and other interregional institutions and through the process of cultural assimilation.

Webb might have chosen either of these Turnerian constructs as a scaffolding for his own most serious work, which began to appear in 1931 with the publication of *The Great Plains: A Study in Institutions and Environment.*[11] But Webb chose neither, perhaps because he lacked rigorous training in American history or perhaps because he had not yet on his own read either of the two Turners.[12] Instead, from his naïveté he forged a sense of the history of American civilization that sounded vaguely Turnerian but which differed fundamentally from both Turnerian models. The similarity stemmed from Webb's depiction of the way in which the culture of a people from one place — in this case Anglo Saxons from the eastern United States — adjusted and adapted in response to the process of moving to a new environment occupied by a people — the plains Indians — formed from and, in Webb's view, marvelously adjusted to that environment. But there the resemblance ends.

The key to understanding the Great Plains, contended Webb, resided in the region's vastness, aridity, levelness, and treelessness, in the success of the plains Indians in adjusting to these conditions by working out a nomadic, pastoral, and warlike way of life, and in the bafflement with which first the Spanish and then Anglo-Saxon Texans and Americans, who carried a cultural baggage of institutions acquired in humid and forested regions, confronted the plains environment. The Spanish, who according to Webb had perfected a method of frontiering suitable to South and Central America, never found a means of settling the plains because their culture discouraged them from making a serious attempt. But the Texans and Americans, by borrowing cultural elements from the Spanish and Indians, and by adapting elements of their own culture, used horses, six-shooters, cattle ranching, windmills, irrigation, and dry farming to conquer the Great Plains, which Webb divided into three sub-regions — the prairie plains, the plains proper, and the high plains between the Rockies and the Cascades. Indeed, for a few short years between 1865 and 1885 these white settlers created a way of life perfectly suited, said Webb, for Anglo-Saxon Americans in this hostile environment: the pastoral, nomadic, and "lawless" culture of open-range cattle ranching that established the Cattle Kingdom. This kingdom, said Webb, rested on an economic system neatly adapted to the Great Plains and to its trading partner, the urban-industrial East. In a few short years, however, it fell, disrupted by the coming of migrants who were encouraged by disastrous eastern policies based on the misguided belief that agriculture might flourish in this arid region, the belief that the desert might be made to bloom.

Despite the destruction of the Cattle Kingdom, wrote Webb, a distinctive plains culture took shape during the late nineteenth and early twentieth centuries, albeit one that rested on shaky rural foundations that left it impoverished when compared with the East. This plains culture exhibited its own way of life, with distinctive occupations, its own modes of cooking, eating, and dressing, and its own folklore, history and political style. And Webb thought this Great Plains culture might yet produce a great and distinctive regional literature. "Desert countries," he wrote, "have always been fertile sources of inspiration" for a literature possessing "mysticism and spiritual quality which have found expression in the lofty and simple preachings of Jesus and Mohammed, both of whom lived in a region so like the Great Plains that the similarities have often been pointed out." Such a literature, he added, would contribute "much to a civilization . . . thus far notorious for its devotion to material things."[13]

Yet Webb in *The Great Plains* did more than outline the history and characteristics of an area he regarded as a distinctive region of the United States. He formulated a social theory of historical discontinuity and of a cultural regionalism of conflict rather than comity. Webb suggested, that is, that some regions of the United States, even though conquered by Anglo-Saxon Americans, could not viably move from the pastoral stage to the urban-industrial stage of civilization. He also suggested that some regions could not be expected either to hold their own in the nation through Congress and interregional associations or through culutral assimilation because in some regions "peculiar" cultural traits would endure and complicate the process of securing regional balance and national coherence.

For Webb, in short, the process of conquering the Great Plains by Anglo-Saxon Americans made the plains neither a part of a culturally homogeneous America, as purported by the first Turner, nor a separate but equal part of an assimilative culturally pluralistic America, as purported by the second Turner. What struck Webb about the brief history of the Anglo-Saxon American Great Plains was its continuing contrast with and persisting differences from the East (conceived either as a region or several regions), its relative poverty, its relative lack of influence in Washington, D.C. and on the dominant industrialized interests of the East, and the failure of the rest of the nation to understand and respect its culture. As a consequence, eastern public and private policy makers had adopted measures and programs that would not work in the Great Plains and encouraged expectations about the Great Plains, especially concerning prospects for a flourishing agriculture, that could not be realized. This and the general intolerance of and tendency to caricature Great Plains culture made it in the 1930s a separate, distinctive, "backward," unequal, misunderstood, and unappreciated part of the United States. For Webb, the Great Plains constituted an aggrieved region whose grievances and culture, if not treated appropriately, would erode its viability and, conceivably, would threaten the coherence of the United States as a democratic urban-industrial and capitalist political entity with a pluralistic culture.

While Webb in *The Great Plains* laid out his own scheme of American development, one which denied the effectiveness of both interregional association through Congress and of cultural assimilation in fostering national coherence, he did not propose solutions to the problems of regionalism and of the Great Plains as he defined it, except to make a plea for tolerance and understanding of the Great Plains by the East. He moved beyond this position, however, in his second major book, published in 1937 in the midst of the Great Depression and in the year following the election of Franklin D. Roosevelt to his second term as President of the United States. Webb called this book *Divided We Stand: The Crisis of a Frontierless Democracy* and both the subtitle and the contents of the volume indicated that by this time Webb had read Turner. The crisis to which the subtitle referred was the passing of the frontier as the dominant force in American history, of the place that had not only yielded such Turnerian frontier traits as practicality and democracy but was also, Webb emphasized, the place that had offered individual economic opportunity for all who would pursue it, including the down and out, troublemakers, and malcontents. And in *Divided We Stand,* Webb asserted, the frontier had created not one (the first Turner) and not a multitude (the second Turner) but just three regions: the North, the South, and the West, regions he sometimes referred to as "nations" confederated as the United States.

In this volume Webb also eschewed the Turnerian view of continuous social development that posited "natural" stages of progress for regions that began with the primitive and ascended to the urban-industrial, for Webb depicted both the West and the South—the former much younger and the latter as old as the North—as agrarian, and the North as industrial. He also discounted once more the effectiveness of interregional associations and assimilation in forging amity, cooperation, and national coherence among the three regions, for he attributed to each region a distinctive cultural consciousness that emerged in frontier days and created a pattern of regional conflict throughout American history that in the 1930s, as in the 1850s and 1860s, threatened the viability of the Union.

To be sure, Webb in this book spent little time tracing the development and describing the non-economic regional characteristics of the three sections. He seems to have regarded these characteristics as so obvious as to require no explication to readers in the 1930s but nonetheless so thoroughly rooted as to be unaffected by regional planning that might in the future yield a modest increase in urban-industrialization in the South and West. Instead, he devoted most of his historical analysis to the emergence in the North of the newly dominant force in American life, the big business corporation, and to an explanation of the ways in which that force after 1870 had reduced the West and South—their city dwellers as well as their farmers—to the status of impoverished colonial dependencies and had constricted economic opportunity, individualism and self-government throughout the United States. In this account, a triple crisis of economic opportunity, democracy, and national coherence approached in the 1890s when the closing of the frontier brought on a depression and made its first mark on national politics in the presidential campaign of Bryan, who led alienated southerners and westerners in their loudest protest against the injustices of northern corporate rule. The crisis receded in the early twentieth century as the automobile and movie industries temporarily mitigated unemployment in the West and South. When it reappeared during the Great Depression, President Franklin D. Roosevelt confronted it, inaugurating a peaceful revolution that sought both to respond to the plight of the West and South and to forge a democratic and centrist path between two looming and ominous alternatives — corporate fascism on the right and communism on the left.

In the final chapter of *Divided We Stand*, entitled "Is There a Way Out?," Webb offered proposals to address the crisis of economic opportunity, democracy, and national coherence. Among other things, he urged Roosevelt to adhere to the vital center and his powerful business opponents to acquiesce in that course. But Webb also anticipated the coming of another and more serious depression. To avert a swing to the right or left before or during such an emergency he offered several suggestions for the long run, none of them calculated to wipe out the fundamental distinctions among the three regions. These explicitly *excluded* three options[14]: first, secession, which he thought no "true American" wanted; second, the turning over of the federal government to finance capital and business corporations, a possibility he sketched in some detail but only as an intellectual exercise, in part to demonstrate that such a scheme might preserve regional diversity but at the price of extinguishing democracy; and third, the imposition of "feudal" tariffs by the South and West on imported northern commodities. Such a protectionist policy, in the unlikely event of its adoption, would provide a stimulus for western and southern manufactures, Webb believed; but the call for which, he asserted, would "create a sensation" and "attract the attention of every northern manufacturer," a traditional and sometimes effective mode of protest by the political "wild jackasses" of the West and South.[15]

Intermingled with these non-proposals, Webb offered three serious suggestions to enhance the prospect of national coherence. These consisted of strengthening interregional political associations, using national planning (although he did not use that term) for regional economic development, and manipulating public opinion to counter alienation, foster good citizenship, and preserve democratic governments. The first two he directed as advice to the West and the South.

Webb thought the West and South should recognize their similar political concerns and traditions — their rural and agrarian interests and their attitude of protest toward the North — and on that recognition create or take control of a political party binding the South and

West, a step that in itself would secure control of the Senate for the beleaguered regions. If that party also adopted a platform appealing to the farmers of the Midwest and labor in the North, Webb added, it could control all three branches of the federal government. Such a platform should advocate the adoption of a constitutional amendment repealing the fourteenth amendment provision that had led to the definition of a corporation as a person and had reserved for the federal government the authority to charter corporations engaged in interstate commerce.

The idea of national planning appeared in Webb's call for the "wider" distribution of "industrial, financial, and manufacturing cities," a step that could be justified as a measure of national defense to prevent the subjugation of the entire United States by the foreign conquest of the ruling great cities of the North, a threat recently dramatized for the nation, said Webb, by the landing on Lake Michigan of Mussolini's amphibian airplanes during the Century of Progress Exposition in Chicago. The idea of national planning also appeared in Webb's recommendation that the North should adopt a "'good neighbor'" policy by which its business corporations would offer to share some of their wealth with the West and South by decentralizing industry through the use of electrical power, by cooperating more with state and national governments, and by more generously passing out their largesses to education in the sections from which the wealth came, the exploited West and South.

In this chapter, too, Webb called for the reuniting of the United States into a national community of diverse regions through the promotion of good citizenship. By this he meant that citizens should become informed, in part by reading books like *Divided We Stand*, so that they could understand the real causes of their economic problems and find adequate solutions, preferably to be carried out by "wise and gradual processes" rather than by "sudden, violent means."[16] Early in the chapter Webb pointed to a reassuringly "growing interest of the people in their government,"[17] and on its last page posed the question of how to enhance and sustain that interest. His book demonstrated, Webb contended, that the solution to the problem of making better citizens ultimately rested in "the adoption of a policy for restoring to all sections and classes of the American democracy a semblance of economic opportunity." Webb belived that the North, "when informed," and its feudal lords would cooperate with the policy because it coincided with their long-term interests; and they would thus "preserve this democracy and save the spiritual values for the individual."[18]

Divided We Stand, like all good books, as we like to say, had its flaws. So, too, did *The Great Plains*, which nonetheless by the late 1930s had won wide acclaim as one of the decade's most popular and influential books. For that reason, it attracted the attention of the Social Science Research Council, which in the late 1930s created a Committee on Appraisal to evalute significant works in the social sciences, and which in 1939 selected *The Great Plains* as the third book for such treatment. For that task the committee selected a panel that included six historians, a geographer, an agricultural economist, a sociologist, and a cultural anthropologist; and it requested a historian, Fred A. Shannon, to write a detailed critique of the book. The book and Shannon's critique were discussed at a panel conference, attended by Shannon and Webb, held at Skytop, Pennsylvania, in 1939. The proceedings of the conference appeared in print in 1940.[19] Shannon's lengthy and thorough critique, though it did not question the validity of the concept of cultural regionalism as a factor in American history and life, proved devastating, at least to Webb, who rejected it as a valid appraisal on the grounds that to accept it "would be to consent to the view that the book I value is really cheap, superficial, erroneous, slightly tainted with dishonesty, and unworthy of the recognition it has already attained."[20]

Nonetheless, *The Great Plains* fared quite well, on the whole, in the course of a full day of often testy discussion at the conference, especially in the remarks of Louis Wirth, who in the 1930s ranked as one of the most prominent sociologists of the University of Chicago school. Indeed, Wirth talked more than any other single participant, with the possible exception of Shannon, who Wirth took to task on several occasions. Wirth, like Webb, felt that Shannon had failed to focus on the book as a whole and therefore, in Wirth's view, had missed the central argument of the book (the inextricable relationship between place, people, and culture) and had missed the central theme of the book (the process of cultural adaptation as people from one place and culture moved into contact with the people of another place and culture). Wirth's interpretation of the book led Webb during the conference to define it as a cultural anthropological study rather than a historical one.[21]

Wirth not only criticized Shannon for misreading the book but also made an effort to explicate his own view of particular points in *The Great Plains*. Wirth, for example, defended Webb's attempt to define a territorial unit by its cultural characteristics, to emphasize its differences from rather than its similarities to the East, and to divide the region into three zones, each of them a part of the culture of the Great Plains but each also exhibiting its own cultural traits. Wirth denied Shannon's suggestion that Webb had succumbed to the geographic and technologic determinisms of the past because the book had stressed the fashion in which easterners adapted such elements of their culture as the revolver, irrigation, the windmill, and land and water laws to their new habitat. Wirth liked Webb's concentration on "certain characteristic aspects of culture" in the book, such as cattle and the range in the section on the Cattle Kingdom but also on cotton and the plantation in a brief reference to the Cotton Kingdom of the antebellum South. Wirth also proposed that the new habitat of the Great Plains modified every institution of the migrating easterners, not just those analyzed by Webb; and specifically suggested that additional research would discover on the Great Plains the appearance of new words in the language, a new dialect, new religious practices, and a distinctive architecture as settlers carried their old culture across what Webb had called "the institutional fault line" along the 98th meridian. And in his concluding comment Wirth lauded Webb's sensitivity to the "process through which land and work, occupation and technology, interact with the institutions, and social organization of the people," the process of cultural adaptation and change.[22]

Though Wirth did not say so at the conference, his comments on *The Great Plains* indicated that he found in the book an analogue to the work of the Chicago school sociologists in the 1920s and 1930s on the modern metropolis. They defined the metropolis as a pluralistic cultural unit with its own way of life. They contended that the metropolis possessed a distinctive social structure composed of an escalating variety of occupational groups produced by the continuing division of labor in industrial society, and of a variety of ethnic groups attracted or driven to the metropolis by the processes of industrialization. They also asserted that the metropolis displayed a characteristic but constantly expanding, shifting, and reorganizing spatial structure composed of commercial, industrial, and residential districts overlain by smaller subcultural areas dominated and defined by occupational or ethnic subcultures. The Chicago school depicted these groups and parts of the metropolis as connected and separated by transportation and communications systems, and portrayed the groups, parts, and systems as so interdependent that a change in one affected all the rest.[23]

The Chicago school not only defined urban life as continually in process but also stressed its tendency to dissolve past cultural and social organizational forms, a process involving a period of community disorganization in particular localities as the characteristic forms of the future took shape. The Chicago school especially emphasized that the modern metropolis eroded "neighborhood," the informal and unorganized expression of neighborly concern the Chicago school associated with the homogeneous village life of the past, something fated to disappear in the urban present and future except in isolated occupational or ethnic areas. This did not mean that the emergence of the modern metropolis would eliminate a vital and distinctive local life, however. According to the Chicago school, local unity and cohesion developed in areas dominated by first, second, and third generation ethnic groups that had successfully forged and sustained institutions of local community in response to the "outside" threat of discrimination. A similar sense of local community and subcultural coherence could also develop in other areas in which city planning or the natural processes of urban growth had separated residential from other land uses and segregated population elements by occupational compatibility. Such homogeneous areas yielded community organizing activities that fostered a competent community consciousness and cooperation on such critically important issues as assuring individuals a home, new experiences, status, affection, and a sense of belonging within their community of residence.

Thus the Chicago school sociologists, like Webb, thought of America as comprising territorial communities that molded the desires, values, aspirations, and personalities of its inhabitants. And just as this way of thinking made it possible for Webb to talk about "the Great Plains" as a pluralistic cultural region, it made it possible for the Chicago school to talk about the metropolis as a pluralistic cultural region. And like Webb, who thought that his regions had problems that threatened the coherence and vitality of the United States as a democratic nation, the Chicago school thought that the metropolis had problems that might yield similar consequences. Indeed, Wirth himself in 1938 assessed the prospects for metropolitan regional culture in an essay on "Urbanism as a Way of Life." This new culture, in Wirth's view, might move in either of two directions. One tendency raised the grim specter of a "mass society" rendered pathologically unstable and susceptible to the appeal of totalitarianism of the right or left by the combination of anomie brought on by the disintegration of local community and of interminable subcultural conflicts among the little regions within the metropolis. But the other tendency raised the brighter hope of a new era of cosmopolitanism, urbanity, and tolerance as the little regions of the metropolitan regions came to understand one another, recognize their mutual interdependence, and to cooperate in forging a metropolitan consciousness that treated each part and group of the metropolis as a separate but equal part of the whole.[24]

This concept of the metropolis and its problems led members of the Chicago school from the 1920s and through the 1930s to advocate comprehensive city planning based on their scientific social theory of modern urban life. Such a comprehensive plan, wrote one member of the Chicago school in 1929, would rest on a "realistic conception" of city life as metropolitan in scope, and as advocates of the plan publicized it to arouse public interest, the plan would give the city "a conception of itself — a self-awareness, a sense of its history and role, a vision of its future — in short, a personality." And only when the city had achieved such self-consciousness, "only when the mosaic of cultural worlds which compose it come to think of themselves not as over against one another, but as related to a vision of the city," could the city act effectively to preserve its coherence and the welfare of its diverse inhabitants carrying out the particular projects and programs in the plan.[25]

As it turns out, comprehensive metropolitan planning caught on in the 1920s and persisted into the 1940s, and the methods and designs of its practitioners rested upon a definition of the metropolis and a mode of analysis similar to those of the Chicago school sociologists. Briefly put, comprehensive metropolitan planning took place when a local agency hired experts on the future of the metropolis as consultants who studied the culture and organization of the metropolis in question and laid out a master plan to guide public and private development for a period of twenty or thirty years. These plans stressed the separation of commercial, industrial, and residential land uses, the segregation of occupational and ethnic subcultures into territorial enclaves, the division and connection of the parts and groups of the region by transportation and communication systems, the provision of educational, social welfare, and civic facilities in the sub-communities of the metropolis, the establishment of elaborate programs to publicize the plan, and the creation of monuments of civic identity and pride as a means of securing intra-metropolitan understanding, tolerance, and cohesion.[26]

Webb, to my knowledge, did not express an interest in comprehensive metropolitan planning in the 1930s and 1940s, but he did continue his work on regionalism, which yielded in 1952 his third major work, *The Great Frontier*, a study of Europe and its frontier lands in the New World, and their prospects. This book suggests that Webb in his three major works told the same story — the story of the formation of regional distinctions and the consequences of regional interaction — and that in each he used a successively larger cast of characters, larger places, and a different major theme. In the first he sought to establish the great plains as a legitimately distinctive region of the United States that deserved understanding and tolerance and that should be treated with policies conforming to its distinctive characteristics. In the second he analyzed the three regions of the United States and focused on the problem of stark regional economic disparities that threatened national coherence and the perpetuation of democracy in a frontierless United States.

In *The Great Frontier* Webb broadened his scope to encompass Western civilization and raised a warning about the imminent disappearance of "individualism" in a frontierless globe dominated by a corporate culture, but especially about the demise of frontier individualism in the United States, the futility of a pervasive nostalgia within the United States for a return to frontier individualism, and the need to develop a corporate individualism. In *The Great Frontier*, the gloomiest of his three major works, Webb did not celebrate the frontier as the source of either a homogeneous America or of a harmoniously pluralistic America of diverse regions, as had Turner. Instead, he consigned the frontier to the dead past by treating it as an aberration, a one-time-only event that had jolted the history of Western civilization out of its normal pattern, defined by Webb in this volume as hostile to the aspirations of individuals for room in which to pursue those things they found interesting, satisfying, and fulfilling. For Webb, the passing of the great frontier in the twentieth century meant a return to normalcy in the last half the twentieth century and beyond.

Webb developed this case in the form of a study of the interaction between The Metropolis — the countries of Europe — and the Great Frontier, the new lands discovered by Europeans at the beginning of the sixteenth century. But he devoted most of his attention to the Great Frontier and especially to the United States as an example of what happened on one frontier of the Great Frontier. He contended that the Great Frontier provided an unprecedented source of new wealth and functioned as the determining factor in producing a new idea, individualism, which manifested itself in the United States chiefly in the development of a democratic polity that concentrated on the facilitating of economic opportunity through laissez-faire capitalism. He also argued that both frontier wealth and frontier individualism insinuated themselves into the Metropolitan way of life. With the passing in the early twentieth century of the frontier in the United States and elsewhere, however, abundance gave way to scarcity, the source of individualism dried up, and frontier capitalism "recrystallized" into a corporate culture, which Webb defined as a culture (medieval or twentieth century) dominated by large bureaucratic institutions that disciplined the lives of individuals living within or residing in territory controlled by such corporations. The stultification of individualism in this corporate culture of scarcity, according to Webb, led to a longing for a return of the old individualism and a nostalgia for the time and the places in which it had flourished most luxuriantly. But Webb regarded both the longing and nostalgia as futile and unrealistic, because that old individualism could only flourish in a culture influenced by the frontier.

Webb thus found himself in a dilemma created by his own cultural determinism. How could the idea and practice of individualism, which he regarded as the more valuable of the two contributions of the Great Frontier to Western civilization, survive in a corporate culture inimical to it? Webb concluded that individualism in the last half of the twentieth century could only emerge from a "sheer act of will" by individuals, a determination to find some level of "self-employment" as an outlet for whatever creative energies they might have. He doubted that most people in the corporate culture of the 1950s could find space in their lives for this sort of self-employment, or that corporate rulers possessed the good sense to provide for it.[27] But he gave two contemporary examples of how it had been done as a subtle suggestion of what voters and others in a corporate culture that still retained the apparatus of democracy might do to broaden opportunities for the exercise of a new individualism, one that revolved around artistic creativity for psychological self-fulfillment rather than the conquest of nature for pecuniary gain.

As his first example Webb described the working life of a hypothetical university professor obligated by the educational function of the institution to teach classes, for which the institution paid his salary and gave him job security through tenure. But the university also gave him time to pursue his hobby or avocation, in this case playing with ideas. Eventually this play led to the production of a book, the mere appearance of which provided "satisfaction entirely apart from any pecuniary gains anticipated" but which also elicited reviews (favorable and unfavorable) and an oocasional letter from New England, old England, or some other "distant land." For the professor, said Webb, this was not a bad life, for it offered him space "for developing the individualism that he has always wanted" and permitted him to have "fun" in "finding a new truth, in developing a philosophy, in saying things in a better way than they have been said before." If the publisher sent a check, added Webb, that would be "fun" too, not so much "for the position of the decimal point but as a sure sign that he has done something that people will approve." Nor did it disturb this professor, claimed Webb, that he found himself, "though voluntarily," bound for life "to a public corporation conducted on a public non-profit basis," for "the public approves of the corporation."[28]

Webb found his second example in the system of public roads, managed in the twentieth century by a non-profit corporation, the state highway department, but which on the individualistic frontier had been planned, constructed, and maintained by citizens. Webb cited a friend of his, a landscape architect, who left private practice to take a job on a modest salary with the highway department. On this job Webb's friend applied his art to public highways — he developed the roadside to prevent erosion and as a preserve where native wild flowers and native shrubbery could grow undisturbed for their "aesthetic and cultural value," planted trees to exert a psychological influence on drivers by slowing them down at dangerous places and providing a sense of security where needed, and designed parks and rest stops where motorists and truckers could pull off and sleep. In so doing the land-scape artchitect, observed Webb, made the public highways so attrac-tive that people "came from all over the nation — came to observe them and to adopt his methods in other states."[29]

The emphasis in *The Great Frontier* on the crisis of the old in-dividualism and its fretting about the future of individual artistic creativity marked the appearance of a second Webb, one struggling to escape from a place-based cultural determinism, that prevailing tendency among social theorists and policy makers between 1920 and 1950 to categorize individuals into groups whose identity, behavior, and prospects stemmed from the place in which they lived, whether it be the Great Plains, the West, South or North, the metropolitan regions of the sociologists and city planners, the Metropolis, the Great Frontier, or the mid-twentieth-century nations of corporatism. The appearance of this second Webb may also be seen as symptomatic of another event, for it coincided with and constituted part of a more general revolt against place-based cultural determinism in the United States, a revolt that manifested itself in laments about the loss of Ameri-can individualism, anxiety about conformity, and a longing for a new kind of individualism, one in which individuals might achieve self-fulfillment by exercising their creative energies in defining themselves.

This "revolt against culture" has also manifested itself, as I have argued elsewhere, in a variety of "practical" ways.[30] The scope of this essay prohibits an enumeration of these ways, let alone an analysis of them. But the tendency has since the 1950s revealed itself in an en-during interest in the second Webb, especially but not exclusively among the "flower children" of the 1960s, and in efforts to turn the formulas of Turner and the first Webb upside down.[31] Instead of acknowledg-ing that place determines the identity of people, participants in the revolt against culture seek to enable people to exercise their creative energies by defining and redefining themselves through engaging in the process of defining their place, including sometimes their work place but more often their neighborhood, region, or nation.

This great reversal — the shift from the notion that place determines the identity of people to the view that "liberated" individuals should invent themselves and design the culture of places — may be seen quite clearly in attempts since 1954 to apply "community action" to the field of metropolitan planning.

Under that impulse, planning agencies abandoned the practice of hiring "expert" consultants to analyze the characteristics and prospects of a particular metropolitan region and to devise a master plan conforming to the current and projected characteristics of the metropolitan region and its peoples. Instead, planning agencies after 1954 sought to devise policies and practices *requiring* the maximum feasible participation of all parties concerned in making and implementing plans, and to facilitate that process by focusing on a unit smaller than a metropolis, by developing comprehensive plans and programs for each of the neighborhoods of the metropolis. Such a process responded to Webb's concern that not many people would be able by a sheer act of will to exercise their artistic creative energies, for it would offer individuals a convenient arena within which to engage in self-conscious planning, an activity that would force them to think about themselves, what they might become, and how they might rehabilitate their neighborhoods along lines that would improve their "quality of life." In this way, individuals might exercise their creative energies in the process of planning and carrying out policies and programs that would make their neighborhoods fit their image of themselves, a formula that laid as heavy a stress on the therapeutic value of participating in the process as on the product of that participation. For that product, after all, was negotiable and subject to change as residents and institutions redefined themselves and as new residents, individual or institutional, moved into the neighborhood and sought changes in the plan to accommodate their view of themselves and of a satisfying and fulfilling quality of life.[32]

This view of planning tended to make it a continuous process in each neighborhood. But it also tended to treat each neighborhood as a discrete locality with several potential identities rather than as a type of neighborhood situated somewhere along a continuum ranging from the new, planned, and "healthy" to the old, unplanned, and "blighted," the distance that in the age of comprehensive metropolitan planning had separated suburb from slum. Liberated individuals, that is, necessarily started to make a plan by asking the question, "who am I" and "who might I become" in this neighborhood, a question they necessarily answered in terms of time and place, in terms of local history and culture.[33] And since the participants in the planning process as liberated individuals lacked a "given" culture they looked to the history of their neighborhood and its accumulated design features for elements they might use in defining themselves so that they might be able to define a future for the neighborhood.

This approach meant that comprehensive neighborhood planners started with an effort to invent a self-identity associated with the history and design of the neighborhood, an approach that made such planning a costly, lengthy, tedious, frustrating and sometimes abortive process. It created a virtually paralyzing dilemma in planning for a new neighborhood, which of course had no history as an urban settlement. It also provided a fertile source for argumentation and conflict in older neighborhoods, including central business districts, which of course had been occupied by a series of occupants and usually a variety of cultural groups, each of which had left its mark on the history and design of the neighborhood. Every older neighborhood, that is, could be seen as having had several histories, especially by liberated individuals uninhibited by a "given" cultural bias that determined what they saw and did not see when they looked at the past and the design of the neighborhood. As a result, the liberated individuals engaged in planning for the future of the neighborhood characteristically described in the plan those histories and designs as a preface to a long argument over which and how much of those histories and designs should be used in the redesign of the neighborhood.

The advent of comprehensive community action neighborhood planning also had other consequences, some of which provided rich opportunities for energetic and imaginative entrepreneurs. It fostered a boom in "local" history and urban historic preservation.[34] It also created a boom for professional planners who no longer functioned as experts in the theory and practice of devising comprehensive metropolitan plans for others to follow, a definition of the profession that had limited the numbers of it practitioners to a small field of consultants and directors of regional planning. Instead, they now served as facilitators in the community action planning process for each neighborhood in each metropolis, a new definition of the profession that now required lots of planners with a new kind of expertise, especially an expertise in neighborhood organizing and conflict management, and also the ability to act as part-time historians or as historical consultants to neighborhood citizen planners, who usually had neither the time to acquire the skills for researching and writing local history nor the time to utilize those skills when they possessed them.

Thus far the revolt against culture may or may not have yielded consequences entirely satisfying or satisfactory to the second Webb, one of the first prophets of the new individualism, or to us. But it appears not to have freed us from the problem that preoccupied the first and second Webb, the problem of who we are and why we are who we are. As Henry D. Shapiro has suggested, the solution to that problem in the age of "place-ism"— the age of the first Webb — may be compressed into a phrase: who you are is where you're from. And "place-ism," adds Shapiro, resembled the "race-ism" of the nineteenth century, both deriving from attempts to understand the reality of human diversity and to classify individuals according to criteria useful for social theory that yielded "a separation of individuals from each other and a denial of all of ourselves in the name of analytic convenience."[35]

Since 1960, however, we have tended to answer the question of who we are by contending that each of us should decide for ourselves,[36] a solution that does not tell us the basis on which to make such a decision and one that also leaves us separated from each other and from time to time denying ourselves as we change our definition of ourselves. Maybe we can or cannot, once and for all time, decide who we really are, but the quest for the whys of who we are may be futile. As a person far wiser than I has observed in another connection, "the whys can be many, entangled with one another or unknowable, if not actually nonexistent."[37] If that is the case, perhaps we should not worry so much about the inescapable human question of who we are and why. Perhaps we should spend more of our time exercising our creative energies in more realizable ways and making sure that our institutions, neighborhoods, regions, and nation provide all of us a chance to explore, develop, and express those creative energies.

That is a view, I like to think, with which the second Webb would concur, for after writing *The Great Frontier* he did not retreat into the pursuit of his own self-fulfillment through creative literature. Indeed, from the 1940s until his death in March of 1963, he spent a good deal of his time renouncing and denouncing the consequences of clinging to both the race-ism and the place-ism that flourished under the cultural group determinisms of the past, including especially the tendency of those -isms to divide us from each other through the imposition of racial, ethnic, and regional segregation.[38] The second Webb, that is, sought to transform the Great Plains and the South into his version of the "Sunbelt" in an effort to show, despite what he had written in the 1930s, that the desert might be made to bloom, that impoverished rural regions might be made to diversify and prosper, and that racial, ethnic, and regional integration might be made to work. This could be done if we chose to liberate ourselves from the conceptual legacies of the past by deciding to make those things happen as part of the process of defining ourselves as autonomous individuals and of redesigning our neighborhoods, our regions, and our nation as democratic communities of individual pluralism.

NOTES

This essay is informed in part by research and writing supported by a grant from the National Endowment for the Humanities for a project entitled "Planning and the Persisting Past: Cincinnati's Over-the-Rhine since 1940," with matching grants from the Ohio Board of Regents' Urban Universities Research Program, the Ohio Board of Regents Linkage Grant Program, and the Murray Seasongood Foundation, Cincinnati, Ohio.

1. This view of the Sunbelt, especially of its cities, is apparent though not stressed in Carl Abbott, *The New Urban America: Growth and Politics in Sunbelt Cities* (Chapel Hill: University of North Carolina Press, 1981). It has also led to the identification of the South and the West as the most forward rather than the most backward regions of the nation, and to the identification of the Frostbelt as the nation's most troubled region, a reversal of the regional taxonomy that predominated between 1920 and 1950. See, for example, David R. Goldfield and Blaine A. Brownell, *Urban America: From Downtown to No Town* (Boston: Houghton Mifflin, 1979), pp. 396–405. For an alternative view see Zane L. Miller and Patricia Mooney Melvin, *The Urbanization of Modern America: A Brief Hisory* (San Diego: Harcourt Brace Jovanovich, 1987), ch. 11, esp. pp. 250–52.

2. Walter Prescott Webb, *Divided We Stand: The Crisis of a Frontierless Democracy* (New York: Farrar & Rinehart, Inc., 1937), pp. 157–59, and *The Great Frontier* (1952; Austin: University of Texas Press, 1975), pp. 5–6, 409, 411.

3. The following discussion of Turner derives from that in Henry D. Shapiro, "The Place of Culture and the Problem of Identity," in Alan Batteau, ed., *Appalachia and America: Autonomy and Regional Dependence* (Lexington: University Press of Kentucky, 1983), pp. 124–31.

4. Frederick Jackson Turner, *The Significance of the Frontier in American History* (New York: Henry Holt and Co., 1920), p. 37, a collection of papers published by

Turner between 1893 and 1920. By this formulation, of course, Turner's Americans had no choice about their identity as American — the frontier determined it for them. For an analysis of the role of the American race in late nineteenth-century histories of American cities and urban studies see the analysis of the U.S. Census Bureau's *Social Statistics of Cities* (1886) in Zane L. Miller, "The Rise of the City," *Hayes Historical Journal* 3, nos. 1, 2 (1980): 73–83.

5. Frederick Jackson Turner, "The Problem of the West" [1896], in Frederick Jackson Turner, *Significance of the Frontier*, pp. 214, 221. I am indebted for this observation about Turner and the Populists to Henry D. Shapiro, who expressed it to me during a conversation on September 7, 1987.

6. The two Turners co-existed, as indicated by Turner's publication in 1920, well after the second Turner began to work on sections, of a set of his essays built around the frontier thesis of 1893. And see Shapiro, "Place of Culture," p. 129.

7. On the switch from racial to ethnic determinism in urban studies see Andrea Tuttle Kornbluh, "From Culture to Cuisine: Twentiety-Century Views of Race and Ethnicity in the City," in Howard Gillette, Jr., and Zane L. Miller, eds., *American Urbanism: A Historiographical Review* (New York: Greenwood Press, 1987), pp. 49–56, and Zane L. Miller, "Cincinnati Germans and the Invention of an Ethnic Group," *Queen City Heritage: The Journal of the Cincinnati Historical Society* vol. 42, 3 (1984): 13–22.

8. A contemporary authority on regionalism argued that it had really never occurred in the United States, except among isolated and temporary settlements of immigrants. He pointed out, however, that a recent effort had been made to see the future development of the United States along regionalistic lines, that of Frederick Jackson Turner, who wrote in 1925: "The significant fact is that sectional self-consciousness and sensitiveness is likely to be increased as time goes on and crystallized sections feel the full influence of their geographic peculiarities, their special interests, and their developed ideals, in a closed and static nation." Hellwig Hintze, "Regionalism," in Edwin R. A. Seligman, ed., *Encyclopedia of the Social Sciences* (New York: Macmillan, 1933), 13:217. The quote is from Frederick Jackson Turner, "The Significance of the Section in American History," *Significance of the Frontier*, p. 45

9. It took Robert E. Park, a Chicago school sociologist, ten paragraphs to define "assimilation" as it was understood in the 1920s and early 1930s. He summarized its meanings in two sentences as "a political rather than a cultural concept" and as "the process or processes by which peoples of diverse racial origins and different cultural heritages, occupying a common territory, achieve a cultural solidarity sufficient at least to sustain a national existence." He noted that a thoroughgoing cultural assimilation as understood by anthropologists seldom took place and that there existed "grades and degrees of assimilation whether or not we are able to measure them." Park listed blacks as the least assimilated group in America but cited Japanese, Chinese, and Appalachians as other examples of relatively unassimilated groups. Park also observed that in a complex modern society every "trade, every profession, every religious sect, has a language and a body of ideas and practices not always and not wholly intelligible to the rest of the world" and that each "may be said to have its own cultural complex." Park concluded by contending that: "Men must live and work and fight together in order to create that community of interest and sentiment which will enable them to meet the common crises with a common will. At the very least there must be such a consciousness of common interest that differences can be discussed, and out of the conflict of interests a genuine public opinion may be formed. Where racial, religious or

other cultural differences are so great that they provoke a racial, caste or class con-
sciouness which makes a full discussion impossible, assimilation does not take place."
Robert E. Park, "Assimilation," in Edwin R. A. Seligman, *Encyclopedia* 1:281–83.

10. For Turner on assimilation see "Is Sectionalism in America Dying Away?"
(1907), in Frederick Jackson Turner, *The Significance of Sections in American History*
(New York: Henry Holt and Co., 1932), pp. 288–90, esp. p. 290. The second Turner
also argued in 1925 that the passing of free lands and the tendency toward urbanization did "not mean that the Eastern industrial urban life will necessarily spread across
the whole nation" because "food must come from somewhere. . . ." If population out-
ran the domestic food suply, suggested Turner, steps should be taken to retain in the
United States "large rural farming interests and sections. The natural advantages of
certain regions for farming, or for forestry, or for pasturage will arrest the tendency
for the Eastern industrial type of society to flow across the continent and thus to produce a consolidated, homogeneous nation free from sections." He added in the foot-
note, however, that future improvements in agricultural machinery and organization
that might reduce the need for farmers would produce a nation of culturally pluralistic
and rival "industrial sections." See his "The Significance of the Section in American
History," (1925) in Turner, *The Significance of Sections*, p. 35.

11. (Boston: Ginn and Co., 1931).

12. For biographical information on Webb I have relied on Necah Stewart Furman, *Walter Prescott Webb: His Life and Impact* (Albuquerque: Univeristy of New
Mexico Press, 1976) and Gregory M. Tobin, ed., *The Making of a History: Walter Prescott Webb and the Great Plains* (Austin: University of Texas Press, 1976).

13. Webb, *The Great Plains*, pp. 514–15.

14. Some American regionalists took secession seriously, however, including the
authors of a pamphlet published in 1935 that advocated the creation of a black state
or nation in the plantation region of the American South with the right to join, or not
to join, the federated United States, just as the Soviet Union, these authors contended,
guaranteed the nations of that union the right of self-determination. See James W. Ford
and James S. Allen, *The Negroes in a Soviet America* (New York: Workers Library
Publishers, June, 1935; reprint, National Economic Council, 1945), pp. 26–27, 30–34.

15. Webb, *Divided We Stand*, p. 229.

16. Ibid., pp. 220–21.

17. Ibid., p. 221.

18. Ibid., pp. 238–39.

19. Fred A. Shannon, *Critiques of Research in the Social Sciences: III. An Appraisal of Walter Prescott Webb's* The Great Plains: A Study in Institutions and Environment, introduction by Arthur M. Schlesinger (New York: Social Science Research
Council, 1940). The Social Science Research Council (SSRC) was organized in 1923
and incorporated in 1924 "to plan, foster, promote, and develop research in the social
field, principally in anthropology, economics, history, political science, psychology, sociology, and statistics." See Shannon, p. v. At the Skytop Conference Arthur M. Schlesinger explained that Webb's book had been selected after a survey of "qualified" historians had been asked to name the four or five most significant works in the field of
history published in the United States since World War I. The survey turned up several
books that stood out from the rest, and the Appraisal Committee chose *The Great Plains*
because it was confined to a single topic, rested on primary sources available for con-
sultation without traveling abroad, offered "certain bold hypotheses, and represented
the 'new history,' " which Schlesinger defined as "a departure from orthodox political

history and an effort at understanding the past with the help of techniques and information derived from the related social disciplines." Shannon, *An Appraisal*, pp. 139–40. On the establishment of the SSRC see Barry D. Karl, *Charles E. Merriam and the Study of Politics* (Chicago: University of Chicago Press, 1974), pp. 118–39, esp. pp. 123–25.

20. Shannon, *An Appraisal*, p. 134.

21. Shannon, *An Appraisal*, p. 152. Webb in *The Great Plains* cited several works by Clark Wissler, the anthropologist who attended the Skytop Conference and who, like Wirth, defended Webb against Shannon. By this time Wissler had been credited with systematizing the concept of "cultural area"— an area "set off from others by relative internal homogeneity of culture and differentiation against the outside." Wissler accomplished this systematization in the work on the American Indian which mapped ten North and five South American cultural areas. A commentator on this work noted that the "most dubious" part of a cultural area was its borders, where it "intergrades with other areas." As a result, said the commentator, Wissler mapped his areas "schematically" and emphasized their "centers," the tracts in which the "culture is most typical and sensitive and which are to be construed as foci of [cultural] radiation." He added that Wissler did not treat the environment as a "cause" of culture but as a factor that stabilized it and tended to bind it to the area, and noted recent questioning of "whether the culture area is applicable to modern civilization and to history." A. L. Kroeber, "Cultural Area," in Seligman, *Encyclopedia* 4:646–47.

22. Shannon, *An Appraisal*, pp. 171, 181, 184, 189, 268.

23. The best introduction to the work of the Chicago school sociologists on the city is Robert E. Park, Ernest W. Burgess, Roderick McKenzie, *The City* (Chicago: University of Chicago Press, 1925). For this essay see especially the contributions by Robert E. Park, "Community Organization and Juvenile Delinquency," pp. 115–16, 119ff.; Ernest W. Burgess, "The Growth of the City," pp. 47–62, and "Can Neighborhood Work Have a Scientific Basis?" esp. pp. 146–47, 153–55. Also see the discussion of the Chicago school sociologists and planning in Alan I. Marcus, "Back to the Present: Historians' Treatment of the City as a Social System during the Reign of the Idea of Community," in Gillette and Miller, *American Urbanism*, pp. 16–19.

24. Louis Wirth, "Urbanism as a Way of Life," *American Journal of Sociology* 44 (July, 1938): 1–24.

25. Harvey Warren Zorbaugh, *The Gold Coast and the Slum: A Sociological Study of Chicago's Near North Side* (Chicago: University of Chicago Press, 1929; Phoenix Edition, 1976), pp. 272–73.

26. See, for example, Zane L. Miller, *Suburb: Neighborhood and Community in Forest Park, Ohio, 1935–1976* (Knoxville: University of Tennessee Press, 1981), pp. 3–27; Robert B. Fairbanks and Zane L. Miller, "The Martial Metropolis: Housing, Planning and Race in Cincinnati, 1940–55," in Roger L. Lotchin, ed., *The Martial Metropolis: U.S. Cities in War and Peace* (New York: Praeger, 1984), pp. 191–222; Marc A. Weiss, *The Rise of the Community Builders: The American Real Estate Industry and Urban Land Planning* (New York: Columbia University Press, 1987), esp. pp. 141–58; Robert B. Fairbanks, *Making Better Citizens: Housing Reform and the Community Development Strategy in Cincinnati, 1890–1960* (Urbana: University of Illinois Press, 1988); Zane L. Miller, Henry D. Shapiro, and Bruce Tucker, "Planning and the Persisting Past: Cincinnati's Over-the-Rhine, 1920–1988" (forthcoming); and Robert B. Fairbanks, "Metropolitan Planning and Downtown Redevelopment: The Cincinnati and Dallas Experiences, 1940–1960," *Planning Perspectives* 2 (Sept., 1987): 237–53.

27. Webb, *The Great Frontier*, p. 139.

28. Ibid., p. 136.

29. Ibid., p. 137.

30. Zane L. Miller, *Suburb*, pp. 46–241; "Cincinnati Germans," pp. 19–22, p. 24 n. 24; The Role and Concept of Neighborhood in American Cities," in Robert Fisher and Peter Romanofsky, eds., *Community Organization for Social Change: A Historical Perspective* (Westport, Conn.: Greenwood Press, 1981), pp. 18–28; "The Politics of Community Change in Cincinnati," *The Public Historian* 5, no. 4 (1983): 17–35; "Self-Fulfillment and the Decline of Civic Territorial Community," *Journal of Community Psychology* 14, no. 4 (1986): 353–64.

31. The University of Texas Press decided in the mid-1970s to keep *The Great Frontier* permanently in print. See Webb, *The Great Frontier*, p. vii.

32. This section of the essay draws on Miller, Shapiro, and Tucker, "Cincinnati's Over-the-Rhine."

33. Shapiro, "Place of Culture," p. 111.

34. On the boom in "local" history see, for example, the essays in Gillette and Miller, *American Urbanism*, and Kathleen Neils Conzen, "Community Studies, Urban History, and American Local History," in Michael Kammen, ed., *The Past before Us: Contemporary Historical Writing in the United States* (Ithaca, N.Y.: Cornell University Press, 1980), pp. 270–91. Community action planning also contributed to the rise of "public" history, including the founding of a journal, *The Public Historian*, as a field of training for professional historians, and the passage of new federal historic preservation legislation that redefined the criteria for historical and architectural significance to include "local" figures, buildings, movements, objects, events, and sites and to provide grants and tax subsidies for local historic preservation activities.

35. Shapiro, "Place of Culture," p. 134.

36. See, for example, Milton M. Gordon, *Assimilation in American Life: The Role of Race, Religion, and National Origins* (New York: Oxford University Press, 1964), esp. pp. 262–65. The appearance of this book was an event symptomatic of the era of the revolt against cultural determinism and the liberated individual, an era also marked by a new civil rights movement that insisted on the right of all individuals to decide who they are and might become, regardless of their race, religion, or regional or national origin. The book addressed the issue of place-based ethnic communality and intergroup relations in an urban industrial society committed to this view of civil rights. Gordon predicted that ethnic communality would eventually disappear in such a society and advocated in the meantime that ethnic communality should be treated with "fluidity and moderation within the context of equal rights for all, regardless of race, religion, or national background, and the option of free democratic choice for both groups and individuals," including the right to decide not to participate in ethnic communality in both primary and secondary social relations. He did not, however, raise the issue of the ultimate fate of American nationality, another form of place-based ethnic communality, in an urban industrial society committed to the view of individualism advocated by the new civil rights movement. For an important study of urban intergroup relations in the period before and during the first few years of the new civil rights movement see Andrea Tuttle Kornbluh, "'The Bowl of Promise': Social Welfare Planners, Cultural Pluralism, and the Metropolitan Community, 1911–1953," Ph.D. diss., University of Cincinnati, 1988.

37. Primo Levi, "Beyond Judgment," *New York Review of Books* 39, no. 20 Dec. 17, 1987, p. 10.

38. Furman, *Walter Prescott Webb*, pp. 159–80.

Essays on Sunbelt Cities and Recent Urban America was composed into type on a Compugraphic digital phototypesetter in ten point Caledonia with three points of spacing between the lines. Caledonia was also selected for display. The book was typeset by Metricomp, Inc., printed offset and bound by Thomson-Shore, Inc. The paper on which this book is printed carries acid-free characteristics for an effective life of at least three hundred years.

TEXAS A&M UNIVERSITY PRESS : COLLEGE STATION